Trading under EEC and US Antitrust laws

Trading under EEC and US Antitrust Laws

ALFRED F. CROTTI
A.B., B.S., LL.B.
Member of the New York Bar
and the US Patent Bar
Fellow, Institute for Foreign and
International Trade Law,
University of Frankfurt,
Frankfurt am Main, W. Germany

London
Butterworths
1977

For Anne Marie and Anthony who, knowing nothing about it, were the greatest help

England	**Butterworth & Co (Publishers) Ltd**
London	88 Kingsway, WC2B 6AB
Australia	**Butterworths Pty Ltd**
Sydney	586 Pacific Highway, Chatswood, NSW 2067
	Also at Melbourne, Brisbane, Adelaide and Perth
Canada	**Butterworth & Co (Canada) Ltd**
Toronto	2265 Midland Avenue, Scarborough M1P 4S1
New Zealand	**Butterworths of New Zealand Ltd**
Wellington	26/28 Waring Taylor Street 1
South Africa	**Butterworth & Co (South Africa) (Pty) Ltd**
Durban	152/154 Gale Street
USA	**Butterworth & Co (Publishers) Inc**
Boston	19 Cummings Park, Woburn, Mass 01801

© Butterworth & Co (Publishers) Ltd   1977

ISBN — 0 406 57170 8

Preface

This book is for those who want to read about the antitrust laws. Its purpose is to explain them so that those who are interested may assess the risk of a particular business activity violating those laws.

The book has been shaped into two parts. The first part is an overview of the field of antitrust in the United States and in Europe. It explains the reasons for the enactment of antitrust law in the United States and in the European Economic Community. Unless one grasps some understanding of why the laws were made, it will always be difficult to understand how courts might interpret them as they do, and how courts might interpret them in future. The first part will, then, explore certain characteristic, indeed essential features of every antitrust offence. Once we are aware of these characteristics, specific business practices can be more easily placed against an antitrust backdrop and assessed as to the applicability of antitrust law.

The second part of the book will be more particular and will deal with areas of normal business activity and the antitrust problems lurking in each of them; and lastly with some procedural and jurisdictional aspects of antitrust enforcement.

January 1977   ALFRED F. CROTTI

Contents

Preface   vii

Table of United States of America Acts   xiii

Table of European Communities Legislation   xiv

Table of Cases   xv

Introduction   1

PART I

General principles of antitrust violations   5
1 The purpose of the antitrust laws   7
    The antitrust conflict   7
    The scope of antitrust laws and administrative advice
       on business practices   9
    Judicial advice on business
       practices—"Reasonableness"   10
    Why the laws came into existence   13
    Personal liability for violations   19

2 What to watch for in a Sherman Act violation   28
    Conspiracy   28
    Intra-enterprise conspiracy   33
    Examples of intracorporate doctrine   50

3 The necessary effect on interstate trade   79
    Why and how much interstate trade needs to be
       affected   80
    Where all the acts are in the same state   82

4 The rule of reason   84
    The cornerstone of the Sherman Act   84
    The interstate effect and the rule of reason   89
    Introduction of the *per se* principle   101

5 The *per se* principle   103

6 Price fixing   105
    Introduction   105
    To what extent does intent play a part   106
    The Trenton Potteries decision   110
    Purpose and/or effect   111
    Trade associations   113

7 Dividing markets   128
    Vertical division of markets—are they *per se* illegal? 131
    In Europe   134
    Exceptions to the *per se* rule   140
    The Schwinn doctrine in foreign commerce   150
    Termination of distributors   152

8 Group boycotts   160
    Dealing in competing products   163
    Secondary boycotts   167

9 Tying arrangements   169
    The relevant market over which a defendant must
        have dominance in a tying arrangement   174
    Coercion as a factor in antitrust illegality   175
    When is a tying arrangement *per se* unlawful?   176
    A purely business view of tying arrangements   179
    Other exceptions to *per se* illegality of tying clauses 184
    In Europe   185

10 Monopolization and abuses of a dominant position   189
    The distinction between ss. 1 and 2 of the Sherman
        Act   193
    The difference between offences in ss. 1 and 2 of the
        Sherman Act   194
    Summary   202

PART II
Trading Practices   207

11   Mergers and acquisitions   209
     Some business reasons why companies merge or
         acquire or are acquired   209
     Merger guidelines of the Department of Justice   212
     Examples   217
     Geographic market   222
     Foreign companies   223
     Foreign entry into the US by way of acquisition   224
     A foreign acquirer   226
     US subsidiaries having foreign parents   228
     American firm acquiring a foreign company   229
     Failing company   230
     Reciprocity   230
     The European Community and elsewhere   233
     Canada   235
     Sherman Act and mergers and acquisitions   235

12   Joint ventures   237
     Foreign joint ventures   243
     The Rolls Royce and Pratt and Whitney Jet Engine
         Development Programme   246
     Mariner International Corporation   250
     Summary   251

13   Use of patents and trademarks   253
     Areas of patent licensing violations in the US   254
     Areas of antitrust vulnerability in the Common Mar-
         ket under art. 85   254
     Viewpoint of the patentee, the government and the
         courts   259

14   The unlawful use of copyright and trademarks   262
     An example of the unlawful use of trademarks in the
         US   269

xii *Contents*

15 The unlawful use of patents to divide markets   273
    Are exclusive licences as such illegal under art. 85?   276

16 The element of coercion in licensing   279

17 The Schwinn principle and licensing   293
    The significance of whether an agreement is a sale or
    a licence of patents   295
    US antitrust law and foreign patent licensing   296

18 Examples of licensing clauses   298
    Example 1   298
    Example 2   299
    Example 3   300
    Example 4   301
    Example: foreign licensor of a process in the US   302

19 US jurisdiction over a foreign person   310

20 Technical assistance (knowhow)   313
    Example of the problem   316

Appendix: Summary of Commission decisions on exemp-
    tions under article 85 (3)   319
    I   Restrictive practices   319
    II   Licensing agreements and industrial property
         rights   333
    III Selective distribution agreements   334
    IV   Cooperation agreements   336

Index   343

Table of United States of America Acts

Antitrust Improvements Act 1976   105
Clayton Act 1914   . . . .   18, 85, 126
  s. 3   . . 164, 169, 174, 177, 190, 279
  4   . . . . 29, 310
  4A   310
ˋ 7   . . 190, 210, 213, 217, 220, 221
    222, 225, 226, 231, 240, 250
Federal Trade Commission Act 1914
    18, 85
National Industrial Recovery Act 1933
    115
Robinson–Patman Act 1936 18, 85, 126

Securities Exchange Act 1934   . .   19
Sherman Act 1890   85
  s. 1   .   13, 15, 29, 30, 38, 56, 64, 66,
    69, 98, 147, 151, 157, 174, 190, 192,
    193, 194, 202, 221, 232, 243
  2 . . .   13, 16, 29, 30, 64, 66, 189,
    192, 193, 194, 202, 217, 221 222
UK Patents Act—
  s. 57   298
Webb Export Trade Act 1918   18

xiii

Table of European Communities Legislation

TREATIES
EEC Treaty (Treaty of Rome) (Cmnd.
5179-II) 13, 92, 128, 138, 190
  art. 5 128
      9 128
     32 128
     30 329
     36 . . . . 263, 265, 329
     85 . 10, 13, 15, 19, 24, 26, 38, 68,
  69, 70, 71, 81, 91, 126, 131, 134, 154,
  155, 158, 160, 186, 187, 188, 190, 233,
  256, 257, 263, 264, 265, 266, 267, 268,
  269, 276, 277, 311, 320, 322, 325,
                              331, 334
        (1) . 91, 153, 155, 156, 158,
  187, 277, 278, 323, 324, 325, 326, 328,
                   329, 330, 332, 333
        (a) 323
        (e) 185, 187
        (3)   26, 90, 91, 95, 104, 126,
  136, 156, 158, 187, 257, 258, 276, 306,
                   322, 324, 327, 329,
                       330, 333, 336

     86 .13, 15, 16, 19, 24, 81, 92, 158,
        160, 188, 190, 191, 196, 197, 198,
        233, 234, 263, 266, 267, 268, 269,
                                 311, 327
        (d) 187

SECONDARY LEGISLATION
REGULATIONS

EEC Council Regulation 17
                         134, 188, 320
  art. 3 24
      4 186
        (2) 185
     16 24
EEC Council Regulation 19/65 . 136
EEC Commission Regulation 67/67
     10, 136, 137, 154, 158, 163, 258, 336

Table of Cases

A

A.C.E.C.—Berliet, *Re*, 17 July 1968, O-J.L 201/7; [1968] C.M.L.R. D35
330, 337
A.C.F. Chemiefarma *v.* E.C. Commission, 41/69, 16 Rec. 661 . . . 319
A.O.I.P.—Beyrard, O.J. L6/8, 13 January 1976 333
Advocaat Zwarte Kip, *Re*, 24 July 1974, O.J. L237/12; [1974] 2
C.M.L.R. D79 329
Agreement of Julien/Van Katwijk, 28 October 1970, O.J. L242/18;
[1970] C.M.L.R. D43 327
Agreement of Prym-Beka, 8 October 1973, O.J. L296/24; [1973]
C.M.L.R. D250 331
Agreements between Manufacturers of Glass Containers, 15 May
1974, O.J. L160/1; [1974] 2 C.M.L.R. D50 . . . . 325, 332
American Column and Lumber Co. *v.* United States, 257 U.S. 377
115, 118, 119, 120, 122
American Tobacco Co. *v.* United States, 328 U.S. 781 . . . 194, 201, 209
Association of German Tile Manufacturers, *Re*, 29 December
1970, O.J. L10/15; [1971] C.M.L.R. D6 332
Automatic Radio Manufacturing Co., Inc. *v.* Hazeltine Research
Inc., 339 U.S. 827 (1950) 280, 281, 282

B

Barr and Levy *v.* WU1/TAS (1975) C.C.H. Trade Cases 60, 198 . . 55
Bayer/Gist–Brocades, *Re,* O.J. L30, 5 February 1976 342
Bayerische Motorenwerke AG (BMW), O.J. L29/1, 14 December 1974
335
Béguelin *v.* G.L. Import Export, 22/71, [1972] C.M.L.R. 81 . . . 39, 70
Belliston *v.* Texaco, Inc., 455, f.2d 175 126
Board of Trade of Chicago *v.* United States, 246 U.S. 231 . . . 87, 108
Boehringer Mannheim GmbH *v.* E.C. Commission, 45/69, [1973]
C.M.L.R. 864 . . . . 319, 320
Bomée-Stichting, *Re*, O.J. L329, 23 December 1975 336
Boro Hall *v.* General Motors, 317 U.S. 695 145

Bronbemaling *v*. Heidemaatschappij, O.J. 249, 25 September 1975 . 334
Buchler & Co. *v*. E.C. Commission, 44/69, 16 Rec. 733 319

C

Cartel in Aniline Dyes, *Re*, [1969] C.M.L.R. D23 71
CEMATEX, *Re*, O.J. L227, 8 October 1971 340
Cementregeling Voor Nederland, *Re*, 18 December 1972, O.J.
    L303/7; [1973] C.M.L.R. D149 328
Centrafarm BV *v*. Sterling Drug, 10/712, [1976] C.M.L.R. 1 275
Central Heating, *Re*, O.J. L264, 23 November 1972 330
Cimbel, *Re*, 22 December 1972, O.J. L303/24; [1973] C.M.L.R. D167   323
Clima–Chappée/Buderus, *Re*, 22 July 1969, O.J. L195/1; [1970]
    C.M.L.R. D7 337
Consten and Grundig Verkaufs GmbH *v*. E.E.C., 56/64, [1966]
    C.M.L.R. 418 . . . . 134, 301
Coöperative Vereeniging "Suiker Unie" U.A. *et alia v*. E.C.
    Commission, 40–48/73, 16 December 1975 16 Rec. 921 326
Coors Co. *v*. F.T.C., 497 F.2d 1178 149

D

Davidson Rubber Co.'s Agreement, *Re*, 9 June 1972, O.J. L143/31;
    [1972] C.M.L.R. D.52 333
Dehydrating Process Co. *v*. A.O. Smith Corpn., 368 U.S. 931 (1961) . 299
Deutsche Philips GmbH, *Re*, 5 October 1973, O.J. L293/40;
    [1973] C.M.L.R. D241 323
Dru-Blondel, *Re*, O.J. 131, 17 July 1965 335
Duro–Dyne/Europair, *Re*, O.J. L29, 3 February 1975 336

E

Eastern States Retail Lumber Dealers' Association *v*. United States,
    234 U.S. 600 164
European Machine Tool Expositions (EEMO)—European
    Committee for Cooperation in the Machine Tool Industry
    (CECIMO), *Re*, O.J. L69, 20 March 1969 340
European Sugar Cartel, *Re*, [1973] C.M.L.R. D65 71
Europemballage Cn. and Continental Can Co. *v*. E.C. Commission,
    6/72, [1973] E.C.R. 215 196

F

Fabrique Nationale d'Armes de Guerre, *Re*, O.J. L134/6, 20 June 1971
    338
Fashion Originators' Guild of America Inc. *v*. Federal Trade
    Commission, 312 U.S. 457 166

Fortner Enterprises Inc. *v.* United States Steel Corpn., 394 U.S. 495   181
Franco-Japanese Ball Bearings Agreement, *Re,* 29 November 1974,
   O.J. L343/19; [1975] 1 C.M.L.R. D8 324
Frubo *v.* E.C. Commission, 71/74, [1975] 1 C.M.L.R. 647   . . . 74, 326

G

G.I.S.A., *Re,* 22 December 1972, O.J. 1972 L 303/45; [1973]
   C.M.L.R. D125 323
G.T.E. Sylvania *v.* Continental T.V., (1974) C.C.H. Trade Cases
   75,072 145
Garrett's, Inc. *v.* Farah Manufacturing Co., Inc. 153
Gas Waterheaters and bath Heaters, *Re,* 3 July 1973, O.J. L217/34;
   [1973] C.M.L.R. D231 332
Glen Manufacturing, Inc. *v.* Perfect Fit Industries, Inc., 324 F.
   Supp. 1133 . . . . 279, 280, 287, 288, 289, 292
Goodyear Italiana–Euram, *Re,* O.J. L38, 12 February 1975 335
Greenville Publishing Co. *v.* Daily Reflector, (1974) C.C.H. Trade
   Cases 75,037 58
Groupements des Fabricants de Papiers Peints de Belgique *v.*
   E.C. Commission, 73/74, 26 November 1975, C.C.H. CMR
   8335 . . . . 325, 332

H

Hawaiian Oke and Liquors, Ltd. *v.* Joseph E. Seagram & Sons, 272
   F. Supp. 915 . . . . 40, 41, 42
Henkel/Colgate, *Re,* O.J. L14/14, 18 January 1972; [1972] C.M.L.R.
   D49 339
Hummel–Isbecque, *Re,* O.J. 156, 23 September 1965 335

I

IFTRA rules of producers of Virgin Aluminium, O.J. L228, 29
   August 1975 . . . . 325, 333
Imperial Chemical Industries, Ltd. *v.* E.C. Commission, 48/69,
   [1972] C.M.L.R. 557 . . . . 74, 118, 320
Instant Delivery Corpn. *v.* City Stores Co., 284 F. Suppl. 941 162
International Business Machines Corpn. *v.* United States, 298 U.S.
   131 178
International Salt Co. *v.* United States, 332 U.S. 392 . . . . 176, 177,
                            180, 181, 186, 187

J

JAZ–Peter Agreement, *Re,* 22 July 1969, O.J. L195/5; [1970]
   C.M.L.R. 129 338

K

Kabelmetal–Luchaire, *Re*, O.J. L222/34, 22 August 1975 333
Kaiser *v.* General Motors Corpn. (U.S. District Court, Eastern
    District of Pennsylvania, No. 71-1242) 144
Kali and Salz A.G. and Kali Chemie A.G.'s Agreement, *Re*,
    [1974] 1 C.M.L.R. D1 . . . . 72, 331
Kiefer–Stewart *v.* Joseph E. Seagram & Sons, 340 U.S. 211 . . 39, 42,
    44, 56, 63
Klor's Inc. *v.* Broadway–Hale Stores, Inc., 359 U.S. 207 166
Knutson *v.* Daily Review, Inc. (CCH 75273) 62

L

Lightweight Papers, *Re*, O.J. L182, 10 August 1972 339

M

Maison Jalatte, *Re*, O.J. 3, 6 January 1966 335
MAN/SAVIEM Agreement, *Re*, 17 January 1972, O.J. L31/29;
    [1974] 2 C.M.L.R. D123 338
Maple Flooring Manufacturers' Association *v.* United States, 268
    U.S. 563 . . . . 119, 121, 122, 124, 125
Mitchel *v.* Reynolds (1711), 1 P. Wms. 181; 21 Digest (Repl.) 319 . . 91

N

Napoleon Liqueurs, *Re*, 1857/74 269
Nederlandse Cement Handelmaatschappij NV, *Re*, [1972]
    C.M.L.R. D94 323
Nederlandse Cement Handelmaatschappij NV, *Re*, 23 December
    1971, O.J. L22/16, [1972] C.M.L.R. D94 328
Northern Pacific Railway Co. *v.* United States, 356 U.S. 1 . . 170, 171,
    176, 179, 180, 186, 187

O

Omega Watches, *Re*, O.J. L242, 5 November 1970; [1970] C.M.L.R.
    D49 335

P

Pacific Engineering and Production Co. *v.* Kerr–McGee Corpn.,
    (1974) C.C.H. Trade Cases 75, 054 60
Parke, Davis *v.* Probel, Reese, 24/67, [1968] C.M.L.R. 47 274
Perma Life Mufflers *v.* International Parts Corpn., 392 U.S. 134 . . 47
Pittsburgh Corning Europe—Formica Belgium Hertel, *Re*, 23
    November 1972, O.J. L272/35; [1973] C.M.L.R. D2 325

Poller *v.* Columbia Broadcasting Inc., 368 U.S. 464 40
Preserved Mushroom Case, 8 January 1975, O.J. L29/26 324

R

Rank/SOPELEM, *Re,* O.J. L29/20, 3 February 1975 340
Rea *v.* Ford Motor Co. (CCH 75029) 54
Reed Brothers, Inc. *v.* Monsanto Co. (U.S. Court of Appeals, Eighth Circuit, No. 74-1695) 142, 144

S

S.A. Cimenteries C.B.R. *v.* E.C. Commission, 8-11/66, [1967] C.M.L.R. 77 322
Siegel *v.* Chicken Delight, 307 F. Supp. 1491 184
Sirdar–Phildar, *Re,* O.J. L125, 16 May 1975 329
Société Commerciale des Potasse et de l'Azote (SCPA) Kali und Salz, *Re,* O.J. L217/3, 6 August 1973 339
Société Technique Minière *v.* Maschinenbau Ulm GmbH, 56/65, [1966] C.M.L.R. 357 134
SOPELEM–Langen, *Re,* O.J. L13/47, 17 January 1972; [1972] C.M.L.R. D77 335
Special Equipment Co. *v.* Coe, 324 U.S. 370 289
Standard Oil Co. of New Jersey *v.* United States, 221 U.S. 1 . . 87, 191
Steers *v.* United States, 192 F.I. 82
Stoves and Heaters, *Re,* O.J. L159, 21 June 1975 326
Suburban Car Rentals *v.* International Telephone and Telegraph, I.T.T. Avis and Avis Rent-a-Car System (1953) 53
Sugar Institute Inc. *v.* United States, 297 U.S. 553 123
Susser *v.* Carvel Corpn., 332 F. 2d 505 183

T

T.V. Signal Co. of Aberdeen *v.* American Telephone and Telegram and Northwestern Bell Telephone Co., (1971) C.C.H. Trade Cases 73, 567 53
Timken Roller Bearing Co. *v.* United States, 341 U.S. 593 (1951) . . 281
Todhunter–Mitchell & Co. *v.* Anheuser-Busch Inc., (1974) C.C.H. Trade Cases 75, 034 150
Transocean Marine Paint Association, *Re,* O.J. 163/10, 20 July 1967; [1967] C.M.L.R. D9 336
Transocean Marine Paint *v.* E.C. Commission, 17/74, [1974] 2 C.M.L.R. 459 337
Transparent-Wrap Machine Corpn. *v.* Stokes and Smith Co., 329 U.S. 637 318
Tripoli *v.* Wella Corpn., 425 F. 2d 932 149

U

UNIDI, *Re*, O.J. L228, 29 August 1975 340
United Reprocessors GmbH/KEWA, *Re*, O.J. L51, 26 February 1976 341
United States *v.* Addyston Pipe and Steel Co., 8 February 1898 . . . 129
United States *v.* Arnold Schwinn & Co., 388 U.S. 350 137
United States *v.* Bausch and Lomb Optical Co., 321 U.S. 707 219
United States *v.* Columbia Steel Co., 334 U.S. 495 212
United States *v.* Consolidated Car-Heating Co., Inc., 20 June 1950,
    U.S. District Court Southern District of N.Y. 293
United States *v.* Container Corpn. of America, 393 U.S. 333 124
United States *v.* E.I. DuPont de Nemours, 351 U.S. 377 199
United States *v.* E. I. DuPont de Nemours & Co., 353 U.S. 586 . . . 220
United States *v.* El Paso Natural Gas Co., 376 U.S. 651 224
United States *v.* General Motors, 384 U.S. 127 145
United States *v.* Grinnel Corpn., 384 U.S. 563 193
United States *v.* Grinnel, 384 U.S. 571 200
United States *v.* Imperial Chemical Industries, Ltd., 100 F. Supp.
    504 (1951) 251, 300
United States *v.* International Harvester, 274 U.S. 693 113
United States *v.* Jerrold Electronics Corpn., 187 F. Supp. 545 . . . 184
United States *v.* E. C. Knight Co., 156 U.S. 1 82
United States *v.* Minnesota Mining and Manufacturing Co., 92 F.
    Supp. 947 243
United States *v.* National Lead Co., 332 U.S. 319 (1947) 300, 318
United States *v.* New York Great A. and P. Tea Co. Inc., 137 F. 2d 459 51
United States *v.* Parke, Davis & Co., 362 U.S. 29 161
United States *v.* Penn–Olin, 378 U.S. 158 . . . . . . 241, 242, 246, 249
United States *v.* Joseph Schlitz Brewing Co., 253 F. Supp. 129 . . . 230
United States *v.* Sealy, 388 U.S. 350 269
United States *v.* Socony-Vacuum Oil Co. Inc., 310 U.S. 150 . . 99, 101,
                                                    107, 108, 113
United States *v.* Timken Roller Bearing Co., 341 U.S. 593 (1951) . . . 42,
                                                    43, 45, 48, 50
United States *v.* Topco, 405 U.S. 596 269
United States *v.* Trenton Potteries, 273 U.S. 392 . . . . . 88, 110, 111
United States *v.* Yellow Cab Co., 332 U.S. 218 . . . . 39, 63

V

Vereeniging van Cementhandelaren *v.* E.C. Commission, 8/72,
    [1973] C.M.L.R. 7 . . . . 73, 323

W

W.E.A. Filipacchi Music S.A., *Re,* 22 December 1972, O.J. L303/52;
    [1973] C.M.L.R. D43 328

White Motor Co. *v.* United States, 372 U.S. 253 . . . . . . 132, 137, 141
Wickens *v.* Evans (1892), 3 Y. & J. 318; 45 Digest (Repl.) 397 129

Z

Zenith Radio Corpn. *v.* Hazeltine Research Inc., 395 U.S. 100, 89
S. Ct. 1562 . . . . 279, 280, 282, 285, 286, 287, 290, 291, 292

Introduction

The antitrust laws were enacted generally to tell the business community what it could not do. In the broadest possible language, the lawmakers proscribed illegal business behaviour without also prescribing safe behaviour. It is not possible to compile an index of every combination of business transaction and find the answer whether it is illegal under the antitrust laws. Imagine the difficulty: assume there is a manufacturer of steel furnaces, or clothing in Bethlehem, Pennsylvania, USA, or in Dundee, Scotland and that he supplies 0.1% or 50% or 100% of the market in his home country or abroad. Assume he has one supplier, or two or more suppliers, and that he distributes his product through one or more distributors or agents, or that he distributes his product himself direct to wholesalers or jobbers, or that he sold to the public without a middleman. Would it not be comforting if such a person could look into an index and turn to a page that would tell him what the courts have decided or would decide about the legality of exactly what his board of directors, or his sales manager wanted to do? The slightest variation of the facts would even then alter the advice obtained. It would, for example, make a difference whether the interested person was not a manufacturer but rather a distributor, agent or retailer. It would make a difference if the matter concerned a new enterprise attempting to enter a competitive market.

No such index is available but no one questions the desirability of having some sort of guide at least to indicate what might be right or wrong action under the antitrust laws.

I

The need for a more practical guide through the anti-trust laws of the US and of Europe has never been more pressing. For the American businessman his need to know about the application of American law as well as of Community law was enhanced by the emergence of the "multinational" corporation.

The size and number of multinational corporations grew dramatically after 1945 and were the cause of some landmark United States Supreme Court decisions which affect even the lesser multinational corporations. The application of US antitrust law to the operations of the multinationals arose probably because more US-based companies expanded into foreign lands by means of subsidiary companies than did foreign-based companies, although the idea of multinational companies was long ago known and established by non-US companies. The multinational development led US interest into the Common Market, hence US interest in Community antitrust law. European businesses expanding abroad similarly have had to come to terms with US law not only because of the reciprocal concern arising from their involvement with US companies but also because of the expansion of their own unilateral business interests into areas within US jurisdiction.

The trading picture is further complicated by the widening application of Community law. Apart from the inherent difficulty of coping with different laws, this development of international (or transnational) business operations is being continuously hampered by fundamental differences in business concepts, for example, between British and American businessmen and business methods and the Commission and European Court of Justice and US courts understanding of them.

Assuming the facts permit or suggest a clear instruction to the businessman that what he is planning will avoid any legal infraction, he still cannot rely on the continuance of that state of affairs. Courts must be free to interpret the law in accordance with economic needs. The relevant market in which the business practice takes place may narrow or widen in time. While this permits the dynamic execution of justice it places all those governed by the law in the uncomfortable position of not being certain that what they do today will be all right tomorrow. Unfortunately, antitrust violations render the agreement or practice invalid, not from the day the court declares it invalid, but from the day the illegal aspect was in force (save for a certain kind of immunity obtained by the Notification procedures provided under reg. 17 of the Treaty of Rome). This feature of the law is especially unpalatable to the European. It is disturbing to him to learn that the agreement he thought was safe was illegal from the day he signed it.

Despite the unsure ground ahead caused by this day-to-day interpretation of the laws, the enforcers have replied that the business community knows fairly well where the edge of the cliff is and if it wants to walk close to it it must be prepared for the consequences. There are very few instances where a corporate director or officer intentionally undertook to violate the antitrust laws. Far more frequent is the case of the businessman acting in good faith later discovering that he has done something illegal.

Part I

General principles
of antitrust violations

Paraphrase — put in other words

The purpose of the antitrust laws

The antitrust laws in the US and in the EEC are aimed at promoting free competition in the market place. They may be paraphrased collectively as declarations of principle that any agreement or cooperative effort or intent by two or more entities which affects or restrains, or is likely to affect or restrain their competitors is illegal. Moreover, anyone who, alone or with another, monopolizes or attempts to monopolize any part of trade is guilty of a crime; and any abusive use of a dominant position in the market is prohibited.

THE ANTITRUST CONFLICT

In order to preserve and foster freedom of competition, the law must curb the right of individuals freely to do business. This seems to be a self-contradiction but it is not. It is an expression of the inherent conflict between the private right to enter into an agreement with one another and the right of the law to prevent injury to the public by the exercise of the private right. This conflict has often puzzled businessmen (and others), so perhaps a brief look at history will help to clarify the apparent inconsistency between public law and private freedom to do business.

It was known in the days of the English common law that certain business restraints were unfair and also harmful to the public at large. Amongst such restraints, for example, was the idea of price fixing. In the US, prior to the enactment of the Sherman Act, the fear was of the power of large companies to fix prices, limit production and divide markets among themselves. At that time there were huge combinations of companies which came to be collected in formations called "trusts". These were prevalent in the industries of railroads and oil, both of which were at that time in a fast growing phase. They were important to the development of the economy in the US, and there was, in fact, fierce competition which disappeared as competitors were acquired and merged and grouped into " " "trusts". The public concern for the activities of these trusts led to the Sherman Act. The initial fear arose simply because of size, as bigness incorporated the power to restrain competition. It was true then, as it is true now, that certain activities carried out by powerful and large organizations may be considered to be illegal restraints of trade whereas the same activities by smaller enterprises may not be considered to be illegal. A competitive economy will always, sooner or later, have to cope with the fear of size itself. After 1890, the courts and the law enforcers mounted a two-pronged attack on restrictive practices. The object was to reduce the size of the trusts and break up the existing monopolies. It was this first attack that led to the dissolution of the great trusts and monopolies in the early days of the Sherman Act. One sees this, for example, in the breaking up of the Standard Oil Company of New Jersey.

The second aspect of the attack was and is to prevent acts which would inhibit competition because such acts could again lead to a concentration and growth of power which would again revive the evil practices which were initially condemned because of bigness. It is odd that as of this writing the United States Civil Aeronautics Authority is contemplating permitting large competing commercial airlines to merge into fewer and bigger units. The EEC Commission is contemplating the same kind of rationalization. In the computer industry, the UK and France encouraged the formation of larger enterprises at the sacrifice of smaller competing companies in order to meet the challenge of American giants such as IBM.

The antitrust laws are double edged because although they are designed to preserve competition, they necessarily preserve the right to grow (by winning the competition) thereby reducing competition. Those who are efficient are given by law the proper climate in which to grow, by themselves being protected by the antitrust laws against those seeking to compete against them by using illegal means. Here then is the inherent conflict: on the one hand the use of law to promote and maintain a free market on the absolute theory that in the end the public good is best served with the best products in the best quantities at the best prices if the market place for them is kept open for the freeplay of competition. Note the areas of interest, i.e. the product, the quantity of the product, the price at which the product is sold and how and where the product is sold. Antitrust enforcement will necessarily concern itself with monitoring business activities affecting each of these. On the other hand, the competition cannot be too free.

THE SCOPE OF ANTITRUST LAWS AND ADMINISTRATIVE ADVICE ON BUSINESS PRACTICES

The nature of the laws requires them to be wide in scope and worded in terms of prohibitive actions. They cannot detail what constitutes safe conduct. In a massive attempt to suggest what might be safe conduct, many fine textbooks and useful weekly publications have been made available. Although these materials are excellent compilations comprehensively covering all aspects of antitrust law, they are not oriented to tell the reader whether his intended business practice is legal. All they can do is report what the courts have ruled to be instances of illegal behaviour and leave it to the reader to interpret history for his own uses.

Spokesmen for the Antitrust Division of the US Department of Justice and for the Directorate-General of Competition in the EEC Commission try to be helpful by indicating, from time to time, the practices which they intend to attack as unlawful but the statements are necessarily broad expressions of policy which serve only to signal areas which may be sensitive. Seldom will the judiciary give a meaningful instruction that a particular business practice will always be free of antitrust problems.

Although the US Federal Trade Commission will give an opinion as to their intentions to prosecute or not prosecute a particular practice, and the Commission will state that a particular practice does not violate Community law or that the practice is exempt from the penalty of the law, all such opinions from the respective authorities are very carefully conditioned on the precise facts given to them in the economic climate of the moment. Any deviation in the practice or in the market can lead to a change in the view of the authorities.

Unlike the US where no broad exemption from the application of the antitrust laws is given (save with respect to certain classes of industries, e.g. labour unions), the Commission in Brussels is empowered under reg. 67/67 to exempt from the application of Community antitrust law (art. 85) groups of exclusive distributorship agreements. This is helpful to indicate that not all exclusive distributorship agreements are illegal and that certain kinds can be excused from the application art. 85. It is not completely helpful because it still does not indicate whether the particular distributorship agreement you are planning to execute comes within the regulation. The same problem occurs with interpreting the decision of a court.

JUDICIAL ADVICE ON BUSINESS PRACTICES—
"REASONABLENESS"

Where the court may seem to have given a clear teaching of the line dividing the legal and illegal, one must be wary. The court shapes the scope and boundaries of its decision so that it will not frustrate the continuing freedom of the judiciary to interpret and apply antitrust laws on particular practices at particular times. Nevertheless the court wants those governed by the laws to understand them. The court will, then, decide on the facts presented to it in order to satisfy justice between the parties but it will quite often also make an apparently unambiguous statement of policy as a guide for future action. Unfortunately those statements are just as often strangely unhelpful because they are so broadly stated that they cannot be translated into practical action except by another decision of the court based on the exact facts of the case itself. For example, the US Supreme Court in 1911 borrowed from the early common law of England and said that not all restraints of trade were illegal, only those that were unreasonable. This came to be called the "rule of reason".

The principle of "reasonableness" seems clear and one has a sense of security about it. But how helpful was the court with that statement? Since 1911 the federal courts have been trying to establish the indicia of reasonableness. They have been doing this by the only fair judicial method, i.e. the ad hoc method of judging each case on its merits. As we shall later see, the courts in the US, appreciating the complicated and difficult task of investigating and weighing all of the economic facts to determine whether a particular practice imposes an unreasonable restraint on trade, invented the *per se* rule. This may yet develop in the Community but the European Court has not gone that far. Briefly, this is a pre-emptive conclusion that a particular practice is a violation without the necessity of inquiring as to its actual effect on trade and competition. For example, price-fixing between competitors is a *per se* violation of the Sherman Act and all that is needed to establish the infraction is to show the fixing of prices by competitors. One might expect that if the same facts were presented to another court the result would be the same. That would not be a safe assumption. Courts will often decide a case for totally different reasons from the earlier one despite the similarity of facts, or will find distinguishing facts in the case at hand and so come to a different result. Note that although the later court may come to a different conclusion from that of the earlier case having similar facts, the principle of law remains inviolate: price-fixing is still bad. This makes even the review of cases and finding of precedents only of limited help to the lawyer and his client. Moreover, it happens with unhappy frequency that one does not find a case having the facts of the particular business situation which has been presented to counsel for advice.

We believe that the only way one might be able to assess the risk of an antitrust violation is to understand the laws. If one is going to carry on a business life it is essential that he reaches this understanding.

Charles W. Robinson, US Under-Secretary for Economic Affairs, in a speech in November 1975 made the case for this understanding:

"We are moving into a world of interdependence, a world that calls for a change in intergovernmental relationships, and certainly for basic changes in the way in which the private sector relates to the Government . . . . I'd like to discuss with you . . . the challenge . . . of forward-looking policies and actions regarding transnational enterprises . . . . I like to think of the transnational enterprise as the international extension of an historical economic development within single countries, particularly within the United States. The development of national corporations in the United States near the end of the last century reduced the distortions arising from separation of regional markets. Early in the 20th century, firms moved their operations from the higher wage areas like New England and the Middle Atlantic to the lower wage South and Midwest. Capital was available at lower interest rates in financial centers such as New York or Boston so firms borrowed there, but used the money elsewhere. Companies increased their efficiency and improved markets by bringing capital and technology to labor because labor was a less mobile factor in production.

This development of national companies was not an unalloyed blessing. Many local and regional firms found that they could not compete; consequently, some died and others were absorbed . . . . Fears grew that competition was dying out, and as a result, we developed antitrust laws to allay these concerns . . . . The transnational enterprise is now facing similar problems on a global scale. As technological leaders, transnational enterprises are now introducing coordinated management, production, and marketing techniques throughout the world . . . . But like our national companies, transnational enterprises have brought problems as well as benefits . . . . Whereas our domestic businesses operated in an environment supported by a consensus of liberal capitalist values, the trans-national enterprise has no such luxury. It is under attack at home and abroad by labor unions, consumer groups, and the general public. These and other groups are suspicious of big business and concerned about the impact of transnational operations on their own welfare. They call for more controls, tougher treatment of foreign source income, and stricter enforcement of antitrust laws internationally."

Mr Robinson was speaking on a global basis. The need to understand the laws translates into a more personal, individual reference.

WHY THE LAWS CAME INTO EXISTENCE

Antitrust concepts in the Community as expressed in arts. 85 and 86 were admittedly at least partially influenced by the US Sherman Act, ss. 1 and 2 respectively, and the economic philosophy that the public is best served by the free play of competitive forces in an open market. This seems to echo the doctrine of laissez faire which is a European concept, not American; but the economic philosophy of both the Community and the US goes, as mentioned above, a step further in believing that free competition is not absolutely free and that competition must be allowed to develop unaffected by agreement between two or more entities or by monopoly of a market seized by one or more persons. Europe, as Europe, saw its first antitrust law in the European Coal and Steel Community Treaty of 1951. Subsequently individual European nations such as France, Germany, Holland, Denmark and Belgium enacted their own laws. It was not until the Treaty of Rome in 1957, however, that Europe created the antitrust laws with which the business community is most concerned. Europe has had considerably less experience with the use of antitrust law than the US, the Sherman Act having been enacted in 1890. One must not, however, make the error of giving too much weight to the US influence. It was not until about twenty years after the Sherman Act came into force that the first significant Supreme Court decision was made interpreting the Act. The first decision in Europe concerning art. 85

came only a few years after the Rome Treaty became effective and although the number of decisions by the European Commission and the European Court of Justice is not enormous, it has become plain that the development and interpretation of antitrust principles in the Community will take its own line. The American influence will probably always be felt and observed and borrowed upon, but not to the extent of causing the Commission of the Court of Justice to come to the same conclusions about what constitutes an unreasonable restraint of trade. In fact, as we shall see, one of the important differences between the US and the Community antitrust laws is that the question of the "reasonableness" of a restraint or of a restraint being illegal in itself (i.e. *per se*, irrespective of its actual effect on competition) does not arise in Community law. There are other fundamental differences that are worth noting in order to understand Community antitrust law.

Whilst Community antitrust law and its basic philosophy were generally patterned on US thinking, the law of the Community was certainly born from a totally different kind of parent. A principal purpose of the Treaty of Rome was to eliminate the national barriers which have divided Europe for centuries. These barriers were largely the natural barriers arising out of the natural right of sovereign nations to make laws governing their own domestic and foreign trade. Among these laws were those instituting import duties and tariffs on wide ranges of goods, and controlling the flow of capital and services from abroad. In the US, such barriers were largely eliminated at the creation of the US as a republic in the Federal Constitution. The Sherman Act is aimed at anticompetitive practices in the private sector. This chief concern of the Community was recognized in 1956, before the Rome Treaty was executed. In what has come to be referred to as the Spaak Report, the first problem mentioned to be solved in the Treaty of Rome in connection with economic competition was that of discrimination, meaning the problem of the effect on competition caused by discrimination by the member states according to nationality or country of residence. The Spaak Report then recited the necessity of establishing basic rules to prevent discrimination in the private sector because obviously the private sector would not be permitted to do what governments themselves were not permitted to do. In the US, the Sherman Act was aimed at anticompetitive practices in the private sector and there is no express provision governing the competitive behaviour of the US Government. On the other hand, art. 90 of the Rome Treaty brings the activities of the governments of the respective member states themselves under the umbrella of the antitrust provisions of the Treaty.

Another fundamental difference between the Community and the US antitrust laws is that the US antitrust laws expressly condemn those restraints of trade, monopolization or attempts to monopolize which affect either interstate commerce within the US or the foreign commerce of the US. The Treaty of Rome does not condemn restraints of external trade with the Community as such, but only effects on trade between the member states themselves. Indeed, arts. 85 and 86 do not use the word "restraint" of foreign commerce at all. All that is required to be a violation of Community antitrust law is that there be some kind of cooperative effort between two or more entities which affects trade between member states (apparently in any way) and which distorts competition within the Community. That is the substance of art. 85. It may be compared with s. 1 of the Sherman Act, with the important qualification that the Sherman Act requires that there be a *restraint* of trade whereas art. 85 becomes applicable even if there is only likely to be any kind of effect on trade and competition, albeit a good one. In this sense, art. 85 is broader in its application than the Sherman Act, s. 1, but it is more forgiving. Under certain conditions showing generally an actual benefit to the public the otherwise illegal act may be declared exempt from the sanctions for violating art. 85. There is no such forgiveness in the Sherman Act. If an act unreasonably restrains trade, there is no escape from punishment. One either does or does not infringe the Sherman Act.

In a comparison of the monopoly provisions of the two sets of laws, i.e. Sherman Act, s. 2 and art. 86 of the Rome Treaty, art. 86 makes no mention of foreign trade with any one or all of the member states of the Community, whereas s. 2 of the Sherman Act does mention the foreign commerce of the US. Article 86 does not condemn monopoly itself but only an abuse of the position of someone in a dominant position. In s. 2 of the Sherman Act, it is the act or attempt of monopolization itself which is condemned irrespective of the presence or absence of an abuse of the monopolistic position. In this sense the situations are reversed and the American Sherman Act, s. 2 is broader in its application than art. 86.

The value of understanding the relationship of Community and US antitrust laws

In view of these fundamental differences between the two great bodies of law one wonders the value in a comparative study of them. One would expect that attention to Community law alone would be sufficient to know about Community law. Trading in America and in Europe has broken through national boundaries and extended between the continents, thus bringing both sets of laws into play in the same transaction. There is the reasonable expectation that interpretation of one body of law will be somewhat influenced by the interpretation of the other. Representatives and observers from the US Antitrust Division are in Brussels and there is an exchange of information between them and members of the Competition Directorate of the Commission.

The value to Americans and Europeans of knowing something about each other's antitrust law is clearly practical. Moreover, especially to a European, it is not so much the factual situation and the result arrived at by a US court that is important but rather the reasoning that went into the decision, particularly the reasoning which would explain why a given set of facts did not amount to an illegal restraint. We say this because the competition required in

Europe is not nearly as stringent as that required in the US. Accordingly Community thinking may disagree with a US court finding a particular set of facts to be a restraint of trade, but there could be something useful in understanding why a US court holds that something is not a restraint of trade, in view of the more stringent view of competition in the US. The author feels therefore that an understanding of both the American and European thinking and, at this stage of development, the American experience in the field of antitrust in a western economy will be helpful, not only because of its practical application in expanding international trade but also in order to understand, by comparison, the separate development of the law and its application.

The core of judicial concern

In every case heard by a US federal court, or the EEC Commission or a national court of a member state of the Community, what is the court concerned with? The maintenance and furtherance of a market economy in which competitors may freely compete and into which new competitors may freely enter. It would be pointless to argue the rightness or wrongness or effectiveness of that principle or to criticize the way the courts have applied it. The decisions are to be understood, not attacked, and unless one clearly grasps the principle of free competition as understood by the courts nothing that follows will have any useful meaning as a guide for action. Countless ingenious schemes will be invented. Some will be examined by the courts and found to be illegal; others will be held not to violate the laws; still others will be found not to be subject to the antitrust laws at all and undoubtedly most schemes will not come to the attention of the courts at all.

Any scheme which is a deliberate attempt to wipe out or reduce competition, regardless of whether the means of doing so are in themselves legal and regardless of whether the effect is a benefit to the public, has an excellent chance of being struck down by the courts.

A summary of the judicial concern

The principle of free competition and condemnation of restraints which unreasonably affect competition was not born in the antitrust laws. It was known in the early English common law, typically in those instances when the buyer of a business required the seller not to enter into competition with him. Where such restrictions were unlimited as to time and place, they were illegal. They were illegal because they were *unreasonable*. They were unreasonable because they went beyond what could be considered to be fair to protect the buyer. It was not necessary for the buyer's protection to require the seller never to engage in competition with the business he had just sold, in the same country, or state, or province, or country, as the case may be. Much more will be said about "reasonableness". It is mentioned now only incidentally, the main point being that antitrust or the undesirability of restraining competition was not invented by the US or the Treaty of Rome.

In 1890 the US Congress felt that the freedom of people to compete with each other was important for the proper development of the country's economy. The abuses of free competition had been so flagrant that the principle had to be enshrined in law and the Sherman Act was enacted, followed by the Clayton Act and the Federal Trade Commission Act.[1] There are two other Acts, the Webb Export Trade Act and the Robinson-Patman Act, that are of interest but they are not as important as the others and will not be discussed here. As this book is a guide, only the most

---

1 The history of the laws is not important to the purpose of this book. There are many fine sources for it, e.g., *Federal Antitrust Laws*, S. Chesterfield Oppenheim and Glen E. Watson, published by West Publishing Company; and *The Attorney General's National Committee to Study the Antitrust Laws*, published in 1955 and available from the Superintendent of Documents, US Government Printing Office. For a fine study of European Community Competition Law, see *The Competition Law of the European Economic Community*. Arved Derringer, published by Commerce Clearing House in 1968, or the up-to-date *EEC Anti-trust Law*. Barounos. Hall and James. London. Butterworths, 1975.

important sections will be dealt with and of these, from the international point of view, the Sherman Act is the most pertinent. Articles 85 and 86 of the Treaty of Rome will be dealt with as they are the most important laws governing competition in the Community.

PERSONAL LIABILITY FOR VIOLATIONS

In the US

If an agreement or activity violates antitrust laws it is illegal and cannot be enforced. Damages arising because of the illegality may be awarded to the injured. A director or officer of any company doing business in or with the US finds himself in a territory mined with laws exposing him to personal liability for his and his company's acts apart, of course, from his company's liabilities for damages to both the government and the public. Some of these laws are the Securities Exchange Act which governs the ways and means of dealing in and offering corporate securities to the US public; various Federal and State pollution laws and the antitrust laws as embodied in the Sherman, Clayton and Robinson–Patman Acts. These are very weighty laws and the liability for infringing them is awesome. The number of actions lodged against directors and corporate officers has more than trebled in the last ten years. Foreign law is considerably weaker than American law in obtaining judgment against directors. The European may not be as sensitive or aware of such liability, but there are signs that Europe may develop in a similar way and lay a similar personal burden on directors and officers of European and American companies for reasons similar to those in the US, i.e. their company's violation of European law.

The imposition of such burdens on directors, even though acting in good faith, may seem irrational unless one understands the philosophy that has developed in the US concerning the social responsibility of companies and the function of the board of directors.

The function of the board in the US is fundamentally

different form its function in Europe. It is interesting that Common Market company law using the two-tier system expressly prohibits the Supervisory Board from intervening in the management of a company. The US is completely contrary.

The company is a creature of each individual state and state laws expressly charge the board of directors with the management of the company. These statutes often contain the explicit commandment: "the corporation shall be managed by a board of directors". It is unfortunate that these words have been literally interpreted, because if one accepts the management analysis that no more than ten people can be directly managed by one person, a company employing 100,000 people would require a board of 10,000. (Arthur Goldberg, former US Secretary of Labor, proposed a separate board very similar to the European Supervisory Board expressly to protect directors, but Roger Blough, an equally eminent man, questions the need or usefulness of such a separate board.) There has always been concern in the US with the placing of responsibility on someone when something "goes wrong". The illogic of holding a man liable for what he may not know or intend must yield to the overriding concern that the American social conscience will not permit use of the impersonal legal identity of the corporation as shelter against responsibility for injury to the public. Someone has to pay and it is not enough to charge only the company itself. The company does not run itself. The board of directors manages it. Therefore the director shall be personally responsible for the acts of the company. It does not matter whether the director is a representative or delegate of the shareowner, or whether his duty and allegiance is to the company in the shape of its employees. It is all the same for executive and non-executive (inside and outside) directors. They are individually and personally liable. But this is an American view under American law; what has it to do with a director of a foreign company or with his company itself resident outside of the US? It does not matter where he or his company is. His company's liability and his personal liability for his own and his company's acts in violation of US law follows everywhere and the US Supreme Court has not hesitated to apply the US antitrust laws to foreign companies and their directors. The more practical difficulty of foreign enforcement of US antitrust law is that of obtaining jurisdiction over the person of the director, but that is a procedural matter with which the book deals later in Chapter 19. The board meeting becomes an extremely sensitive event when one is aware of personal liability of directors. If the board approves a contract or act illegal under US law, even though unaware of the illegality, each director present can be held accountable.

The liability of the director is not absolute. The law does recognize that it depends on certain standards of conduct. The individual states enacted laws to reflect what is known generally as the "business judgment rule". It varies from state to state, but the intent was to set a standard so that a businessman would not be liable for using ordinary good business judgment. Of course, if the statutory standard is low, the director will have a wide scope of error in which to manage his company. The law of Pennsylvania is representative of other state laws setting the standard: "The Director shall exercise his duties with that diligence and care which ordinarily prudent men would exercise under similar circumstances in like positions". This has often been attacked as a very low standard for a director's behaviour if only because he should be something more than ordinarily prudent. There is in fact a trend to place a higher standard of conduct on executive directors than on non-executive directors. The federal antitrust laws are more explicit and forceful and no doubt the evolution of European Community company law will deal with the matter.

The antitrust statutes expressly allow criminal suits by the Federal Government and private civil actions which provide for treble damages to be awarded to a successful complainant who has been damaged by antitrust illegalities. Damages as high as $400,000,000 have resulted directly from an antitrust judgment. Criminal penalties against directors provide personal fines of up to $100,000 and imprisonment of up to three years. The corporation can be fined up to $1,000,000.

When interviewed,[2] US District Judge Charles B. Renfrew distinguished the degree of severity among various types of antitrust offences and advocated prison sentences as well as fines for directors guilty of "hard core" cases. He specifically described price-fixing as a "hard core" case and was firm in the view that directors must be punished for such wanton damage to the public.

The antitrust laws are uniquely perilous because their interpretation and application is subject to the changing view and needs of the market and the concentration of competition in a given market at a given time. By "concentration" is meant the number of competitors in a relevant market. A high concentration means few competitors. By "relevant market" is meant the kind of products in competition with each other. This is an over-simplified but workable definition of an important part of antitrust law—the battlefield where competitors tactics are judged.

Antitrust law requires careful crystal-ball gazing. There is no sure guide for right action and there is no "due diligence" standard needed. Good intentions mean nothing. The public good may be well served by the action of companies in competition with each other and agree to fix prices, but no evidence of a good effect is permitted to be introduced although such evidence may be used in the Common Market and may save an otherwise illegal and invalid agreement. The director has no defence to such an allegation. If he has agreed to fix prices or approved of price-fixing with a competitor, he is guilty. If his company has fixed prices with a competitor and he did not know about it but should have known about it, he is liable. The Supreme Court, however, established that a director is subject to criminal prosecution only if he knowingly participated in effecting the violation, whether or not he was acting in his representative capacity as director. The fea-

---

2 Bureau of National Affairs, *Antitrust and Trade Regulation Report*, 19 November, 1974, No. 689.

ture of "knowingly" participating is necessary for criminal liability, but it is not unknown for the courts to derive such knowledge from the facts.

Private civil actions for damages as high as treble the actual amount of damage against the corporation and its directors are also provided by law. These actions may be lodged by individuals, classes of persons such as shareholders, or by groups of individuals or companies injured by the illegal acts. In private suits, the complaining party is seeking the pot of gold of treble damages. Despite the personal liability of a director, the plaintiff knows that the director is unlikely to be able to pay the probably enormous sum of treble damages. Accordingly, the private complainant is not seriously seeking the director's head, but it is still not a pleasant experience to be named a defendant and have to endure the ordeal of public exposure for a wrong and to go through the drudgery of giving evidence.

In the Common Market

Neither the Common Market nor any of the individual member states has reached the degeee of sophistication of the US in holding directors and corporate officers personally liable for antitrust violations by the enterprises for whom they work; but the Commission has not been reluctant in fining companies for infringement of the competition statutes. In fact, Mr Albert Borschette, the Community's Commissioner in charge of antitrust admitted[3] after having been chastised by the European Court, that the Commission had been overly severe in imposing fines.

As the purpose of the imposition of fines is purely punishment for the violation, the Commission can levy them even for past activities which are no longer continuing. The Commission is not restricted to fining only enterprises domiciled within the Common Market. So long as an effect

---

3 *The Times*, 4 February, 1976.

on competition occurs between member states of the Common Market, the perpetration of the activity causing the effect can be anywhere. In this respect the extraterritorial reach of the competition law of the Common Market is similar to that of the US Sherman Act.

The Commission has the authority under art. 16 of reg. 17 to impose daily penalties on offending enterprises until they cease the offending activity. The US antitrust statutes expressly permit third parties to sue for damages resulting from violations of US antitrust laws. The Treaty of Rome does not contain any such express right of action by private individuals and enterprises to sue for damages resulting from violation of art. 85 or 86; however, under art. 3 of reg. 17, any individual may request the Commission to require the offending party to terminate the infringing practice. The right of individuals to sue for damage because of an illegal act under art. 85 or 86 arises from general legal principles permitting an injured party to obtain some remedy for damages resulting from the fact that an agreement or practice violating art. 85 or 86 is invalid. The civil and administrative results are therefore the fines and penalties already mentioned (imposed by the Commission) and damages for injury (imposed by the national courts of the member states).

Administrative protection against antitrust actions by private individuals

There is a rough parallel between procedures in the US and in the Community to help an offending party protect himself from attack by members of the public injured by his anticompetitive acts. Ordinarily in America if the government succeeds in obtaining a court judgment that an antitrust defendant is guilty of the offences charged, the path is substantially eased for an individual to sue and recover damages from the guilty party. Any individual injured by the defendant's adjudicated action can use the judgment obtained by the government as indisputable proof of the defendant's guilt. The plaintiff then needs only to prove his injury and amount of damage and that it was caused by the defendant's guilty actions.

It is a well-used tactic for a defendant, prior to the beginning of judicial proceedings against him by the government, to come to an arrangement with the government whereby, for one thing, he stops the offending activity. Many other conditions are normally demanded by the government, but the object of the exercise is to avoid a long and costly trial whose outcome may be uncertain. At the same time, the government is satisfied that the violation will not continue. The government and the defendant then present their settlement agreement to the court, because they must obtain the court's agreement or "consent" to dismiss the action. The court must be satisfied that justice is being done and it is not an automatic result that the court will consent. It could happen that the court feels the alleged offence to be so heinous that the defendant should be tried. The same is true for the government. The government certainly is not bound to settle the issue with the defendant. In blatant price-fixing cases rarely will the government agree to discontinue suit in favour of a settlement. The government will want the defendant tried and probably convicted and fined and possibly imprisoned.

It is a considerable advantage for the defendant to obtain a "consent decree" in cases where he is doubtful of mounting a winning defence. If the consent decree were not obtained and the defendant were found guilty, we repeat that the door would then be open for any private person, believing himself to have been injured by the acts of the defendant who had been tried in court, to sue the defendant privately and to rely on the judgment of the court in the government's case to prove the fact of antitrust violation.

If the defendant had obtained a consent decree, the same private person would have to produce all of the proofs of antitrust violation, as well as his injury and damage. A consent decree is not an admission of guilt which can be used by a private person as *ipso facto* proof that an antitrust violation has occurred. One finds frequent use of consent decrees.

In the Community there is no administrative procedure protecting an antitrust lawbreaker from being sued by a private person, but the well-known procedure of notification to obtain a declaration from the Commission either that the agreement does not violate the law or that it does violate the law but is exempt from penalty makes it difficult for a private litigant to prove a successful case for damages against the accused party. The European Court is the ultimate arbiter of whether an agreement or practice violates Community law. A private litigant cannot have a national court decide contrary to the European Court. If the European Court holds an agreement to be void, the result is a matter primarily between the parties but a third party can bring his own suit in a national court for damages, and he can use the European Court's decision to prove the violation which caused his damage. In the Community there is no equivalent of the US consent decree, but if the Commission grants a negative clearance a national court hearing a private action cannot reverse the Commission and find an antitrust violation.

In the Common Market the procedure of notifying a doubtful agreement to the Commission relieves the parties to the agreement only from fines and penalties by the Commission for the time prior to notification (if the agreement is notified after its entry into force). In any case, there would be no fines or penalties for the time following notification, until the Commission decides that the agreement does violate art. 85 and cannot be saved by the exemption in art. 85(3).

In the US, the consent decree, whilst not an admission of guilt, is neither a declaration that the agreement or practice in question does not violate the law. It is worth remembering that both in the Common Market and in the US, private persons always have the right to bring their own private legal actions against a party who they believe has violated antitrust law and have been damaged because of the violation. The consent decree in the US and the notification procedures in the Common Market simply regulate the disputed matter as between the accused party and the government authorities.

There is an important exception to this in the Community. Notification of an agreement to the Commission can mitigate the size of retroactive damages that may be awarded to a private person. An interesting effect of notification is that the agreement may not be held to be void until it is so declared by the Commission. As a result the damages flowing naturally because an agreement is void will be measured only from the time it has been declared void. On the other hand, if the agreement has not been notified and is later found to be void (by the Commission or the European Court of Justice or a national court), that agreement is deemed to be void from the moment the offending parts of the agreement became effective, i.e. normally from the date the agreement was signed by the parties. Consequently damages would be measured retroactively from the date of the agreement.

There has been some debate about whether the Commission should be notified of an agreement. The argument against notification is that its contents are made public. Even if the agreement is not notified one can always argue legality. The reasons for notification have already been given.

Having been introduced to the general purpose of the Antitrust Laws and to a practical need to understand them, one must become aware of the signs of an antitrust violation.

2

What to watch for in a Sherman Act violation

CONSPIRACY

The law protects the right of individuals to be free to compete, which is not the same thing as preserving a freely competitive market. What the business community might consider to be normal business practice could be considered by the courts to be abnormal because it restricts or inhibits competition. To this the businessman could quite logically reply, "Of course, it is in our interest to hold down competition. What's wrong with that? That is simply a business fact of life that every man who is in business for profit recognizes and knows quite well". So long as his objective is to return a profit to his shareholders, he will continue to seek ways to realize that profit and no one seriously doubts that profits are enhanced when competition is controlled.

On the other hand, no one seriously challenges the rightness of laws and judgments that prevent unjust ways of doing business. The difficulty arises when a business decision made in good faith and with good intentions is retroactively declared illegal for reasons invented by the court and unsuspected by the guilty party. In order to anticipate liability and guilt, one must have some idea of what constitutes a violation of the antitrust laws.

What are the parts of a business practice that qualify it as illegal under those laws?

Here is what the Sherman Act says constitutes a violation.

Section 1:

> "Every contract, combination in the form of trust or otherwise, or conspiracy, in restraint of trade or commerce among several States, or with foreign nations, is declared to be illegal . . .".

Section 2:

> "Every person who shall monopolize, or attempt to monopolize, or combine or conspire with any other person or persons, to monopolize any part of the trade or commerce among the several States, or with foreign nations, shall be deemed guilty . . .".

(Each section also provides for fines and imprisonment for violations. As mentioned earlier, individuals may be fined up to $100,000 and imprisoned for up to three years. Companies may be fined up to $1,000,000. The criminal sanctions are imposed by the Federal Government through the Department of Justice or the Federal Trade Commission itself. The public, however, can proceed against violators on an individual civil basis. Section 4 of the Clayton Act provides "Any person who shall be injured in his business or property by reasons of anything forbidden in the antitrust laws may sue therefore in any district court of the United States . . . and shall recover threefold the damages by him sustained, and the cost of the suit, including a reasonable attorney's fee".)

The characteristic essentials for every s. 1 violation are (1) a contract, combination or conspiracy, meaning that more than one entity must be involved; (2) a restraint, meaning the act itself that impedes or would impede competition; and (3) the restraint must affect or be likely to affect trade or commerce between two or more states of the US or between any part of the US and a foreign nation.

Of the three characteristics the one that is limited only by the imagination of man is the restraining act itself. All court cases are individual examples of such acts. As emphasized earlier, there is little value in simply collecting all of the examples. Moreover, having knowledge of the restraining acts themselves is meaningful only if the other two characteristics are present; otherwise there is no violation. For example, price-fixing is a restraining act but in itself it is not a violation because obviously a manufacturer can set the price at which he wants to sell his product (provided he has not set his price below cost for the specific purpose of driving out competition); but if the price of a product is fixed by agreement between the manufacturer and a competitor, it is a violation if the required effect on interstate trade is present.

The element, therefore, that is perhaps most important for the reader to understand at the outset is when it is that he is entering a collaboration with another. He will want to know at what point his liaison with others in the market creates the contract, combination or conspiracy that establishes the ground for a possible violation. Although the variety of restraining acts is almost infinite, one essential characteristic in every violation involving Sherman Act s.1 and part of s.2 is some form of cooperation or coordinated action between two or more parties.

There is no need to discuss what constitutes a "contract" because this has been well established by the laws of virtually every country. The contract can, of course, be found by a court whether it is oral or written. The presence of a combination or conspiracy is not always as clear. They assume many disguises.

Combination or conspiracy

The interesting feature of a combination or conspiracy is that an act may be legal when done by one person or by one company, but if it is done in combination with or in conspiracy with another entity it can become illegal.

Although the words "combination" and "conspiracy" are used in the Sherman Act, the distinctions between them are negligible. For the purpose of this book they can be considered to be equivalent.

The "conspiracy" differs from a contract in that, among other things, it does not require an exchange of promises or obligations between the conspirators. Joe Bloggs and John Jones, two furniture manufacturers, simply agree not to supply Harry Smith, a wholesaler. There is no contract between Bloggs and Jones and neither one can compel the other to boycott Smith, but there is a conspiracy between Bloggs and Jones.

The very word "conspiracy" connotes something illegal, hidden and difficult to prove. In fact it is seldom that the Federal authorities obtain clear direct proof of the existence of a conspiracy but this is a question of the burden of proof rather than the establishment of the fact of the conspiracy itself.

The courts have been able to infer from circumstantial facts the existence of a conspiracy. A typical symptom (but not proof) of a conspiracy is when one finds in the market that prices of competitors seem to approximate each other. It is true, of course, that in the course of normal competitive play in the market-place, one supplier's pricing of a particular product may influence a competitor, totally independently, to adjust his price accordingly. Such instances may arise naturally where there is a price leader in a market of a standardized product with only a few competitors. The problem of illegality arises when the competitors themselves "conspire", i.e. agree, to arrange approximation of their respective prices.

Apart from Community and American federal antitrust law, in every country that has even a semblance of an antitrust law price-fixing by competitors is condemned. It is, perhaps, the most sensitive of all violations and the courts will search carefully for any sign of agreement between competitors influencing or effecting a common pricing policy.

It is one thing for an officer or director of a company to conspire deliberately with a competitor to do something. It is another thing to discover in what sense a court will infer a conspiracy from facts that may not have been intended to violate antitrust law. This has been called "consciously parallel" behaviour of unrelated competitors and we will discuss it presently. First we will deal with the timely question of when a conspiracy exists within a corporate structure itself.

Conspiracy within a corporate group

The Attorney General's National Committee to Study the Antitrust Laws published in 1955 and updated in the later supplement published in 1968 and prepared by the Antitrust Law Section of the American Bar Association said the following:

> "In recent years two problems have emerged from the cases treating conspiracy under the Sherman Act. The first is the extent to which the conduct of corporations linked by common ties of ownership and control, or actions by fellow employees of the same corporation, can constitute a conspiracy. The second is the extent to which 'consciously parallel' behavior of two or more legally independent and separately controlled business enterprises is evidence that their action was the product of conspiracy".

Of the two problems recited by the Committee in 1955, the first would seem by far to be the one which has attracted the most attention and which is perhaps today the most important. The conduct of corporations linked by common ownership or control would be expected to come under intensive scrutiny of the antitrust laws since 1955 because of the growth of the multinational corporation. Certain events since 1955 caused the parent companies of great multinational companies to exercise closer control of their foreign subsidiaries. The improvements in communications and transportation made such control easier.

Mr Robinson stated the problem well in his address, part of which is quoted at the beginning of Chapter 1. The attention given to American companies by Central and South American governments after 1959, and the rise of the Third World countries and their increasing control of their natural resources and raw materials compelled multinational companies to coordinate the functions of the related members of the group.

The increasing interest of foreign governments in requiring establishment of local companies (as opposed to exporting raw materials and importing finished goods) also caused foreign parent corporations to create subsidiaries in those countries. In order to operate them efficiently for the profitability of the group the elements of control, cooperation and coordination had to be introduced.

This created fertile ground for antitrust violations because as multinationals proliferated it was not in their interest to compete with each other. It is not surprising that cases since 1955 involve the coordinated activities of parent and subsidiaries, and among the subsidiaries themselves *vis-à-vis* competitors. This was the framework and setting for the so-called "intra-enterprise conspiracy". Because of the timeliness of this particular aspect of conspiracy somewhat more than passing mention will be given to it. It will be appreciated that this chapter will not go into the legality or illegality of the particular acts of the company, but rather to a consideration of how an illegal conspiracy itself can be found within a corporate structure. As will be seen, the picture developing from court decisions must lead to a reassessment by corporations of their ways of doing business with their subsidiaries and affiliated companies abroad. In the course of discussion of "intra-enterprise" conspiracy, the reader will understand the concept of conspiracy itself, as it may apply to totally unrelated enterprises.

INTRA-ENTERPRISE CONSPIRACY

The US Attorney General's National Committee grouped under three headings the conspiratorial situations that could occur between parties who are not separated from each other both legally and economically, i.e. the "intraenterprise conspiracy":

(i) conspiracy solely between a corporation and its officers or between its officers acting on its behalf;

(ii) conspiracy solely between a parent corporation and its subsidiaries or between two or more such subsidiaries.

(iii) conspiracy solely between two or more corporations, the stock in each of which is owned by the same natural person or persons.

If this section is going to be helpful to the reader, it will be necessary to begin by understanding what is meant by a "conspiracy" in the sense of the law. The Oxford Dictionary defines it as an "act of conspiring (in good or bad sense) . . .". The word "conspire" is defined as being "to combine privily for unlawful purpose . . .". The key feature of a conspiracy is the mutual agreement of two or more individuals for a common purpose which is illegal or which has an illegal effect. The conspiracy notion can reach within a company and taint its officers and directors with liability, as mentioned in Chapter 1. In the instance of a company having done something illegal, all those who participated in the crime are guilty of criminal conspiracy.

Conspiracy is itself illegal; it is itself the crime, regardless that the act planned never occurs. The mere act of conspiring is illegal. How does this apply to normal business planning and discussion within a company? This is the first heading of the Attorney General's Committee's deliberations on intra-enterprise conspiracy.

Conspiracy solely between a corporation and its officers or between its officers acting on its behalf

Where a group of corporate officers acting within their capacity as corporate officers cause their company to act in restraint of trade they would not be held guilty of a conspiracy in restraint of trade although their company would be guilty of the illegality. The officers could be held to be personally liable; but that is not "conspiracy". Their personal liability arises because of the Agency principle, i.e. the officers are agents of the company and are therefore responsible for the company's acts. There cannot be a conspiracy solely between a corporation and its officers. In 1955 the Attorney General's National Committee itself admitted that "restraining trade is not illegal, but only contracting, combining and conspiring in restraint of trade" is illegal. The clear inference from this is what goes on strictly within the company as a plan to restrain trade, not involving the cooperation of any person or entity outside of the company, would not be an illegal conspiracy because the situation would lack the element of having at least two separate and independent entities "conspiring".

This has come to be called the "single trader" doctrine. It is a catch phrase which only recognizes the fact that it is impossible for any individual to conspire with himself, and that a corporation and its officers and directors are viewed as being a single entity. The practicality of this recognition is obvious. It would be unrealistic, if not impossible, for a company to carry on business if its own employees could not discuss with each other what it is that they wish to do, regardless of the legality or illegality of the plans. At this point we are considering only the fact of discussion and not the carrying through of the illegality. If the illegality is actually effected, then the corporation itself would be guilty and whether it would be under a charge of conspiracy is immaterial.

Since 1955 the intra-enterprise conspiracy interpretations by the courts have upheld the single trader insulation against liability for conspiracy, i.e. concerted action between the company and its officers or among officers acting on behalf of the company; or between affiliated companies; or between the corporation and divisions within the corporation. However, since 1955 the single trader doctrine has been attacked and the courts seem to be eager to find traces of extracorporate contacts in order to get round the "single trader" protective screen. The single trader doctrine has been upheld where the facts involved action only between the company itself and its officers or among the officers themselves acting on the corporation's behalf. No case has been decided which has found any restraint-of-trade guilt in those situations.

Conspiracy solely between a parent corporation and its subsidiaries or between two or more such subsidiaries

For the same reason, i.e. the necessity of permitting normal business procedures within the company and among its officers, no case has been found establishing the existence of any conspiracy where the activity has been simply and solely between a company and its subsidiary or even between the company and affiliated corporations, and the activity concerned only internal matters.

By a "subsidiary" in the American sense is meant a corporation limited by shares which is wholly or virtually completely owned by a parent, or a company with a majority of the voting capital shares owned by a parent and a minority of the voting capital shares held by non-competitors of the parent—held only for investment. Again, as with the relationship between a company and its employees, so is there a practical aspect to this immunity in dealings between the parent and its subsidiary or between affiliated corporations. In many cases, the normal relationship between a parent and its subsidiary is not so much an agreement between the two as control by the parent of the subsidiary's operation. The parent-subsidiary relationship is looked at as a single entity, although unlike the company-employee "single trader" structure, a parent and subsidiary can lose their "single trader" immunity and can be held to conspire with each other.

The courts have never been entirely happy having to recognize the single trader "one family" nature of parent and subsidiaries. Each is, in fact, a separate legal entity and should arguably be treated as a separate individual. On the other hand, the separate legal entity of a subsidiary has been seen as simply a legal fiction because of the legal ownership of the subsidiary by a parent. After all, it has been argued, legal ownership is at least the power to control and, having that power, the parent and the subsidiary cannot be considered really to be separate entities. This is the view that the courts have taken in granting single trader immunity from the conspiracy aspect of the antitrust laws.

As we shall see, the principle is being sniped at by the courts—and not only by the courts, but also by the US Department of Justice.

On 25 October, 1972, Wilbur L. Fugate, Chief of the Foreign Commerce Section of the Antitrust Division of the US Department of Justice, in a speech about multinational companies, gave his view of the Attorney General's Committee 1955 Report's conclusions relating to the relationship of parent and subsidiary companies. He said: "As a matter of caution, the Committee's conclusion as to the law, which I think is essentially correct today, should be only stated definitely as to *wholly owned* foreign subsidiaries, and as to any actions of the parent taken through corporate control and not by contractual arrangements" (our emphasis).

Earlier, on 22 February, 1971, in a letter to the General Counsel of the Federal Reserve System about the application of the intracorporate conspiracy doctrine, Richard W. McLaren, Chief of the Antitrust Division, said:

"The Department of Justice has adopted a policy of using the intra-enterprise conspiracy doctrine to challenge . . . practices engaged in by commonly-controlled firms only where the practice has a coercive or restrictive effect on outsiders. As a result we . . . do not expect to challenge internal arrangements within a corporate group as to prices or markets for the products or services of the corporation within the group; this is a traditional corporate management function".

Mr McLaren then footnotes this passage:

"The discussion assumes that the parent company holds a majority of the stock in each subsidiary involved in any such agreements".

Mr McLaren differs from Mr Fugate in that he requires only a majority shareholding by the parent company in order for the intracorporate enterprise doctrine to be effective against an allegation of conspiracy. Mr Fugate wants the parent to own all of the shares of the subsidiary.

Mr McLaren in addition requires a "coercive or restrictive effect on outsiders". The courts have held Mr McLaren's view; but Mr Fugate's view should not be easily dismissed. Note especially his observation about the nature of the cooperation between parent and subsidiary. He distinguishes between the actual control and dictation by a parent of the subsidiary's actions, and an express agreement between the parent and subsidiary. In the latter instance there would be, according to Mr Fugate, a conspiracy. Perhaps he speaks academically and that, in fact, a parent does not need the agreement of the subsidiary. Realistically, it is difficult to imagine a subsidiary disobeying the command of its parent, so Mr Fugate's precondition of an express agreement between parent and subsidiary before a conspiracy can occur is somewhat fanciful.

Intra-enterprise conspiracy in the Common Market

The problem of identity of parent and subsidiary was finally settled in the Common Market in 1971. It had been difficult to determine what constituted an "enterprise" in the Common Market within the meaning of art. 85. One can make a general analogy or parallel between the Sherman Act, s. 1 and art. 85 of the Treaty of Rome. The history of the development of art. 85 indicates clearly that the drafters were strongly influenced by the Sherman Act. Article 85 requires more than one enterprise in order to establish the agreement or the concerted action that would be a violation. After wrestling with the legal problem of a clear definition of what constitutes separate enterprises, and accordingly cutting through the fiction of two separate legal entities, both the Commission and the European Court of Justice have established that the test of whether two enterprises are really separate is largely decided by the degree of economic control one has over the other. Simply stated, it means that if a parent company actually controls the activity and decisions of its subsidiary, and the subsidiary does not enjoy economic independence from the parent then an agreement between the two cannot be said to be a conspiracy as their activity would be tantamount to a company conspiring with itself and this is not possible.[1] Although this is simple in the saying of it, it is quite another matter when the question of economic control has to be determined from the facts. As mentioned earlier, it is hard to imagine a subsidiary embarking on a course of business conduct independently of its parent's wishes.

US court decisions about conspiracy

The first important Supreme Court ruling cracking the protection afforded by the intracorporate shell formed from the interrelationship of legally separate but commonly owned companies was in 1947, *United States* v. *Yellow Cab Co.*, 332 U.S. 218. The court said:

> "The test of illegality under the Act is the presence or absence of an unreasonable restraint on interstate commerce. Such a restraint may result as readily from a conspiracy among those who are affiliated or integrate under common ownership as from a conspiracy among those who are otherwise independent. . . . The corporate inter-relationships of the conspirators in other words, are not determinative of the application of the Sherman Act".

So the court opened the attack on the "one entity" or "single trader" theory of parent-subsidiary relationships.

In 1951, the Supreme Court reinforced its Yellow Cab decision and in *Kiefer-Stewart* v. *Joseph E. Seagram & Sons*, 340 U.S. 211, it again dealt with a defence against a conspiracy charge by rejecting the argument that the defendants were protected under the single trader doctrine because the defendants were legally separate corporations having a common parent. The court ignored the legally separate identities and based its decision on the fact that the affiliated corporations held themselves out to be competitors with each other.

---

1 Case 22/71: *Beguelin* v. *G. L. Import and Export*, [1972] C.M.L.R. 81, European Court of Justice, 25 November, 1971.

It understandably became difficult for companies to decide what kind of structure would permit them to operate as a cohesive business group without encountering antitrust problems. This does not mean to suggest that corporate structures are decided on this basis. Of course they are not. The General Electric Company and Radio Corporation of America believed in a management philosophy of decentralization into autonomous divisions and subsidiaries each with its own profit and loss responsibility, not for antitrust considerations, but for business efficiency. Yet Sherman Act problems have arisen with such structures and the conspiracy notion seems naturally to have attached itself to those structures.

Although the court removed the protective coat of "common ownership" from affiliated but legally separate companies, it never held that a corporation and its divisions could conspire. Indeed, all of the reported cases held the other way, i.e. a corporation and its unincorporated division cannot be guilty of conspiring with each other, even though the division may itself have acted autonomously. This was established by the court in 1962 in *Poller* v. *Columbia Broadcasting Inc.*, 368 U.S. 464.

It might be suspected that some companies would have learned something from the net effect of the Keifer-Stewart and the Poller cases and simply converted existing subsidiaries into divisions. It might also be suspected that the courts would not be hoodwinked by the legal fiction of transformations of subsidiaries into divisions in order to avoid the antitrust laws. Both suspicions met in 1967 in *Hawaiian Oke and Liquors Ltd.* v. *Joseph E. Seagram & Sons*, 272 F. Supp. 915.

Joseph E. Seagram & Sons was one of those companies who felt they had learned something from the earlier 1951 Kiefer-Stewart decision in which itself was a party. Seagram distributed several famous brands of spirits, e.g. Calverts, through subsidiaries. Probably influenced by the Kiefer-Stewart decision. Seagram intentionally changed the legal structure of the subsidiaries to that of divisions in an apparent attempt to create a "single trader" situation.

Seagram relied on the Poller decision. The lower court, the District Court, would have none of that. It held the view that there was an unlawful conspiracy, despite the divisional structure of the conspirators, because each had held itself out as a separate entity doing business on its own with each having its own identity. Among the facts which influenced the court's decision were that each of the Seagram divisions had its own sales organisation and made its own decisions as to marketing and distribution and, in fact, acted entirely independently of the other divisions. Each of the divisions had its own distinctive name and product that had come to be associated in the public mind as competitive products. All in all, the evidence indicated economically and socially independent entities. The court therefore ignored the common ownership and the legally inseparate existence of the divisions. In other words, the court went to the substance of the relationship and not to the form.

The decision was reversed on appeal. It would seem that although the Supreme Court will not accept in itself the mere fact of common ownership of subsidiary companies as protection against a conspiracy charge, it will also not accept that unincorporated divisions of a company are not protected against a conspiracy charge.

The instruction seems clear that if a company wants to indulge in perhaps borderline anticompetitive planning, it might safely do it by dividing itself into operating divisions without separate legal identities. Despite the apparently clear holding of the Supreme Court, one cannot help suspecting that economic and competitive reality could well influence a later court to overrule this view and perhaps judge the issue whether a company and its parts are conspiring illegally more on the merits than on the form of the entities.

It may be prudent to note the words of Chief Judge Pence who was overruled by the Supreme Court in the *Hawaiian Oke* case. His words may yet more accurately forecast the development of conspiracy tests within corporate structures:

"No recorded opinions have dealt with an alleged horizontal conspiracy among the unincorporated divisions of a single corporation . . . whether a division is capable of conspiring depends upon the peculiar facts demonstrated . . . . Is each facet of the unincorporated division's operation in fact, for all purposes, controlled or directed from above, or is it endowed with separable, self-generated and moving power to act in the pertinent area of economic activity? . . . If the division operated independently in directing the relevant business activity, then it is a separate business entity under the antitrust laws. There is nothing sacrosanct about the unincorporated aspect of corporate divisions."

Apart from the *Hawaiian Oke* case the Supreme Court decisions since the *Yellow Cab* case have developed in a manner going beyond the plain structure of the corporate defendant to determine whether a conspiracy is established within the corporate formation. Whilst granting the point that a company must be allowed to make internal decisions without having to worry about being accused of illegality conspiring, the courts have been qualifying that immunity. The plain fact is that the law is loathe to let justice be decided by matters of form. If a company does something of substance which the court feels *should* be punished as an antitrust violation, the court will find a way to justify such a ruling. For example, the courts have introduced the qualification that the planning must concern only internal matters. Only these should be exempt from antitrust conspiracy violations because subsidiaries and divisions obviously cannot be required to compete with each other.

In their efforts to expose and invalidate otherwise illegal intracorporate activities, the courts have gone into what effect particular intracorporate activities have on extracorporate competition. Probably the most important case illustrating the principle of what kind of intracorporate acts would be dangerous is one of the great landmark Supreme Court cases, *United States* v. *Timken Roller Bearing Co.*, 341 U.S. 593 (1951). It is interesting that the Timken decision was made at about the same time as the *Kiefer-Stewart* v. *Seagram* decision. Both decisions were of extreme interest to the United States business community and, indeed, in the case of the Timken case, the international business community as well because Timken cast a very serious cloud over the business relationships between corporations and their foreign subsidiaries. For example, certainly the Timken decision raised the fear that a parent company in discussing prices or establishing prices or markets for and between its subsidiaries would be committing an unlawful act, at least in the form of a conspiracy in violation of s. 1. A closer look at the Timken case will illustrate the early warnings by the Supreme Court that intracorporate acts affecting competition with unrelated persons can be US antitrust violations.

U.S. v. *Timken Roller Bearing Co.*, 341 U.S. 593

The US brought a civil action against Timken Roller Bearing Co., an Ohio corporation (American Timken) charging that it conspired with British Timken Ltd. and Société Anonyme Française Timken to restrain interstate and foreign commerce by eliminating competition in the manufacture and sale of antifraction bearings in the world market.

In 1909 American Timken and the predecessor of British Timken Ltd. agreed to divide world markets. In 1927 an Englishman named Dewar along with American Timken bought all of British Timken's shares. British Timken's shares were then offered publicly. The result was that American Timken, at the time of trial, owned 30% of British Timken and Dewar owned 24%. In 1928 American Timken and Dewar established French Timken, all of the shares of the French company being owned by them. Thereafter, American Timken, British Timken and French Timken cooperated and coordinated their business activities so that each enjoyed certain geographic markets. Although each could sell into another's territory, the prices of those products were fixed by agreement among them. They also agreed to eliminate competition among themselves and with others and agreed to restrict imports and exports with the US.

Among the defences was that their actions were a necessary incident to a legally constituted joint venture; the joint venturers being American Timken and Dewar; the joint venture being their joint activities in each of the companies and, presumably, the actions of the companies among themselves. The court had little difficulty in dismissing this defence. The feature of the activity which seems to have tilted the scales against the defence of joint venturers was that the principal purpose of the restrictive agreements among the parties was not a necessary and reasonable ancillary act to the joint venture but rather simply for American Timken, British Timken and French Timken "to avoid all competition among themselves *or with others*" (our emphasis). There is an important observation to be made of the court's precise language. Later the court in the same decision made a small change in wording that is significant. The court said: "The fact that there is common ownership or control of the contracting corporations does not liberate them from the impact of the antitrust laws". (The court cited the *Kiefer-Stewart* v. *Seagram* decision mentioned above.) "Nor do we find any support in reason or authority for the proposition that agreements between legally separate persons and companies to suppress competition among themselves *and* others [our italics] can be justified by labeling the project a 'joint venture'. Perhaps every agreement and combination to restrain trade could be so labeled."

In the earlier instance the court said that the related companies conspired to avoid competition among themselves *or* with others. Later it said they conspired to suppress competition among themselves *and* others. The distinction is important because if the first wording is taken to define what related but separate companies can do, it would seem that related companies under common ownership would be compelled to compete with each other. That, of course, would place a substantial and probably impractical burden on parent and subsidiary companies. The court itself suggested later that the illegality was in the suppression of competition not only between the subsidiaries and parent themselves but the suppression of competition of third parties by agreement among the related companies. More accurately, the court indicated that the illegality arose because of agreement among the related companies to suppress competition among themselves *and* others.

This decision upset American companies because it implied that a US company with a foreign subsidiary could be accused of conspiracy if it used the subsidiary to divide markets with the parent. In the *Timken* case, Justice Jackson's dissenting opinion states the confusion well:

> "It is admitted that if Timken had, within its own corporate organization, set up separate departments to operate plants in France and Great Britain, as well as in the United States, that would not be a conspiracy; we must have two entities to have a conspiracy."

Thus, although a single American producer, of course, could not compete with itself either abroad or at home, and could determine prices and allot territories, that would not be a violation of the Act, because a corporation cannot conspire with itself. Thus, the court applied the well-established conspiracy doctrine that that which would not be illegal for Timken to do alone may be illegal as a conspiracy when done by two legally separate persons. Jackson went on:

> "The doctrine now applied to foreign commerce is that foreign subsidiaries organized by an American corporation are 'separate persons' and any arrangement between them and the parent corporation to do that which is legal for the parent alone is an unlawful conspiracy. I think that result places too much weight on labels.
>
> But if we apply the most strict conspiracy doctrine, we still have the question whether the arrangement is an unreasonable restraint of trade or a method and means of carrying on competition in trade. Timken did not sit down with competitors and divide an existing market between them. It has at all times in all places, had powerful rivals. It was not effectively meeting their competition in foreign markets, and so it joined others in creating a British subsidiary to go after business best reachable through such a concern and a French one to exploit

French markets. Of course, in doing so, *it allotted appropriate territory to each and none was to enter into competition with the other or with the* parent. Since many foreign governments prohibit or handicap American corporations from owning plants, entering into contracts, or engaging in business directly, this seemed the only practical way of waging competition in those areas. The philosophy of the government adopted by the court, is that Timken's conduct is conspiracy to restrain trade solely because the venture made use of subsidiaries. It is forbidden thus to deal with and utilize subsidiaries to exploit foreign territories, because 'parent and subsidiary corporations must accept the consequences of maintaining separate corporate entities' . . . . But not all agreements are conspiracies and not all restraints of trade are unlawful. In a world of tariffs, trade barriers, empires of domestic preferences . . . I think a rule that it is a restraint of trade to enter a foreign market through a separate subsidiary of limited scope is virtually to foreclose foreign commerce . . . . It is one thing for competitors or a parent and its subsidiaries to divide the US domestic market which is an economic and legal unit; it is another for an industry to recognize that foreign markets consist of many legal and economic units to go after each through separate means. I think this decision will restrain more trade than it will make free".

Justice Jackson raised some provocative points. Note that he did not say that Timken conspired against third parties. Presumably the agreement amongst them did relate to third parties; certainly it directly restricted imports and exports with the US. Jackson indicated that if they had all been US companies, a division of the domestic market might have been a violation, but Jackson suggests it was all right for the Timken companies to agree because it was the only way they could do business abroad.

The majority opinion written by Justice Black answered Justice Jackson's point that the arrangement was necessary to compete in the foreign market:

"We also reject the suggestion that the Sherman Act should not be enforced in this case because what the appellant has done is reasonable in view of current foreign trade conditions. The argument in this regard seems to be that tariffs, quota restrictions and the like are now such that the export and import of antifriction bearings can no longer be expected as a practical matter; that appellant cannot successfully sell its American-made goods abroad; and that the only way it can profit from business in England, France and other countries is through the ownership of stock in companies organized and manufacturing there. This position ignores the fact that the provisions in the Sherman Act against restraints of foreign trade are based on the assumption, and reflect the policy, that export and import trade in commodities is both possible and desirable. Those provisions of the Act are wholly inconsistent with appellant's argument that American business must be left free to participate in international cartels, that free foreign commerce in goods must be sacrificed in order to foster export of American dollars for investment in foreign factories which sell abroad. Acceptance of appellant's view would make the Sherman Act a dead letter insofar as it prohibits contracts and conspiracies in restraint of foreign trade. If such a drastic change is to be made in the statute, Congress is the one to do it".

It would be pointless to argue the merits of this decision. It was written in 1951 when the US economy was not threatened by foreign trade and when US investment abroad was still small relative to the avalanche of foreign investment that followed in the late 1950s and the 1960s. The decision does not adequately deal with the issue of intracorporate immunity from the law. The decision also ignores the fact, properly raised by Timken, that in many countries it was necessary, i.e. required by local law, for a foreigner to invest in the establishment of an enterprise in that country in order to obtain permission to do business there. Thus the establishment of subsidiaries can also be effected because of need to comply with law and not necessarily as a subterfuge to circumvent US antitrust laws. The words of the court in 1951 seemed to be echoed in the 1968 decision *Perma Life Mufflers* v. *International Parts Corpn.*, 392 U.S. 134: ". . . since the parties . . . availed themselves of the privilege of doing business through separate corporations, the fact of common ownership could not save them from any of the obligations that the law imposes on separate entities".

The difficulty with the *Timken* case as a guide is that it suggests it is something bordering on illegality to have subsidiaries abroad (the court suggests straightforward imports and exports are more desirable) and something still more illegal for subsidiaries and their parent to agree not to compete among themselves. The 1955 Attorney General's Committee strongly recommended that the *Timken* case should be taken to mean that intracorporate members could not conspire against third parties, i.e. non-members of the corporate family.

Both *Antitrust Law Developments* prepared and published by the American Bar Association and *Federal Antitrust Laws* by S. Chesterfield Oppenheim and Glen E. Watson state that the substance of the Supreme Court decisions in connection with the question of finding conspiracy within a corporate body is that the court will strike down "concerted action between a parent and subsidiary or between otherwise related corporations when the challenged conduct has a purpose or effect of unreasonably restraining the trade of unrelated competitors, customers, or suppliers". The Oppenheim book simply states that the court will strike down such action if the purpose or effect is "coercion or unreasonable restraint on the trade of strangers to those acting in concert".

Conspiracy when competition of third parties is restrained

It would seem that no action between parent and subsidiary or between sister companies which is aimed at defeating competition of third parties will escape the application of the Sherman Act.

The question whether a parent controls or does not control a subsidiary has no meaning if their concerted act is an unreasonable restraint of trade of third parties. This result must seem odd to a businessman because it makes it very difficult for a parent and subsidiary to plan competitive action against third party strangers. Inasmuch as it is part of normal business to compete with competitors and to defeat the competition, it would seem to be a strange interpretation to condemn a parent and subsidiary for conspiring to affect the trade of a competitor. The company, as a whole, would be a poor competitor indeed if its subsidiary parts did not cooperate to blunt the competition of that third party. The only explanation that makes sense of the enigma is, as stated before, the courts will not be impeded by "corporate structural form" from finding an antitrust violation.

What, for instance, would the view be if the parent and subsidiary did not hold themselves out as being autonomous (as in the Seagram cases involving subsidiaries as well as divisions)? Would the court still find illegality if the required restraint on third parties was established? If the answer is affirmative, then the validity of the "single trader" doctrine is in doubt because it would not be difficult to find that the actions of a parent and subsidiary affect unrelated competitors. If the court ignores the legal separation of the related companies, it is not a long step to ignoring the corporate "one-ness" in the composite parts of commonly owned divisions—if the effect or intent of their activities is to beat down the competition.

Presumably, if a company, e.g. a subsidiary, proceeds on its own to violate the law, there would be no "conspiracy" implicating the parent. Mr Fugate, in his October 1972 address, suggested the distinction that a wholly owned subsidiary acting under the corporate control of its parent should be entitled to "single trader" protection but not if it entered into contractual relations with the parent.

In a multinational world it is highly unlikely that subsidiaries will be permitted to act wholly independently of a central, controlling parent. The subsidiaries may have autonomous profit and loss responsibility, but it must be doubtful that their common owner would permit them to compete with each other, or act with respect to third parties in the market to the economic detriment of the whole interrelated structure. In the end the questions must narrow to precisely what kind of control it is that is being exercised by one party over the other, and what kind of restraint on unrelated competition resulted from that control.

Summary

Accordingly, the intracorporate or single trader insulation against an antitrust conspiracy charge is a creature under attack. The tests so far applied by the courts concern the actual legal inseparableness of the company and its parts, e.g. company and its divisions. In that case there cannot be a conspiracy. The courts will search for weakness in the single trader fortress as soon as the company group is composed of parent and subsidiary relationships, because the courts will grasp the fact of legally separate identities to construct the two entities necessary for conspiracy. Even then it will not yet be enough to establish conspiracy because the courts must recognize the business reality that a parent and subsidiary cannot be required to compete with each other (although Justices Black and Douglas in the *Timken* case came perilously close to saying just that, where the parent chooses to establish a foreign subsidiary instead of simply exporting abroad direct).

Then the Kiefer-Stewart and Timken cases introduced the illegality that subsidiaries and parent could not agree in such a way as to restrain third party competition. Since then the courts have searched the many arrangements within and between related companies for a flaw in the "bloodlines" that would annul their status as a single trader or intracorporate structure.

EXAMPLES OF INTRACORPORATE DOCTRINE

It is often difficult, moreover, to evaluate whether a proposed intracorporate act falls within the net of conspiracy. A lawful act could be used as part of an unlawful conspiracy. The characteristics to watch for are the intent and purpose of the proposed action in light of third parties. The practical problem of conspiracy can easily arise, e.g. in the structure of chain store operations, most typically, chain food stores.

As the individual stores are related to each other and normally are under common control, their coordinated activities will be sensitive to the conspiratorial aspect of the Sherman Act.

In a landmark case precisely on this point, *U.S. v. N.Y. Great A and P Tea Co., Inc.*, 137 F.2d 459, the government alleged that companies and subsidiaries connected with the chain had "instituted practices designed . . . to make the conspiracy effective". (Thus preparing the ground to establish the intended end result as the test of legality, and not merely the means used.) The court said that it made no difference what specific forms of action were used in the conspiracy and that all methods and forms, even though legal in themselves, became illegal because the intended end was illegal.

How have these tests been applied in respect of related companies and their liability for conspiracy under the Sherman Act? What is the prognosis for the continued viability of the intracorporate single trader doctrine?

Richard McLaren in 1971, then Chief of the US Antitrust Division, set the stage when he said that the Department of Justice would pursue only those situations in which "the commonly controlled firms have pooled their power in a manner which has adverse competitive effects in independent business entities". In this statement we see the difficulty, mentioned in the preface of this book, with general statements, however sincerely intended to be a useful guide for business practices. Mr McLaren does not use the word "unreasonable" to define the kind of coercive or restrictive effect that will create the illegal conspiracy. His wording is broad enough to cover the situation where a parent and subsidiaries could internally and properly agree to sell a product at a fixed low price to increase sales volume and make greater use of their respective production facilities, or simply to clear stock to make way for a new model product. Yet that coordinated action could very well have a coercive and restrictive effect on outside competition. Mr McLaren then seemed to cure that defect when he reaffirmed the policy established in 1955 by the Attorney General's National Committee to Study the Antitrust Laws:

"...concerted action between a parent and subsidiary or between subsidiaries which has for its purpose or effect coercion or *unreasonable* restraint [our italics] on the trade of strangers to those acting in concert is prohibited by section 1. Nothing in these opinions should be interpreted as justifying the conclusion that concerted action solely between a parent and subsidiary or subsidiaries, the purpose and effect of which is not coercive restraint of the trade of strangers to the corporate family, violates section 1. Where such concerted action restrains no trade and is designed to restrain no trade other than that of the parent and its subsidiaries, section 1 is not violated".

As a statement of policy those words are fine. As an instruction outlining the scope of permissible action of interrelated companies it is not and indeed cannot be satisfactory. A selective sampling of the views of the federal courts on particular facts might give some recognizable shape to what to expect as dangerous ground.

In one case a parent and subsidiary agreed a policy to limit use of their facilities. A third party who had been denied use of the facilities sued the parent and the subsidiary for conspiring against outsiders. One of the defences was that there could be no intracorporate conspiracy where the parent and the subsidiary were not in competition with each other (an unlikely event, in any case) or where the parent and the subsidiary were not in a buyer-seller relationship. These defences did not succeed. In fact, there had been earlier decisions denying such limitations in finding intracorporate conspiracy, so one cannot rely on the absence of an arm's-length relationship between the parent and subsidiary to avoid a conspiracy violation. In this particular case the court did not rule that there *had* been an intracorporate conspiracy, but simply that the defence presented did not persuade the court that there was no intracorporate conspiracy. In the same case the defendants said that there could not have been a conspiracy because the parent did not know that the subsidiary had refused to offer the facilities to plaintiff. This defence was struck down on the ground that although the parent might not have known of this particular instance, the parent and subsidiary had agreed a policy and the instance was simply a carrying-out of the policy: *TV Signal Co. of Aberdeen* v. *American Telephone and Telegram and Northwestern Bell Tel. Co.*

It is important to distinguish between a parent dictating to a subsidiary, e.g. what price to charge for resale by customers of the subsidiary, and an agreement between the parent and the subsidiary as to resale prices. It sometimes happens that a parent company may wish to terminate a distributorship with a third party in order to distribute through its own subsidiary. Thus a parent and its subsidiary distributor could be vulnerable to a charge that they conspired as to what price a purchaser from the subsidiary should resell products purchased from the subsidiary. The illegal act is the fixing of prices charged by the purchaser from the distributor. There would, of course, be no illegality for a parent and subsidiary to fix prices at which the subsidiary sold products obtained from the parent.

A further essential feature of the violation is that the accused must have "conspired". Apparently, if the parent and subsidiary simply discussed business problems and the parent alone decided what the subsidiary should do, there would be no conspiracy. It would then have been a normal decision made by a parent directing the operation of its subsidiary. Perhaps the subsidiary had disagreed with the parent's plan, but had to yield because it was directed to obey. In that event it would be arguable that there had been no conspiracy because the essential element of a common plan would not have been present. The plan would not have been "common" or agreed.

An example of a parent and subsidiary being guilty of conspiracy because of injury to a third party is given in *Suburban Car Rentals* v. *International Telephone and Telegraph, ITT Avis and Avis Rent-a-Car System* (1953). Avis Rent-a-Car was wholly owned by Avis Inc. (a holding company) which itself was wholly owned by ITT. Suburban was the exclusive licensee of Avis in the car rental business for a small part of Westchester County, a part of New York. Suburban wanted to extend its operation and sought another licence for an adjoining city of Westchester County but was refused by the licensor Avis on the ground that Avis itself wanted to operate there. Suburban sued, alleging conspiracy to exclude licensees from big urban areas in order to retain those areas for themselves. The interesting part of the defence of no conspiracy was that defendants were related and subsidiary companies, i.e. the intracorporate doctrine, and what they had agreed to do was no more or less than what an individual licensor could freely do. A licensor can unilaterally select and terminate a licensee and can refuse to licence. The court reiterated the principle that runs through all of antitrust: what may be legal when done by one person acting unilaterally may be illegal when done by two or more in agreement. The attempt to establish the licence refusal as the unilateral act of one person failed. The court ignored the intracorporate relationship and held that it could be an illegal conspiracy for parent and subsidiary to refuse to licence a third party. The implication of this decision is plain. It is dangerous for related companies to favour themselves by refusing to deal with a third party.

Another facet of the intracorporate conspiracy doctrine as applied to a franchising operation was struck in *Rea* v. *Ford Motor Co.* (CCH 75029). The pertinent facts are that Ford distributed its cars in three principal ways: by sales to independent dealers; by sales of its own company-owned dealers; and by sales to dealer-development stores (Ford would give the franchise to an independent person and finance the operation permitting the dealer to buy the entire investment out of profits). Less than 3% of Ford's sales were to its own dealer companies and dealer development companies. Nevertheless a complaint was filed that Ford was pursuing "a plan to operate its company-owned and dealer development stores in such a way as to impose an unreasonable restraint on interstate trade and for the purpose of driving independently owned Ford dealers out of the business of selling Ford automobiles". The evidence actually concentrated on the activities of Ford in a section of the city of Pittsburgh. The complaint was that Ford would operate its own dealers at a loss in order to divert sales of competitors cars to Ford. However, in the process of doing this Ford also diverted sales from its independent dealer franchises and would then take over the dealership itself. The court said "... automobile manufacturers are subject to the structures of the antitrust laws in the operation of their wholly owned outlets, and *where a violation of those laws causes injury to the business of a competitor*, they will be liable for damages". We have italicized the passage which seems to have the wrong end of the stick. The court seems to be presuming the violation of the antitrust laws and then actual injury to competitors. In all of the Supreme Court cases, the offence of conspiracy is the conspiracy itself. Either what is intended is itself wrong or what is intended is all right in itself but has an illegal result. The court in the Ford case would have been more accurate had it held that Ford's plan to operate at a loss was a violation *because* it caused injury. To put it another way: would Ford's action have been illegal if there had not been an injury to the independent dealer?

An obvious and sensitive question is whether a parent and its subsidiary might fix prices but avoid the antitrust evil of price-fixing by sheltering the act in the "single trader" or intracorporate doctrine. A very influential and experienced federal court, the US District Court for the Southern District of New York, had to deal with this question in February 1975 in *Barr and Levy* v. *WUI/TAS*.

Defendant was a telephone answering service with many subsidiaries throughout the country. It was accused of conspiring with its subsidiaries to fix the prices for their services. In fact they had agreed to increase their prices and two of their subscribers, Barr and Levy, sued them under the antitrust laws. The critical point of interest here is that illegality was alleged in the act of the parent and subsidiaries agreeing on what price the subsidiaries should charge for their telephone answering service. One would expect this to be a normal business practice so that subsidiaries would not act discordantly to the disadvantage of themselves and their parent. We caution the reader that the court has not yet ruled on the issue, the case having come before it for other reasons, but the court did say something worth noting: "It is well settled that a corporation may violate Section 1 of the Sherman Act by conspiring with its subsidiary corporations to fix prices". The court then referred to the *Kiefer-Stewart* v. *Seagram* case mentioned earlier in this section, but we think the court may have been slightly off the mark in that reference because the price-fixing aspect in Kiefer-Stewart is not analogous to what was done by the defendants here.

In Kiefer-Stewart, the subsidiaries and parent had agreed on fixing a maximum price at which wholesale purchasers of spirits from the subsidiaries might sell. The subsidiaries would refuse to sell to wholesalers who would not agree to the maximum price they should sell to customers. The Supreme Court struck this down as a conspiracy but it is not entirely clear what the particular evil was that established the conspiracy. One could suspect that the court considered the price-fixing aspect to be illegal because it was the fixing of a *resale* price and not the price at which the subsidiaries themselves sold to the wholesalers. The Attorney General's National Committee in 1955 said the price-fixing or market division between subsidiaries would not be a violation because it would serve no useful purpose to require subsidiaries to compete with each other. Moreover the court in Kiefer-Stewart had another clearer violation to rely upon, namely, the agreement among subsidiaries to refuse to sell to third parties. This is a violation in which the court could have found conspiracy without reference to the resale price-fixing. But we emphasize that the Supreme Court did not condemn all price-fixing between parent and subsidiary, as suggested by the Southern District Court in New York. It is probably still safe to assume that a parent and subsidiary can establish prices at which the subsidiaries may sell so long as the fixing of prices does not have the purpose or effect of unreasonably restraining the trade of third parties!

The issue of control by parent over subsidiary

In at least one case the parent company tried to break down the separate entity structure between itself and its subsidiary by alleging that it exerted such control over the subsidiary that the separate legal identity was fictitious and the reality was that they were one and the same enterprise. The subsidiary had been operating as a division of the parent although it was separately incorporated in Oregon. The parent was a Japanese company. The Japanese parent exerted great control over the activities of the US subsidiary. The president of the subsidiary who was a member of the board of the subsidiary was also a member of the Japanese parent board. The district court ignored the significance of control and held that notwithstanding the control, the parent and subsidiary could conspire. The court quoted the Supreme Court:

> "It is now settled law that if a corporation chooses to conduct parts of its business through subsidiary or affiliated corporations, and conspires with them to do something that independent entities cannot conspire to do . . . it is no defense that the corporations are in reality a single economic entity . . . common ownership and control does not liberate corporations from the impact of the antitrust laws".

When conspiracy can exist between a company and its officers

The presence of a member of the parent company on the board of its subsidiary is a common business practice and it can reopen the interesting question whether it is possible for a corporation to conspire with its own officers. The principle is that no conspiracy is possible because if such conspiratorial liability did exist, it would be virtually impossible for a company to make decisions freely, and the intracorporate immunity or "single trader" doctrine would evaporate. But there are situations in which a company and its officers can be guilty of antitrust conspiracy. The exception to the general rule may be generally stated to be that there can be conspiracy between a company and its officers or directors when the officer or director has an independent personal interest in having the corporation achieve its illegal objective. There have been at least two cases illustrating this exception to the general rule.

In *Greenville Publishing Co.* v. *Daily Reflector*, there was only one daily newspaper in the town of Greenville, North Carolina. Another unrelated publisher began to publish and distribute a shoppers' guide called the *Advocate*. The *Advocate* contained only advertisements. The daily news-paper began to publish its own advertisement paper, the *Reflector Shoppers' Guide* separately from the newspaper itself. However, the pricing policy used by the newspaper was alleged by the unrelated publisher of the *Advocate* to be an antitrust violation because it was intended to have the effect and did have the effect of driving the *Advocate* out of business thus leaving the newspaper with a monopoly in shoppers' guides. The part of the case of present interest was the allegation of a conspiracy between the newspaper company and its president, director and shareowner to adjust the pricing policy so as to force the *Advocate* out of business. The old question arose: was it possible for a company to conspire with its own officers? On appeal the court said that it was possible because the president had an independent interest in improving the profitability of the *Shoppers' Guide*. The president was affiliated personally with another weekly newspaper and he had an arrange-ment with it under which he received $5.00 for each page it printed and that if its advertising revenues reached a cer-tain amount he would receive in addition a percentage of the revenue. That other weekly newspaper with which he was affiliated sold advertising to Greenville merchants so the court reasoned that it would be to the president's benefit, personally, if the *Advocate* went out of business because his other newspaper would gain the advertise-ments which would have gone into the *Advocate*. That separate and independent interest was sufficient for the court to rule that the president could conspire with the *Reflector*, his own corporation.

The principle of "independent interest" used to establish a conspiracy between a company and one of its own officers can take strange forms with serious implications for those having interests such as management or controlling share interests in more than one company. An example or an analogous application of the principle occurred in Fort Wayne, Indiana.

The *Fort Wayne Journal-Gazetter* and the *Fort Wayne News-Sentinel* are separately owned and incorporated newspapers. Fort Wayne Newspapers, Inc. is a company acting as a business agency for the two newspapers. Fort Wayne Newspapers, Inc. is two-thirds owned by the News-Sentinel and one-third owned by the Journal-Gazetter. Fort Wayne Newspapers, Inc., on its own, decided to restrict the kind of advertising that would appear in the two newspapers for whom it acted as business agent. Advertisements for unrated or X-rated motion picture films would be restricted. One such motion picture exhibitor objected and sued all three corporations alleging conspiracy in restraint of trade; in particular, a conspiracy to exclude him from advertising in the two newspapers. The court could find no evidence that the companies conspired among themselves although it did say that conspiracy would not be precluded simply because of the interlocking ownership of Fort Wayne Newspapers by the two newspapers (a "single trader" situation). The court said further, "It is difficult to say that *any* action taken by Fort Wayne Newspapers is not done in concert with the other two corporations". The court's problem was to find *two* separate identities to establish the conspiracy.

The court found them, in a way that causes some concern. Miss Helene Foellinger was the majority owner and publisher of the *News-Sentinel*. She was also president of Fort Wayne Newspapers, Inc. In this dual-role, she functioned in different capacities for the different corporations. The court recognized the doctrine that a company cannot conspire with its own officers and it admitted that Miss Foellinger could not conspire with herself, but the court nevertheless did construct an argument establishing that she did manage to conspire with herself, in her dual roles. When she, as president of Fort Wayne Newspapers, Inc., was discussing with other Fort Wayne Newspapers, Inc. employees the new advertising policy to be used by the two newspapers she was, in fact, also a representative of the *News-Sentinel.* She could not, therefore, have been acting solely in her capacity as president of Fort Wayne Newspapers, Inc. and had to have been representing the *News-Sentinel* as well. There were the two separate entities combined in Miss Foellinger. As it happened, the court ruled against the motion picture exhibitor for other reasons, but the court's finding of the separate personalities necessary for conspiracy must cause some concern to those persons who are members of the board of more than one company.

The lower courts sometimes confuse the issue of when intracorporate entities can be liable for conspiracy with each other even though they may be separate legal entities, such as subsidiary corporations. An example of the confusion was seen in *Pacific Engineering and Production Co. v. Kerr–McGee Corp.* Kerr–McGee Corp owned all of the shares of Kerr–McGee Chemical Corporation. Pacific Engineering sued them for, among other things, conspiracy to obtain a monopoly. The essential to be proved was a joint agreement between parent and subsidiary to monopolize. It would have been entirely proper for parent and subsidiary to plan and control and coordinate their business activities. The evil enters when the planning, control and coordination is intended for or results in an illegal result, e.g. monopoly or monopolization.

The court took a slightly off-centre view of the conspiracy issue. It said:

> "... if there were any evidence to add to the facts presented, we would be justified in finding that an agreement existed between Kerr–McGee Corporation and Kerr–McGee Chemical Corporation whereby Kerr–McGee Corporation approved of or aided Kerr–McGee Chemical Corporation in its monopolistic activities".

The court is confusing conspiracy here. The test is not whether the parent approves or aids its subsidiary. If this were so then in practically all cases in which a subsidiary violates antitrust law the parent would be liable as a conspirator because it it highly unlikely that the parent would not know or approve the subsidiary's action. The test is whether the parent and the subsidiary mutually agreed. It may be, but it is not clear, that the court had in mind a situation like that of Miss Foellinger. Mr James J. Kelly was, at the time, executive vice-president and a director of Kerr–McGee Corporation and also president of Kerr–McGee Chemical Corporation. Could the court have felt that in this dual capacity he was conspiring with himself in the same way that Miss Foellinger did as representative for Fort Wayne Newspapers, Inc. and the *Fort Wayne News-Sentinel*?

Another aspect of the "independent interest" idea to establish conspiracy between an employee such as a corporate officer and his own company can be seen where one party might be considered to be an independent businessman. This kind of independent status for someone who would otherwise be a straightforward employee can occur, e.g., in petrol station operations where the station operator has an agreement with the oil company to operate the station. If he is an employee of the oil company he cannot be guilty of conspiring with the oil company to fix prices. On the other hand, if he is an independent businessman operating the station under franchise from the oil company, he and the company could be conspirators because they would then be separate, unrelated entities. The same reasoning applies to agencies. One must take care to establish the relationship properly. If the agent is an independent agency, conspiracy is possible. If the agent is really employed by the principal on a salary and commission basis, conspiracy is more difficult to establish. In this respect the degree of control becomes an important consideration, the more control exerted by the principal over the agent the less is his independence.

The matter of finding two persons to establish a conspiracy has, as we have seen, taken strange and ingenious convoluted thinking, e.g., the status of Miss Foellinger as president of Fort Wayne Newspapers, Inc., and majority shareholder of the Fort Wayne *News-Sentinel*. It will be remembered that Newspapers, Inc. decided to exclude certain advertising from the *News-Sentinel* and from the *Fort Wayne Journal-Gazetter*, two separate newspaper companies. The court held that when Miss Foellinger met other staff members of Newspapers, Inc. to make the exclusionary decision, she was at the same time wearing the hat of the separately incorporated *News-Sentinel* and, therefore, constituted the separate entities for the conspiracy. One might come to the opposite conclusion on the facts. In other words Miss Foellinger could just as well have been seen as the common owner of Newspapers, Inc. and the *News-Sentinel*, thus putting the relationship in the "single trader" or common ownership class, thereby taking the matter in the opposite direction from the court and absolving her of conspiracy because by virtue of her common ownership-type status, there would have been no separate persons and no conspiracy would have been possible.

Such a case did in fact occur in the District Court in California, *Knutson* v. *Daily Review, Inc.* (CCH 75273). This case also involved the newspaper business. The defendants were two separate corporations, The Daily Review, Inc. and the Bay Area Publishing Co., both California companies, each of which published several newspapers. The Daily Review wholly owned the Bay Area Publishing Co. These companies were sued by their distributors. The reasons for the suit are not important but one of the issues was whether the two companies conspired to restrain trade unreasonably.

Floyd Sparks was the controlling shareholder of the *Daily Review*, its president as well as the president of the Bay Area Publishing Co. Sparks decided to change his distribution system for all newspapers published by companies owned or controlled by him. His distributors objected to the change and this led to the law suit. It was his sole decision so on the face of it there was not the prerequisite two or more persons necessary for a conspiracy; however, both the *Daily Review* and the Bay Area Publishing Company notified their respective dealers of the changes, and the allegation was that these two companies conspired to restrain the plaintiffs. The two companies replied that there could be no combination or conspiracy between them because the decisions were made by only Mr Sparks, the common president and controlling owner of the two companies. The court agreed with defendants. The plaintiffs tried to argue that when the common owner of more than one corporation makes the same decision at the same time for each of the corporations, that act establishes the required conspiracy. In support of this, the defendants cited the *Yellow Cab* and *Seagram* cases mentioned above. The court took the view that those cases disclosed only that common ownership could not be relied on as a shield from the application of the antitrust laws, precisely the opposite contention from the proposition by the plaintiff that those cases support the view that common ownership alone establishes the existence of the conspiracy. The court seemed to think that if Mr Sparks had discussed and decided the objectionable course of action with other corporate officers or agents, there would have been a conspiracy. The court was not clear as to whether the officers or agents would have to be from each of the companies. It would seem that this case comes to the opposite result from the Fort Wayne and Miss Foellinger case. The decisive and distinguishing feature may have been that Miss Foellinger discussed the policy change with other employees whereas Mr Sparks did not.

Conspiracy among companies formed into associations

In the forming of associations among competitors to facilitate a reasonable and efficient development of a market, several hybrid structures have been invented. When these associations or groups of competitors are charged with conspiracy (usually to fix prices, divide markets or regulate customers), a favourite defence is that they are joined within a single unit or are somehow related as an intracorporate structure. If this defence succeeds, that is the end of the matter and it becomes irrelevant whether there has been or intended an unreasonable restraint as among

themselves, but it is doubtful if the association would escape
the law if their intent is against third party competition.

Metro MLS, Inc. was a company organized in the state of
Virginia. All of its shareowners were real estate brokers,
each being separately established as a broker in the business
of selling, leasing and managing property in the state of
Virginia. Within Metro MLS, Inc. the members exchanged
information about properties for sale. They called this a
"multiple listing service". The US accused the members of
conspiracy to fix and maintain fees for the sale of land, to
restrict membership in Metro and to restrain competition.
They defended that a corporation cannot be accused of
conspiracy with its own officers and shareowners when they
act for the corporation and not for their own individual
purposes. Note the attempt to thwart the allegation of the
brokers individually, having an "independent business
interest".

The court rejected the defence and held that the real
estate brokers could not escape the conspiracy charge by
forming a corporation. The court indicated, however, that
the incorporation would have succeeded in the defence if
the officers and agents had maintained no separate business
identity from the corporation. The test would seem to be: is
the organization an aggregation of different businesses? If
it is, then the defence of "single trader" would probably fail.
Note the absence of common ownership of the different
members.

Summary

In s. 1 of the Sherman Act the conspiracy must be to restrain
trade unreasonably. In s. 2 of the same Act the conspiracy
must be to monopolize. These are two separate offences but
the test for the existence of the conspiracy itself is the same.
In our multinational corporation world where companies
operate through subsidiaries in different countries, it is
obviously important to understand when a parent and its
subsidiaries or the subsidiaries themselves may make decisions without the threat of a Sherman Act conspiracy viola-

tion. In less than a multinational enterprise, the problem and the worry is the same, i.e. when will business plans and decisions among officers of a company, its divisions and subsidiaries suddenly become illegal conspiracies? When are there two separate entities involved in a plan, thus creating the first ingredient for a conspiracy violation itself—the actors on the stage?

In addition to the presence of two or more persons or business enterprises there must be a common plan or scheme between them. This must be distinguished from the command by a parent to its subsidiary to do something. In such instances of straight-forward control and instruction by the parent, the question would be a matter of parent liability, along with the subsidiary, for the subsidiary's illegal action on the master-servant theory of liability. In a conspiracy it is not necessary that the plan or decision be acted upon or, even if carried out, that it be successful. The evil is the conspiracy itself. A conspiracy has another uncomfortable attribute. Once the conspiracy has been established, every conspirator becomes liable for the acts of his co-conspirators in the carrying out of the conspiracy. Members of trade associations and consortia in joint or common undertakings might take note of this point.

It has been established that a corporation cannot be guilty of conspiring with its own officers but this needs to be looked at more closely. We have seen instances where conspiracy has been found within a company when, e.g., the board of directors includes people having a business identity separate from that of the company of which they are a board member. Accordingly even within a company one must examine the extracurricular interests of the personnel concerned with decisions and planning of the company. It was thought that a company acting through agents could not be accused of conspiring with its own agent, but even this arrangement must be judged cautiously. If the agent has some vestige of independence, he could be considered to have a sufficiently separate business identity to take the matter out from under the protection of the single trader concept. Although subsidiaries and parent are not required to compete with each other, the danger area is entered when the related companies agree on joint action with respect to unrelated third parties. The question arises whether parties who have agreed on a joint plan of action in a common business scheme can be guilty of conspiracy to violate the laws when they had no intent to violate them. The answer is that liability does not depend only on whether the intent or purpose was to violate the laws but also on whether the intent or purpose would have the effect of violating the law.

Conspiracy under s. 2 of the Sherman Act is concerned with monopoly and monopolization. In its broadest meaning, monopoly differs from the restraint of trade in s. 1 in that it is possible to have a restraint of trade which falls short of monopoly. Monopoly and monopolization mean power to affect competition within a certain business market area. Section 2 conspiracy requires that at least one member of the conspiracy has the power to exclude actual or potential competition in the market relevant to the activity of the conspiracy. Monopoly and monopoly power as an antitrust offence is discussed below. We mention it here only in relation to the discussion of conspiracy. In all other respects, the test for the existence of a conspiracy is the same for both ss. 1 and 2 Sherman Act violations.

Having introduced the element of combination or conspiracy as a building block for antitrust violations, we must now deal with the problem of how the courts find indirect evidence of a conspiracy. As business practices become more sophisticated, the availability of direct, clear evidence of conspiracy becomes less frequent. A popular symptom of an underlying conspiracy is consciously parallel behaviour of competitors.

Conscious parallelism

The authorities and the courts have learned to diagnose conspiracy from certain symptoms in business behaviour. When the quality and number of such items of circumstantial evidence gain sufficient weight, the courts have declared the existence of a conspiracy. "Conscious parallelism" is the term given to the similar business patterns of the different entities suspected of conspiring. There may have been, e.g., a certain sameness in their pricing and attitudes towards suppliers and customers which would support the claim that they were acting so consciously in parallel that it could have occurred as a result of conspiracy. "Conscious parallelism", therefore, is not illegal in itself but it is evidence of the underlying violation, conspiracy.

It is not an illegal conspiracy or, indeed, a conspiracy at all simply because independent traders in competition arrive at the same decisions. This often happens in a standardized market with an oligopolistic structure. Economic facts can provide economic justification of common action without this amounting to a conspiracy. In the problem of finding evidence of a conspiracy, there must first be a conspiracy. If there is no conspiracy, the mere presence of indicia that seem to point to conspiracy is not enough. Appreciating the problem, the Attorney General's National Committee in 1955, after surveying the facts of business practices, proposed the following questions as a test for conspiracy:

"How pervasive is the uniformity? (of action by the competitors)

Does it extend to price alone or to all other terms and conditions of sale?

How nearly identical is the uniformity?

How long has the uniformity continued?

What is the time lag, if any, between a change by one competitor and that of the other or others?

Is the product involved homogeneous or differentiated?

In the case of price uniformity, have the defendants raised as well as lowered prices in parallel fashion?

Can the conduct, no matter how uniform, be adequately explained by independent business justification?

Upon the answers to questions like these depends the weight to be accorded parallel action in any given case".

In order to evaluate a company's risk of being held to be a conspirator, one should obviously be prudent in communications with competitors, particularly the activities within one's own trade association. Maintaining an independent approach to business decisions is clearly help-ful; interdependent activity is harmful. The area most found to be sensitive to this kind of informal, unspoken but implicit mutuality of agreement among competitors is pric-ing. A dangerous event is when competitors meet and after a discussion about prices (rises or falls) they pursue a common pricing policy. That is reasonably suspect as being more than the natural result of price leadership. It is all right for competitors to experience similar business prob-lems and to solve them in a like fashion. This can be and often is a phenomenon of business in a competitive indus-try. The point is that the competitors should not mutually agree on the common course of action. That is conspiracy.

Is there a European equivalent of the American conspi-racy violation?

What to watch for in a violation of art. 85

Here is what art. 85 of the Rome Treaty says is an illegal anticompetitive act in the EEC:

> "1. The following shall be prohibited as incompatible with the common market: all agreements between undertakings, decisions by associations of undertakings and concerted practices which may affect trade between Member States and which have as their objective or effect the prevention, restriction or distortion of competition within the common market . . .".

One senses the overtones of the Sherman Act. Similar elements are required to establish the violation. For exam-ple, more than one person in agreement with another is an essential building block for a violation. An effect on inter-state trade and competition is another. There is no difficulty in understanding the operation of both bodies of law in respect of the necessity of a "contract" (in the Sherman Act) and an "agreement" (in Europe). Both in the US and in Europe, the legal concept of a contract is very similar. Furthermore, as a practical matter, there should be no quibbling about what one means by an "agreement". An agreement is wider in scope than the legally more technical requirements for the existence of a contract. Nevertheless one understands by an agreement something which, quite simply, has been agreed by two or more parties.

Difficulty is met when one tries to find in art. 85 an equivalent to the "conspiracy" mentioned in the Sherman Act. Can it be latent in the "concerted practices" recited in art. 85?

The question is not put as an academic exercise. The answer is important in trading because if a trader does not have an agreement that is in restraint of trade, it may not be possible for him to be doing something illegal under a principle analogous to the American conspiracy doctrine because a conspiracy is nonetheless an "agreement". Under the American conspiracy doctrine, an agreement among the conspirators must exist, albeit not necessarily a contract. One cannot have a conspiracy without agreement among the conspirators. It is not so clear that the same is true in Europe and, as we shall see, the European Court of Justice and the Commission and, indeed, even the Advocate-General are not certain as to the liability of parties once their activity is outside the scope of an agreement. We repeat: in the absence of an agreement there can be no conspiracy in America and, in fact, no violation of s. 1 of the Sherman Act.

There is a strong suspicion in Europe that a violation of art. 85 can occur without an "agreement" among the offenders and that art. 85 therefore casts a far wider net than does the Sherman Act. In America, the conspiracy itself can be the offence, even in the absence of an overt act to carry through the intended practice. It is not certain that the same would be true in Europe.

For example, in America a group of dress manufacturers might secretly agree not to sell their dresses to certain wholesalers or to sell them only at a certain price. Their agreement might not require the exchange of obligations and assurances that they will do what they agreed to do. They might not even carry through their agreed action. Nevertheless, they would be guilty of "conspiracy".

Europe seems to look at the matter differently. For one thing, art. 85 expressly uses two different expressions, "agreements" and "concerted practices". If "concerted practices" required an agreement among the practitioners, why include the expression "concerted practices" at all? The concerted practice would have been covered by the umbrella of "agreements". It must, then, mean something else, and to that extent it is not like the American conspiracy.

We think that there is uncertainty at the moment in Europe as to what constitutes an art. 85 violation in the absence of an agreement among the parties; but we also think that there is a hybrid developing from the dialogue between the Commission and the Court that will emerge as a requirement for quasi-agreement (where there is none) in order to create a "concerted practices" violation. We appreciate that such a statement is unhelpful because it does not indicate what a "quasi-agreement" is.

Perhaps a tour of some of the European court cases will clarify what we cannot make clear in a simple declaratory sentence. There are actually only two important cases that have dealt with the problem of identifying and distinguishing "concerted practices" from "agreements". We must first dismiss from the European scene a couple of American characteristics relating to the necessity of having at least two separate entities to have a violation.

So far there is no European equivalent to the American "intracorporate conspiracy". Generally speaking, the test for establishing whether there are two separate enterprises or a unity of enterprises in Europe has been satisfactorily settled. As spelled out in the Beguelin case (case 22/71: *Beguelin* v. *G. L. Import and Export*, 25 November, 1971), when a parent and subsidiary are legally separate companies, but the subsidiary is not, in fact, economically independent of the parent, the two companies are considered to be one enterprise. Accordingly, they cannot be guilty of a "concerted practice". Moreover, Europe has not yet adopted the American view of finding liability of corporate directors and officers for an illegal "concerted practice" by their company.

There still remains the question of when companies are considered to be engaged in a concerted practice. In what follows, try to be aware of signs of a conscious agreement among the parties. If that exists there is not really a concerted practice. The matter would be covered by the "agreements" mentioned in art. 85 so the Court need not look further for a "concerted practice".

The Court of Justice set the theme on 24 July, 1969 in *Re Cartel in Aniline Dyes*, [1969] C.M.L.R.D. 23 when it said:

> "If Article 85 distinguishes the concept of 'concerted practice' from that of 'agreements' . . . this is done with the object of bringing under the prohibitions of this Article a form of coordination between enterprises which, without going so far as to amount to an agreement properly so called, knowingly substitutes a practical co-operation between them for the risks of competition.
>
> By its very nature, the concerted practice does not combine all the elements of agreement, but may, inter alia, result from a co-ordination which becomes apparent from the behavior of the participants".

So it was in 1969 that the Court began its struggle with "concerted practices", particularly in trying to establish that it is something other than an agreement among the accused parties. Yet the Court *had* to base liability on some kind of mutual knowledge and assent because fairness demands that one cannot be guilty of a concerted practice with another if there had not been some form of consent or agreement, tacit or otherwise. The cases consistently wriggled on the horns of that special dilemma.

In a decision dated 2 January, 1973, *Re European Sugar Cartel*, [1973] C.M.L.R.D. 65 the Commission attacked the main producers of sugar in the Community, alleging that sharing of their respective markets and importing only through sales organisations under their control were illegal concerted practices, although there was no "agreement" in the usual sense.

The Commission endorsed the Aniline Dyes and Sugar Cartel decisions in its Third Report on Competition Policy, 1974. Whilst identifying an illegal concerted practice, it asserted that the "sales of products by undertakings which are normally competitors can lose their competitive effect when they are carried out on the basis of the co-ordination and, in particular, if the distribution of products from various sources is carried out by a joint organisation".

It can be expected that in due course the Commission will uncover many instances of concerted practices because traditionally in Europe competitors do not reduce their understandings and agreements to direct formal documents. In the absence of direct evidence, the Commission and the Court will have to infer illegal agreements and concerted practices from factual behaviour.

The Commission intervened on such a basis in the potassium salt business. This was a Commission decision on 11 May, 1973 in the matter of *Re agreement of Kali and Salz A.G. and Kali Chemie A.G.*, [1974] 1 C.M.L.R. D1, a German company, which became a monopoly seller of potassium salts which were mined in France. Kali and Salz acted as the agency for the largest producers of potassium salt in the Community. This fact caught the interest of the Commission who then pondered the effects of that kind of monopoly on the market. The Commission found that there was joint agreement on the quantities and the quality of potassium salts to be exported by each of the companies. The Commission also found circumstantial evidence sufficient to convince them that there was coordination of the deliveries and distribution of these products.

The particular evidence was the fact that there were joint distributors in Holland and in Italy for the producers, the necessary conclusion from this fact being that there had to be an agreement not to compete in those markets. As a result there was coordination of the prices and sales terms in Holland and in Italy. The oral agreement was between the French company S.C.P.A. and Kali and Salz. The French company had appointed a subsidiary of Kali and Salz to represent it in Germany and the Commission felt that this was obviously a concerted practice between the two undertakings because it was unlikely that a subsidiary would apply a sales policy in conflict with the interests of its group's trading policy.

Note the Commission's reliance on "co-ordination" of the competitors' activity and its influence of the existence of an agreement from circumstantial evidence. Despite attempts to deny the need of an agreement to support a concerted action case, the Commission felt compelled to speak in terms of an agreement being present.

Earlier in 1972 the Commission had looked into the activities of the two German potassium salt producers, Kali and Salz and also Kali-Chemie. In that instance, there was direct evidence in the form of agreements between the two companies which, although not contracts in the American sense, were nevertheless written agreements indicating a common course of action which was illegal.

In the course of developing criteria to identify a "concerted practice" separately from an "agreement", the Commission and the Court borrowed the "conscious parallelism" features from the US. But the Europeans gave it more subtle meaning and sophisticated usage. By way of introducing this difficult topic we will first illustrate the way the Commission and the Court dealt with price-fixing by trade associations.

In Case 8/72: *Vereeniging von Cementhandelaren v. E. C. Commission,* [1973] C.M.L.R.7, a totally Dutch association of cement dealers recommended prices at which its members should sell certain quantities of cement. There was no agreement about following these prices and the members were not bound by the recommendations. There were no restrictions on imports or exports. Nevertheless, the Commission and the Court agreed this was an illegal concerted practice because simply by recommending prices the association members were made capable of adjusting prices uniformly.

Apparently the Commission and the Court have little difficulty in finding concerted practices to fix prices where businessmen form themselves into national trade associations. This was seen also in Case 71/74: *Frubo v. E. C. Commission*, [1975] 1 C.M.L.R. 647, where fruit and vegetable merchants formed an association providing that all fruit and vegetables had to be bought by their members at auction. Although there was no agreement on fixing prices, this was condemned as a concerted practice having a price-fixing effect.

Possibly the most dramatically explicit example of the confusion about what constitutes a concerted practice is seen in Case 48/69: *Imperial Chemical Industries, Ltd.* v. *E.C. Commission*, [1972] C.M.L.R. 557.

The Commission and the Court had to deal with unclear alleged concerted practices by dyestuff manufacturers in the UK and throughout Europe. There was no obvious association or express recommendation of prices such as in the two Dutch cases; however, the pricing by the manufacturers on three separate occasions seemed to follow a uniform pattern. The major issue was whether there had been a concerted practice in pricing by the manufacturers. Both the Commission and the Court dismissed the US precedents on evidence of a conspiracy and "conscious parallelism". In the US there must be evidence of an intent with concerted action and a common design among competitors. The Commission referred vaguely to a "shared intent" regardless of whether it resulted in action by other parties.

The Commission stated flatly that the mere exchanging of pricing information is sufficient to amount to a concerted practice by competitors to fix prices because it consciously eliminates "the risk of not knowing their future market behaviour . . . and in doing so co-ordinate their conduct. . . . The dyestuffs manufacturers followed a uniform course of conduct in their pricing. On that basis alone it sufficiently proved the existence of concerted practices . . .". The Commission apparently believed that any prior consultation, regardless of the absence of a common design or intent by all of the parties is sufficient to be a concerted practice fixing prices if only because it "eliminates the risk of not knowing their future market behaviour" and permits coordinated conduct. Again there is the uncertainty as to whether the Commission, if only subconsciously, was gripped by the need to find some sign of mutual assent. How can their action be "co-ordinated" in the absence of assent? Perhaps one can give assent without this amounting to an agreement?

The Court was equally unclear but not so sweeping. The court was unwilling to accept the Commission's extreme view and although it agreed with the Commission, it did so on grounds closely resembling those for the US "conspiracy". The Court, unlike the Commission, inferred from the "consciously parallel" behaviour in pricing that there *was* an intent and a common design to fix prices. This is quite different from the Commission's opinion. Yet, the Court also followed the Commission's thrust that by announcing prices, the manufacturers eliminated the risk of not knowing about future conduct.

The Court was clearly confused by the Commission's absolute condemnation based almost solely on the ground that the manufacturers announced their prices and were thereby able to adopt a uniform pricing policy. Such a view would eliminate the need to have people acting "in concert" since all that would be needed would be separate and individual pricing activity that was nevertheless similar or uniform. The court accepted this and yet muddied the principle by suggesting there had to be a concerted act by the manufacturers. The court said, "that they did not act otherwise *than in* concert is corroborated"; and later "it is hard to imagine that such parallel conduct . . . could come about without some *prior arrangement*"; and still later "the only explanation . . . is that the enterprises *had the same intention*, i.e. to improve the price level . . ." (our italics). The Court also required that an actual effect on competition should result.

The Advocate-General very nearly adopted the US view and advised the Court that parallel conduct was insufficient in itself to establish a concerted practice; that there had to be an intent of the parties to act together and there had to be a causal connection between the common intent of the ies and their conduct. Moreover, and very significantly, the Advocate-General said that there need not be an actual effect on competition and that the offence would occur if the parties only attempted to establish uniform pricing.

We think that this particular area of "concerted practices" of Common Market law is still confused and unsettled, but we suspect that the view of the Advocate-General will eventually be the standard for determining a concerted practice.

The need for an effect on trade

Article 85 requires that there be either an effect on trade between member states or an activity which is likely to affect trade between the member states. In other words, if the activity, i.e. the concerted practice, has not been put into practice at all it would be impossible for trade to be affected between member states. Accordingly the simple plotting or scheming by competitors to do something illegal would not be a violation of Community antitrust law because unless some action is taken there could be no likelihood of trade being affected. As indicated in the ICI case discussed above, the Commission unsuccessfully took the opposite position.

In the US on the other hand it is the conspiracy itself which is illegal irrespective of its being successfully completed or indeed anything being done at all. In view of the expansion of international trade, this aspect perhaps needs a bit more comment in connection with the US aspect of conspiracy either within the US or abroad.

It was long ago held in the US that a conspiracy in the US to do acts in another country, or between a US person and a foreign person, would not come within the US antitrust laws unless the conspiracy actually affected the foreign commerce of the US and there were overt activities which were put into operation within the US. Obviously this is a very sensitive point because of the diplomatic implications in the application of the US law to acts done by foreign persons. The general rule is that the conspiracy is illegal regardless of where the conspiracy takes place if the conspiracy is intended to restrain American foreign commerce and actually results in such restraints. In this respect, therefore, the conspiracy doctrine is modified because where the conspiracy takes place within the US, it is irrelevant whether there is actually any effect on inter-state trade, nor is it necessary that the conspiracy actually be put into effect. On the other hand, whether the conspiracy takes place abroad or within the US and only foreign trade is concerned, there must be the intent and the actual effect of restraint on the foreign trade before the conspiracy is illegal.

In the ICI case decided by the European Court of Justice, both the Commission and the Court were somewhat unclear as to whether there had to be an actual effect on trade resulting from the concerted practice. We think that the confusion in the courts arose because both the Commission and the Court had very carefully considered the development of the conspiracy doctrine in the US and were trying to establish a parallel within the Community, even though no such parallel was possible.

As suggested earlier, an analogy between the US conspiracy and the Community's concerted practice is virtually impossible because in the US Sherman Act the element of agreement is necessary; whereas in art. 85 the words "agreement" and "concerted practice" are mutually exclusive. A contract or agreement certainly is an expression of intent but the law requires an overt act or a real threat of restraint. Conspiracy is itself illegal and intent alone is sufficient in its makeup to condemn it as illegal.

Logic compels the European Court to view a concerted practice as something other than an agreement. Yet one simply cannot escape the necessity to find the element of an agreement in a concerted practice. One must allow the possibility that two or more parties could not be guilty of a concerted practice if they did not have an intent to perform uniformly. This in itself carries at least the implication of some kind of tacit agreement among the people involved. Both the Commission and the Court wrestled with the problem of trying to establish that the concerted practice need not be an agreement and that it would itself violate the law even though it were not carried through. The expression "shared intent" was used and in several places the decision referred to the intention of the parties. The Advocate-General apparently saw the problem in establishing the concerted practice as a violation irrespective of any effect on trade and took the position that such an effect would have to occur before the violation could be established. One wonders why the Court did not simply rely on the wording of art. 85 because the article itself states as a requirement that the business practice either be likely to affect or actually affect trade and competition. If the concerted practice is never put into effect, it is difficult to conceive its being likely to affect trade at all, in which case "intent" has no meaning to art. 85. As we mentioned earlier we think that the Commission and the Court place themselves in this unnecessarily confused view of intent and whether or not an effect on trade is necessary because they were trying to parallel the conspiracy theory of the US.

We have now dealt with the first essential in the violation of either great body of law. If we now assume that we have the requisite two separate legal and economic entities either entering into an agreement, or acting in a conspiracy or taking part in a concerted practice, the next practical question that one would want to know the answer to is the subject of the next chapter.

3
The necessary effect on interstate trade

We have dealt with the first essential in the answer to the question, "When does a violation occur?" We have omitted discussion of monopolization and have looked into the necessity of having two or more people in agreement or acting in concert to do something in restraint of trade. That is not yet enough to spark an illegal restraint of trade under the antitrust law. The "trade" that is meant is that which occurs between any two states of the US, between any part of the US and a foreign country, or between any two countries who are members of the Common Market. The antitrust law is brought into play when trade and competition in interstate or international commerce are affected or are likely to be affected unreasonably.

It is not always easy for corporate planners to evaluate the interstate or international effect of what they intend to do. Of course, it is no problem when the company, knowing that it enjoys a significant share of the market in its product, agrees with a major competitor to restrict production or to control prices or to divide up territories into which they will sell. The planners know they are entering an area of antitrust problems because their actions must have an effect on interstate trade and competition. There are perhaps more instances in which the corporate planners and managers will embark on what they consider to be a normal business arrangement which in itself has no taint of illegality but which later on may be proved to have an adverse effect on trade and competition. If there is no such effect and if it is not likely that there will be such an effect, then regardless of the competitive restraint caused by the particular course of action, there will be no federal antitrust violation under American antitrust law. The necessity of having an actual effect needs qualification.

It will be recalled from previous discussion concerning conspiracy in the US that the conspiracy itself is a violation irrespective of an unsuccessful effect on trade and competition and irrespective of whether any overt act at all took place to implement the conspiracy. Accordingly, if in the US two parties agree and intend an action to affect competition, that in itself would be a violation under the Sherman Act. As already discussed in connection with a parallel situation in Europe, it is not at all certain that the wrongful intent and purpose can itself be illegal if there is no effect on trade and competition or no likelihood of there being such an effect. Apart from the narrow issue of conspiracy itself being a US violation, the general rule applies but there must be either an effect on trade and competition or the likelihood of there being such an effect between states of the US or in the foreign commerce of the US or between the member states of the EEC.

WHY AND HOW MUCH INTERSTATE TRADE NEEDS TO BE AFFECTED

This effect on or intention to affect interstate trade or foreign commerce is necessary in the US because without it there is neither a violation of the Sherman Act nor can the federal courts of the US have jurisdiction over the matter. The interstate and foreign commerce effect establishes the matter as being within federal jurisdiction under the cover of the Commerce Clause of the US Constitution. Similarly in Europe, the interstate effect is necessary for the Commission in Brussels and the European Court of Justice to have jurisdiction over the subject matter.

As the Sherman Act itself uses the expression "trade or commerce among the several states, or with foreign nations", it will be necessary to begin by discovering what is meant by "trade or commerce". Trade or commerce in *what*? The safest course is to consider that all business activity is involved and it is not simply limited to the production and the distribution or commercial movement of goods. Services are also covered. All sorts of financial advisory services, banking and insurance are covered. Some items are excluded but these are few and in order to avoid unnecessary discussion, we will keep to the more practical aspects and we repeat that the prudent course is simply to take the view that all business is covered. Watch for the exceptions rather than attempt a recital of all inclusions.

The effect on interstate trade or commerce relates to the flow of goods or services across state (or national) boundaries. That effect is necessary to impose the jurisdiction of the Sherman Act or, indeed, any federal antitrust laws, and the Rome Treaty's arts. 85 and 86.

In the US if the offending acts are purely local, i.e. the business conduct takes place totally within one state, the test is whether that conduct causes an effect on the flow of interstate trade. The effect also must be measured in relation to a relevant market, meaning a product or service in competition with similar products or services. Thus, if a defendant is accused of illegal practice under s. 1 of the Sherman Act and that person is involved in the manufacture of shoes, the relevant market may be shoes generally, or ladies' shoes, or shoes of a particular type.

A business practice under Sherman Act scrutiny must either occur in the stream of interstate commerce or, if the practice takes place wholly in one state (two competing doughnut manufacturers in Wyoming agree to fix prices at which they sell their doughnuts in the town of East Gravel Switch Junction, population 300) must *substantially* affect interstate commerce. Despite the particular instance of acts taking place wholly within one state, the effect or threatened effect on interstate commerce or trade is not the determining factor as to whether a violation occurred. It is possible that the business practice concerned could very well affect interstate trade substantially and yet not be "undue" or "unreasonable". We are dealing with the trade or commerce test simply to indicate that unless this test is met the business practice itself would not be illegal under the Sherman Act (save for "conspiracy"). Except for the qualification that business activity which takes place solely within one state must *substantially* affect interstate commerce, the amount of interstate commerce which is involved is not relevant because the Sherman Act declares the character of the restraint to be a violation and not the amount of the commerce affected.

This was clearly established by the Supreme Court in a Sherman Act case in 1911 (*Steers* v. *United States*, 192 F.I.). In that case only the shipment by one shipper to another state of the US was involved and the court held that the Sherman Act applied even though there was only the single shipment. The substantiality aspect of the restraint has to do not with the amount of the commerce that is affected by the act but rather with the effectiveness of the act in impeding commerce, however small the amount of commerce may be that is affected. In general terms, therefore, regardless of the particular business scheme, if the direct effect of that scheme is to obliterate a single competitor from the roll of competitors in interstate commerce, it could be a Sherman Act violation. In that instance it would be no defence to say that what was done affected only one individual.

The very first case to reach the US Supreme Court under the Sherman Act had to deal with this issue of the effect or lack of effect on interstate commerce, in so far as the issue determined whether the Sherman Act was applicable at all. This was in 1895 and the case was *United States* v. *E. C. Knight Co.*, 156 U.S.I.

In that case the restraint involved manufacture and as all of the manufacturing restraint occurred within one state, the Supreme Court held that the Sherman Act did not apply. That decision was distinguished so many times that eventually it lost its effectiveness and was overruled.

WHERE ALL THE ACTS ARE IN THE SAME STATE

The development from the Knight case was first that the Sherman Act would apply even to totally intrastate activity if the result of that activity had a substantial effect upon interstate commerce. If there is no aspect of or substantial effect upon interstate commerce then the intrastate activity does not fall within the Sherman Act. The reader will immediately see the enormous scope the court is allowed in deciding whether interstate commerce has been substantially affected or is likely to be so. Indeed, the Supreme Court did not hesitate to expand its notion of when and where and how much of interstate commerce is effected.

In Chapter 2 on conspiracy, we mentioned the Yellow Cab Company case. An incident in that case will illustrate what we mean. Two of the defendant cab companies had agreed not to compete with another transportation company. The agreement was concerned with providing taxi-cab transportation for passengers between railway stations in the City of Chicago in the State of Illinois. The Court held that such transportation of passengers and their luggage "is clearly a part of the stream of interstate commerce". The clear meaning from this is that even if the conduct is entirely within one state, if the particular restraint is on a part of what the court has called a "stream" of interstate commerce the interstate commerce test would seem to be met. It is safer to assume at all times that if the acts under scrutiny are so offensive to fair play, the court will find interstate commerce affected, or the court will not be thwarted by a defence that interstate commerce has not been affected.

Whenever one speaks of an effect on interstate trade, one must become embroiled with economic analysis of the market in the trade concerned. As mentioned above, one of the reasons why the *per se* doctrine was instituted was to preclude the necessity of the very often complex, difficult and tedious examination of the conduct of the defendant in the full glare of the rule of reason to determine whether the threatened effect or actual effect on competition is prohibited by the Sherman Act. We can think of no other aspect of the entire body of the US antitrust law which is more important than this concept.

4

The rule of reason

THE CORNERSTONE OF THE SHERMAN ACT

Having identified the agreement or concerted action of two or more persons, and the interstate effect, we now must answer the manager's query: "My actions were normal business practices. What do you mean they could be considered to be 'unreasonable'?" He will then be told that the violation will occur when what he plans to do will have an *undue* restraint on trade and competition. He will then ask what "undue" means, and when anything is considered to be a "restraint" at all. His adviser tries to answer these questions and finds himself driven into a long string of detailed explanation of every facet of the plan to look especially for a reasonable justification for the restraint on trade or the threat of such restraint—and the quality of the restraint. It is largely the quality of the restraint on trade and competition that makes it "undue" or "unreasonable"; not necessarily the "quantity" of the trade and competition affected. That is the standard which has been used to guide the courts in their interpretation of s. 1 of the Sherman Act.

What standard does the court use to measure "Undue-ness" of a restraint under the Sherman Act?

Having established the effect on trade in the relevant market, the final question for the court is whether the conduct under attack unduly restrains that trade. It would be helpful if there could be one uniform test to measure the quality and degree of undueness of the conduct before a particular act is declared illegal. Unfortunately, the test varies among the different antitrust laws in the US. For example, there is a different test for each of the Sherman Act, the Clayton Act, the Robinson–Patman Act, and the Federal Trade Commission Act. In fact, there are variations within the individual competition laws in the individual states of the US. Moreover, even within each of the Acts there is a different test depending on the particular business conduct under scrutiny. As mentioned before, the test as declared by the court where the Sherman Act is concerned is that of reasonableness of the business practice under investigation.

On the other hand, the Clayton Act itself states the tests that are required. For example, the Clayton Act expressly deals with price discrimination and condemns price discrimination when the effect of it "may be substantially to lessen competition or tend to create a monopoly in any line of commerce, or to injure, destroy, or prevent competition with any person who either grants or knowingly receives the benefit of such discrimination . . .". There are other parts of the Clayton Act which state nothing at all about the effects on competition; certain sections condemn the practices and transactions described regardless of their effect on competition.

The Sherman Act is not so explicit as the Clayton Act. It does not require that the offending practice "substantially" lessen competition; it mentions nothing at all about the effect on competition. All that the Act requires is a restraint of trade. The Sherman Act's rule of reason arose because the courts recognized that a restraint of trade could necessarily accompany many business transactions that are perfectly normal. The rule of reason was instituted to measure whether the restraint of trade or competition was reasonable under the circumstances in which the business conduct took place. In other words, the Sherman Act will allow a lessening or even elimination of competition or trade if this is the result of a reasonable business practice.

This is quite different from the requirements in the Clayton Act. As a matter of further interest, the Clayton Act, which is generally considered to be the second most important of the body of US antitrust law, applies only to persons, corporations or companies who are themselves engaged in interstate or foreign commerce of the US. The Clayton Act would probably not reach an Englishman who agrees with a Belgian to restrict exports to the US or to fix prices of the products which they sell to the US unless they had been dealing in the foreign commerce of the US. This is why virtually all of the cases which appear in the US courts involving international business come under the jurisdiction of the Sherman Act. The Sherman Act does not limit its applicability only to those people or companies who are engaged in interstate or foreign commerce of the US.

Because it expresses its test for the offence, the Clayton Act has no need for rule of reason. So long as the identified business practice may substantially lessen competition, it is illegal. Accordingly, in assessing what it is that one plans to do in business, one must first see whether the practice is expressly named in the Clayton Act as being a violation and then one must assess whether there will be a substantial affect on interstate commerce. It is not so easy to evaluate the risk in a Sherman Act violation so this needs to be looked into more closely. The Sherman Act (indeed all US antitrust law) only applies to practices which must somehow be connected directly or indirectly with interstate or foreign commerce.

The Sherman Act is, as we have seen, uncomplicated. Its wording simply condemns all restraints of trade in interstate or foreign commerce. It makes no allowance for a perhaps good effect (for the public) resulting from control of competition. But the courts have said that not all restraints are bad because, generally speaking, some restraint of competition can occur quite naturally in the ordinary course of business trading. It would be unreasonable to condemn out of hand the doing of all business which restrains competition. It would, on the other hand, be reasonable to weigh the restraint, and the kind of restraint, to judge whether it is a reasonable effect in the framework of the business giving rise to the restraint. The concept of the rule of reason as a standard for interpreting the Sherman Act was introduced by the Supreme Court in 1911 in *Standard Oil Co. of New Jersey* v. *United States*, 221 U.S. 1; but it was Justice Brandeis in 1918 in *Board of Trade of Chicago* v. *U.S.*, 246 U.S. 231 who outlined the kind of evidence needed to apply the rule and the framework of evidence within which someone accused of a violation might justify the restraint on competition brought about by his particular way of doing business.

Statement of the rule

Board of Trade of Chicago v. *U.S.* involved a regulation enacted by the Commodity Exchange in the city of Chicago. It said that there could be no commodity trading between the close of business one day and the opening of business the next day except at a price equal to the closing bid of the preceding day. The US government attacked the regulation but gave no evidence of any effect on trade or competition. Its position was simply that it was a Sherman Act violation for persons in positions of strength to fix prices and the regulation, in effect, was an agreement to fix prices. If the government prevailed, the defendant could have made no defence showing a beneficial effect from the regulation. It would have been a *per se* Sherman Act illegality. But Justice Brandeis here gave the first and most famous discourse on the rule of reason.

> ". . . the legalization of an agreement or regulation cannot be determined by so simple a test as whether it restrains competition. Every agreement concerning trade, every regulation of trade, restrains. To bind, to restrain, is of their very essence. The true test of legality is whether the restraint imposed is such as merely regulates and perhaps thereby promotes competition or whether it is such as may suppress or even destroy competition. To determine that question the court must ordinarily consider the facts peculiar to the business to which the restraint is applied; its condition before and after the restraint was imposed; the nature of the restraint and its effect, actual or probable. The history of the restraint, the evil believed to exist, the reason for adopting the particular remedy, the purpose or end sought to be attained, are all relevant facts."

Justice Brandeis gave more than a colourful description of the rule of reason. He indicated that the rule of reason might not come into play if the restraint was intended or resulted in the suppression or destruction of competition. The rule imposed by the Commodities Exchange was not aimed at suppressing or destroying competition. Evidence had been given to show it had a regulating effect and the government had not supplied any evidence that the regulation had the effect of either suppressing or destroying competition. The very fact that the court required such evidence illustrated the operation of the rule of reason. In that instance, if the government had shown an adverse effect on competition because of the regulation, the court might have come to a different result.

The rule of reason can be better understood when seen in contrast with the principle of *per se* illegality, and the criticality of purpose and intent. For this comparison let us look at a Supreme Court case decided nine years later, *U.S. v. Trenton Potteries*, 273 U.S. 392. This decision is generally regarded as one of the great legacies left by the Supreme Court as a guide for later *per se* decisions. The Sanitary Potters Association controlled 82% of the vitreous pottery fixtures, bathrooms and lavatories in America. It was an association of competing manufacturers. They agreed to fix prices and to limit sales in interstate commerce. This was not disputed, but the potters wanted the court to charge the jury with an instruction that their agreement to fix prices and limit sales should not be illegal unless they unreasonably restrained interstate commerce. In other words, the potters were seeking judgment of what they had done on the basis of reasonableness, i.e. the rule of reason. On the other hand, the government created in the clearest way possible the issue for the court whether the rule of reason could be considered at all, because the fixing of prices was itself inherently unreasonable. The Supreme Court agreed with the government and made the declaration which distinguishes *per se* violations from acts which need to be examined for unreasonableness before they can be declared to be violations.

"The aim and result of every price-fixing agreement, if effective, is the elimination of one form of competition. The power to fix prices, whether reasonably exercised or not, involves power to control the market and to fix arbitrary and unreasonable prices. The reasonable price fixed today may through economic and business changes become the unreasonable price of tomorrow. Once established, it may be maintained unchanged because of the absence of competition secured by the agreement for a price reasonable when fixed. Agreements which created such potential power may well be held to be in themselves unreasonable or unlawful restraints, without the necessity of minute inquiry whether a particular price is reasonable or unreasonable as fixed and without placing on the government in enforcing the Sherman Law the burden of ascertaining from day to day whether it has become unreasonable through the mere variation of economic conditions . . .".

Note the distinction from the Board of Trade case. In that case, there was no agreement to fix prices. The objective was simple regulation of a practice. In *Trenton Potteries* the agreement was to fix prices. The court in the potteries case indicated another essential for Sherman Act impropriety, namely, the defendants must have the power to fix prices. This particular feature of power in the market place is repeated in other landmark cases which we will study in this chapter.

THE INTERSTATE EFFECT AND THE RULE OF REASON

Whether we concern ourselves with a rule of reason to judge the legality of a restraint or take the direct route to condemnation via the *per se* doctrine, we must find the essential effect on interstate trade. This is true in both the US and in Europe. But what weight is given to the interstate effect to decide reasonableness or, indeed, *per se* invalidity? Is any weight at all given to the interstate effect for these purposes?

In Chapter 3 we saw that in the US the effect on interstate trade is necessary in order to give to the federal courts jurisdiction over the challenged business conduct. The interstate effect itself is not the most significant factor determining the legality of the restraining conduct. The most significant evidence to determine legality is whether, all factors being considered, the restraining effect was reasonable and necessary to attain the legitimate aim of the business transaction, or was a legitimate exercise toward a valid business objective. That, in short, is the rule of reason.

It is safe to say, on the other hand, that if one's business practice is itself illegal, or if the business objective is illegal (even if the means of getting there is legal), one would be liable for *per se* illegality with no recourse to a rule of reason. That, in short, is the *per se* doctrine. Those sketchy statements of the rule of reason and of the *per se* doctrine are most unprofessional and deceptively simple, but we think they are practical thumbnail definitions.

In Europe

In the Common Market the interstate effect is something more than just a jurisdictional requirement. It is of the essence of the rules of competition. It is a determining factor of legality, much more so than in America. Article 85 itself plainly says that any effect on interstate trade will bring the agreement within its ambit and will render such agreement automatically null and void. No court decision is needed. On the other hand if the agreement or activity has an otherwise good purpose and effect that benefits trade in certain ways and does not damage competition too badly (see art. 85 (3) for details) then the offending conduct can be declared to be clear of nullity and voidness. This provision has been debated to be Europe's rule of reason. If it is, it is not like that of the US. Note, e.g., that the European view can make price-fixing legal. This cannot happen in the US. There can be no evidence of a beneficial or stabilizing effect from price-fixing, or from limitation of production or division of markets in America. Yet, in Europe, any such evidence is permissible to exempt an agreement from the sanction of art. 82 (2). It is the pragmatic desire of the Community to improve the free flow of trade within the Community. The US is more committed to economic principle than to actual short-term benefits from conscious control of competitive forces. One might say that the rule of reason is everywhere present in Europe or, to put it another way, there is no such thing as *per se* illegality.

There is a significant difference between the powers of American courts and European courts in the application of the rule of reason. Neither the European Court of Justice nor the national courts in Europe can exercise the rule of reason. That is to say, those courts cannot judge that an agreement falls within the prohibition of art. 85 and yet not be a violation of the article, on the ground that the effect on trade is "reasonable". The European courts can only decide whether the matter before them comes within art. 85(1). If it does, there is an infringement of the law. Only the Commission in Brussels can bestow the forgiveness of art. 85(3). This is why the notification procedure is important. In America, there is no machinery outside of the courts for applying the rule of reason. The preliminary advice given by the Federal Trade Commission or the Antitrust Division of the Department of Justice is only a statement that they do or do not intend to proceed against the kind of practice which has been presented to them for comment. This is not an imprimatur of absolute safety.

The idea that the public does not benefit from controlled competition did not originate in America. It was stated in 1711 in England, *Mitchel* v. *Reynolds* 1 P.Wms. 181, "corporations ... are perpetually labouring for exclusive advantages in trade, and to reduce it into as few hands as possible". Accordingly, in America, the amount of interstate trade affected is immaterial where the offence has as its direct purpose or effect a restraint on interstate trade and competition. Only enough interstate trade is needed in those cases to establish jurisdiction. The reason for this goes back in US history of antitrust legislation.

Direct restraints on competition may have only negligible adverse competitive effects today, but they can lead to monopoly power—and that is where legislation began in 1890 with the Sherman Act. It was aimed at incapacitating monopoly power. The quotation from the *Trenton*

Potteries case given above strongly makes this point. The little things that operate as a run-up to monopolization are what the courts fear. Monopolization is the ultimate evil. Europe has not yet reached this kind of sophisticated awareness. In fact, there is nothing in the Treaty of Rome forbidding monopolization; only *abuses* of already established monopoly positions. One must observe, however, that what the Treaty failed to make clear, the Commission is trying to remedy. The Commission has attempted and will attempt to have the Court of Justice declare that acts of monopolization or obtaining a monopoly (e.g. through merger) are within art. 86.

Intent and the rule of reason

The motive and intent of a businessman are generally not important in establishing a Sherman Act violation. Of course, with *per se* violations, motive and intent play no part at all. However, intent can be a factor if the particular business conduct has only a probability of restraining trade. It often happens that a course of behaviour in business is taken that is not obviously or necessarily restrictive of competition, but might be. In such cases, the intent of the parties is important. If they intend to restrict competition, for example, then what was uncertain becomes bad. In cases of conspiracy, as discussed in an earlier chapter, the intent of the conspirators is still more decisive of illegality because even if there is no actual unreasonable restraint of trade in fact, the conspirators would be guilty because of the mere intent to bring about the restraint. Save for these exceptions, intent is not a factor because the court judges on the basis of the "necessary result" of the practice. Following this reasoning, one appreciates that where the necessary result of an agreement is an unreasonable restraint of trade, intent will in any event be inferred. A safe general rule is not to rely on the plea "I didn't mean it to have that result".

Despite the constantly repeated admonition of the courts, the law professors and spokesmen of the Antitrust Department and of the Federal Trade Commission, businessmen consistently miss the point of antitrust philosophy and continue to rely on the unacceptable argument that what they did was a good thing for the public. There are hundreds of federal judgments hammering the message home that if the intent or result is to restrain trade unreasonably it makes no difference that the public good is enhanced. The action is illegal. There is no need to chart those cases to illustrate what the courts held to be unreasonable. It would be more useful to take the opposite approach and discuss two landmark cases which apparently restricted competition, yet the Supreme Court held one of them to be legal, and the other one to be illegal. From such a comparison one might catch a glimpse of what purpose and result in business will influence the courts' judgments about reasonableness.

The use of a common selling agency

1933 was a bad economic year nearly everywhere in the world. Among the worst affected industries was the coal industry in that part of the US known as the Appalachian region. This roughly comprises the states of Virginia, West Virginia, Kentucky and Tennessee. This is an area which American literature has used as a setting for stories of human misery and povery. Due in part to the increased production stimulated by the 1914–18 War, and the general economic decline leading to less coal consumption by industry, and the increased competition from other natural energy sources such as gas and oil, there was an over-production of bituminous coal in the Appalachian region. There was surplus coal, called "distress" coal, being that coal which was produced but which remained unsold. Coal producers were offering the same coal to different selling outlets with the result that the same batch of coal was competing with itself. The Appalachian coal producers decided to do something about eliminating and correcting this unfavourable condition and established a common selling agency called Appalachian Coals Inc. The coal producers owned all of the shares of this company and each of them entered into an exclusive agency agreement with the company for the sale of virtually all of their coal production in the Appalachian region. There was no agreement limiting production (which would have been a common method of curing overproduction and therefore stabilizing prices); and there was no restriction on the prices at which the selling company sold coal. It had complete discretion to negotiate the best price in open competition with coal produced and sold by others.

The government attacked this arrangement on two main grounds: it gave the selling company the power "substantially to affect and control the price of bituminous coal in many interstate markets", and it eliminated competition among the coal producers themselves. Ordinarily, on these facts (the coal producers accounted for the production of over 74% of the coal mined in the Appalachian region), the court would have simply declared a *per se* violation of the Sherman Act, but it did not. Why?

The defendants had argued that they had not intended to control prices but rather that their purpose was to promote interstate commerce by eliminating the destructive practices that had prevailed in the industry. (Note: this is the constant refrain of all defendants to price-fixing charges.) Defendants argued and the court agreed that the selling company, although it had the power to fix the prices at which it sold the coal for its principals, did not have the power to dominate or fix the price of coal in any market and that the price of coal would be set in the natural manner in an open competitive market.

This was a crucial point, we think, in the court's decision. It was a question of fact whether Appalachian Coals Inc. had the power to fix the market price of coal. If that power had been present, the court might well have found a *per se* violation—on the same reasoning of the court in the *Trenton Potteries* case quoted above. Moreover, the court found no intent to fix prices, although it had already affirmed the *Trenton Potteries* principle that good intentions will not save an otherwise illegal practice. The key distinction was the court's belief that the selling agency did not have the power or the intent to fix the market price and had to compete openly with other coal. But the government countered this with the argument that nonetheless the very fact of having a common selling agency for the coal producers would tend to stabilize market prices "and to raise them to a higher level than would otherwise obtain".

Even on this basis, the court would have been justified in finding a *per se* violation because of the necessary price-stabilizing result of the actions of the selling agency. The court dodged the issue by shifting the emphasis to the necessity of *proving* that such a tendency would have resulted. The court again refused to see *per se* characteristics. Possibly, if an intent to stabilize prices had been found, the court would have held otherwise. The court made a frank comment reflecting its concern with the economic condition of the time (a factor which normally would not influence a court in a *per se* violation). It said, in connection with the stabilizing of prices argument advanced by the government, "But the facts found do not establish, and the evidence fails to show, that any effect will be produced which in the circumstances of this industry will be detrimental to fair competition". Again, we can only observe that arguments of favourable or unfavourable effects on competition are not accepted in price-fixing cases. Clearly, the court was determined not to find a *per se* violation.

The court likened the action of the coal producers to the formation of partnerships and enterprises integrating to promote competition, rather than a conspiracy of competitors to fix prices. It seems that the court must have been influenced by the economic depression of the times because it said:

> "A co-operative enterprise, otherwise free from objection, which carries with it no monopolistic menace, is not to be condemned as an undue restraint merely because it may effect a change in market conditions, where the change would be in mitigation of recognized evils and would not impair, but rather foster, fair competitive opportunities".

(These words are substantially echoed in the exemption clause 85(3) of the Rome Treaty.) The court summed up its view of lack of evil intent and lack of power to fix prices as the saving features of the *Appalachian* case:

> "Putting an end to injurious practices, and the consequent improvement of the competitive position of a group of producers is not a less worthy aim and may be entirely consonant with the public interest, where the group must still meet effective competition in a fair market and neither seeks nor is able to effect a domination of prices".

While the principles of the *Appalachian* case are probably sound, we think that in practice the use of a common selling agency by a group of competitors making up a substantial part of a production industry is perilous ground if only because of the elimination of competition among themselves. Note also that in the Common Market, in the Kalie Chemie series of cases,[1] the Commission raised strong objections of the anticompetitive effects of competitors using a common selling agency. No doubt the sympathy of the court with the economic disadvantages of overproduction in an era of economic depression helped it to a favourable decision for Appalachian Coals Inc. But this kind of argument did not work seven years later in another matter involving a natural energy producing substance: petrol. Note the distinctions in *United States* v. *Socony-Vacuum Oil Co. Inc.* 310 U.S. 150.

The use of a common buying scheme

In this case, as in the Appalachian matter, the business traders were concerned with a deteriorating condition in their business. As we shall see, good motives will not cure an antitrust defect. The key factor is the way traders in an industry go about correcting imbalances. We have seen how the coal producers did this in the Appalachian region. They created a common selling company which sold their coal. In the case we will now consider the major oil companies created a common *buying* scheme to stabilize a deteriorating situation. The Supreme Court condemned the practice

---

1 Pages 72, 73.

as a *per se* price-fixing violation. Why did the court take what was apparently a view contradictory to theirs in the *Appalachian* case?

After 1926 and continuing to 1935 there was overproduction of petrol and it was selling at below the cost of refining it. Overproduction was wasteful because it reduced the productive capacity of the oil fields and drove down oil prices below cost of production. When this happened the oil wells were abandoned and once abandoned it became difficult or impossible to begin production again in the same wells. Individual states attempted to legislate production to avoid this effect but the producers circumvented state laws and produced oil unlawfully. This came to be called "hot oil". The hot oil sold at much lower prices than the legal oil. The resultant hot petrol refined from hot oil sold at a price less than the cost of refining legal petrol from legal crude oil. The independent refiners of legal oil could not stop their operations because to do so would cause them to lose their connections with the producers of crude oil and their customers for refined petrol. They had to sell petrol as soon as they produced it because they had no storage facilities. The result was that they sold their legal petrol at prices that depressed the market. This petrol was called "distress petrol" (note the analogy with "distress coal" in the *Appalachian* case).

The federal government attempted to remedy the situation through a Petroleum Administrative Board to plan and coordinate the production and purchase of crude oil and petrol, principally by allocating the amount of crude which each refiner could produce. In this way the government hoped to increase the price of petrol. Nevertheless the flow of hot oil continued. A voluntary effort was sought to remedy the situation and the major oil producers and refiners agreed a programme under which the major oil companies would purchase the production of the refiners, each company agreeing to buy from its assigned refiner. Each company then sold the petrol in tank cars to its own retail outlets and to jobbers who, in turn, would sell to independent retail outlets.

The key observation here is that the companies agreed to buy their respective petrol at the going fair market price. This would naturally affect the price of the tank cars of petrol sold to jobbers. This, in turn, would affect the retail petrol prices.

The government attacked the programmes as a Sherman Act s. 1 price-fixing conspiracy. There was much evidence showing that the intent of the oil companies was to stabilize the retail market. There was direct evidence by one of the defendants that "if we were going to have general stabilization in retail markets, we must have some sort of a firm market in the tank car market". The companies then sopped up the distress petrol from the refiner at a "fair going market price". But there was no agreement to fix prices. They bought on the open market. The refiners informed the oil companies regularly as to the amount of distress petrol available and the companies then advised as to how much they would buy from whom. This information of the available distress petrol was handled by a committee of three men who found purchasers for it. It was this committee who watched the current prices of petrol and tried to persuade the companies to pay whatever the fair market price was. Apparently actual price fixing did not occur and the oil companies did not attempt to fix the price at which they bought.

Two things to observe at this point: although the buying oil companies did not fix prices, neither did they compete in purchasing prices, and the refiners had guaranteed buyers. As it happened, the second point was ignored by the court, but the first had more significance, although even that was not the decisive factor.

The intent and power to stabilize prices—illegality

There was no evidence that the companies' concerted action in purchasing distress petrol had the effect of fixing or, indeed, controlling the retail prices at all. It was enough for the court that the evidence showed an intent by the oil companies to stabilize retail prices. No evidence was needed to show that the prices actually were affected. So long as the companies controlled a substantial part of the commerce in petrol and had the power to raise prices, that would be enough to constitute a violation. The narrower point was that it was unnecessary that the action of the companies cause the price rise. The court believed that it was in itself illegal to intend to stabilize prices and, consequently, no evidence of the actual effect was necessary. In distinguishing from the *Appalachian* case, the court noted that there the intent had nothing to do with stabilization of prices. As that purpose or intent was missing the matter was not capable of self-determination on the *per se* theory and needed recourse to proof of an unreasonable effect on trade, i.e. a rule of reason test. The court quoted some wording from the *Appalachian* case which, with respect, might be interpreted by the most untrained mind to be a magic wand with which the court could forgive almost any concerted activity among competitors which might effect prices:

"The fact that the correction of abuses may tend to stabilize a business, or to produce fairer price levels, does not mean that the abuses should go uncorrected or that cooperative endeavour to correct them necessarily constitutes an unreasonable restraint of trade. The intelligent conduct of commerce through the acquisition of full information of all relevant facts may properly be sought by the cooperation of those engaged in trade, although stabilization of trade and more reasonable prices may be the result".

What went wrong with the oil companies? Their buying programmes had the direct purpose and aim of raising and maintaining the spot prices of tank cars to jobbers and others. That was the first red signal to the court. Another was the court's view that the purpose of doing this was to stabilize the retail price of petrol. The third was that the oil companies had the power to stabilize prices.

The oil companies fought hard to defend their actions. They argued that they had no power or purpose to suppress competition; that there was no elimination of competition in the spot tank car market; that those prices were in fact determined by competition and their purchases depended on the open spot market prices. The court ignored this argument. It was satisfied that the purpose was to raise prices, despite the companies' protestation there was evidence showing only that their actions may have contributed to stabilizing prices. That was nonetheless sufficient to convince the court that they collectively did have sufficient power to affect prices, although it may have only been a contributing and not a determining factor. We think that the fundamental evil was that the oil companies agreed to buy at a market price. Even though they did not agree to fix a price, their agreement had the direct effect of contributing to putting a floor on the price. The court said that this had an effect on competition because it interfered with the play of supply and demand. The court suggested that no proof of an actual price effect was necessary because this was a conspiracy indictment and it is the conspiracy, i.e. the illegal purpose itself that is at fault, not the concrete success or failure of the conspiracy.[2]

As mentioned earlier, some power is required before two or more persons can be found guilty of a violation such as found in the *Socony-Vacuum* case. It is not likely that Smith and Jones, each the sole owner of his own hardware store in Bethesda, Maryland could be condemned under the Sherman Act if they agree not to sell light bulbs below a certain price.

> "Where the machinery for price fixing is an agreement on the prices to be charged or paid for the commodity in the interstate or foreign channels of trade, the power to fix prices exists if the combination has control of a substantial part of the commerce in that commodity."

Thus, both in the *Appalachian* and *Socony* cases, the motives of the defendants were noble but in one case the concerted action through a common selling agent was all right and in the other the concerted action in buying was not all right. Both sets of defendants had the power to affect prices because each combination controlled a substantial

---

2 See pages 28–68 for the "conspiracy" aspect of the Sherman Act.

part of interstate commerce in coal or in petrol, and control presumes possession of the power. (Conversely, if control were not present, the purpose and effect would have to be proved.) The difference was that the purpose and intent of the oil companies was at least to influence stabilization of prices, whereas this was not the purpose or intent of the coal producers. And so the rule of reason was raised for the coal producers, but was ignored for the oil companies.

No one doubts the competitors prefer to trade in a price-stable atmosphere. It is not unusual that they are motivated by good thoughts in planning various schemes, even price-fixing, to stabilize the price climate and that they have no intent to destroy competition.

The rule of reason, however, will not be supported by good intentions if the intentions themselves are to restrain competition. On the other hand the intention to affect competition will be sufficient to attract the attention of the Sherman Act even if the effect itself never transpires. One reads this precept in the *Socony-Vacuum* case.

INTRODUCTION OF THE *PER SE* PRINCIPLE

There are limits to the extent that the rule of reason can be explained. One might state its principle and why it was devised by the courts, but it would be impossible to give it any kind of contour so that one might know what particular business conduct might be defended by argument about the reasonableness of the conduct under legal attack. Reasonableness is whatever one wants to make of it. On one thing everyone agrees—it takes a lot of time and effort for the court, the plaintiff and the defendant to prove and argue what is reasonable.

With the same ingenuity that devised the rule of reason, the court created a tool to lighten everyone's burden of deciding whether something is reasonable. It approached the issue from another direction and outlined areas which were plainly illegal without the necessity of inquiring whether practices within the areas were reasonable. The court said that business practices are illegal under the

Sherman Act, without recourse to the rule of reason, if because of their nature or necessary effect, or because of their clear objective, they injuriously restrain trade. The courts found that certain practices by their nature must restrain competition and cannot be explained away on the grounds of reasonableness. These are *per se* violations.

As a practical matter, the reader is well advised to become familiar with *per se* violations. The initial aim of law enforcement officials and private individuals is to establish their target as a *per se* violation. It saves them a great deal of trouble in assembling proof of unreasonableness. It also substantially destroys the defence, because the defendant cannot introduce evidence to show that what he did was reasonable and necessary to his business purpose. The courts are sympathetic to attempts to find *per se* evidence because it saves them a great deal of time and effort. Knowledge of the *per se* principle is easier to assimilate because the principle can be divided into compartments of business activity which are recognizable; their very statement indicates their boundaries of application.

5

The *per se* principle

Any agreement or individual attempt or agreement to attempt to monopolize or do an act of monopolization which has as its purpose and/or its necessary effect a restraint of interstate or foreign commerce is illegal, and no evidence of a beneficial or incidental effect, i.e. reasonableness, will remedy the illegality. The hallmark of *per se* violations is found in the answers to the questions, "What is the principal thrust or necessary effect of the proposed practice? Is it aimed at affecting competition in some way?"

The practices which have been established as illegal are:

(*a*) price-fixing among competitors;
(*b*) resale price-fixing agreements with distributors;
(*c*) division of market territories among competitors;
(*d*) group boycotts;
(*e*) tying arrangements.

It can be seen that each of these groups of practices must result in a restraint of trade. If competitors fix prices, they self-evidently have at least restrained price competition among themselves. If a supplier agrees with his distributor as to the price the distributor will charge for the goods, competition is eliminated between the distributor and others selling the goods.

In a division of markets, competition is eliminated among the parties in the allocated markets. A boycott effectively removes the boycotted person as a competitor, as well as competition among the boycotters themselves in respect of that person. In a tying arrangement, competition in the "tied" product is eliminated in that the tied party cannot obtain that product from a third person.

It is obvious that there can be an infinite number of variations in business practices within each of the *per se* categories; nevertheless it is useful to know that if the result of the practice places it within any one of the categories, that practice will be a Sherman Act violation. These practices are also condemned in the Common Market but, unlike the US view, they are not *per se* illegal, because they might be exempt under art. 85(3). Unlike the Commission in Brussels, no US court has the power to bestow legality on what is illegal. This needs to be done by Congressional legislation.

Unfortunately the *per se* doctrine has been interpreted to mean that whatever falls into one of the *per se* categories is always absolutely and without further investigation, wrong. This is not correct. For example, there must be the effect on interstate or foreign commerce, or the Sherman Act does not apply at all. The effect on trade does not have to be substantial in a *per se* action (except for tying arrangements as we shall see). Apart from having to prove the interstate or foreign commerce effect, there are other items of proof that are necessary *before* the court can hold that the matter under examination is *per se* illegal. As we deal with each of the categories, it will become apparent that paradoxically there is some reasonableness needed to lay the groundwork to support a decision that something is *per se* illegal. Let us look at price-fixing.

6

Price-fixing

Price-fixing is the cardinal sin and the core of virtually every antitrust transgression in the US and Europe. The antitrust laws are concerned with trade and commerce. Trade and commerce are possible because of a monetary system and the monetary system functions by means of pricing. In every category of *per se* violations mentioned above the underlying evil, the element that makes the category illegal is the fact that the practice affects prices. So much so is this true in America that a Bill introduced in Congress, the Antitrust Improvements Act (H.R. 8532, formerly S. 1284) proposes permitting individual state attorney generals to bring legal action under the antitrust laws on behalf of citizens of their particular state. The Bill proposes to permit such actions for only wilful price-fixing.[1] One might concentrate only on price-fixing and arrive at all of the *per se* categories.

But we mean illegal price-fixing. Not all price-fixing is illegal. It is the agreement between at least two parties in purpose or affect to fix prices that is wrong. It is the decision of a party attempting to monopolize or being in a monopoly position to fix the price of his product in order to affect competition or for any reason inconsistent with fair business practices, that is wrong. The concept is ancient and simple to understand. The great task of the courts and the litigants is to determine whether the business practice being challenged constitutes price-fixing. For the purposes of this chapter we will leave aside jurisdictional questions such as the necessary interstate effect (which was partially discussed

---

1 This has been enacted with wider provisions.

earlier) and deal with the substance of price-fixing violations.

There is no problem where an agreement is found among competitors blatantly agreeing to fix prices. In our more sophisticated times, rarely are such agreements found. More realistically, price-fixing purposes or intent or effects are disguised in the fabric of otherwise apparently valid agreements, written or oral, or concerted practices and actions. It is in the set of facts comprising such situations that the courts search for *per se* illegal price-fixing. The inflexible theory of antitrust is that prices are determined fairly only by the free play of competition. Accordingly, it follows that any business purpose directly intended to affect competition will affect prices and will be *per se* illegal. This is why, for example, group boycotts, divisions of territorial markets and tying arrangements are illegal: they control or attempt to control competitors, and ultimately prices must be affected. No doubt most businessmen would like to be able to control prices and no doubt most ingenious schemes have been invented to accomplish the illegality in a legal way. In this cat-and-mouse game between private enterprise and the courts, certain indicia of lurking price-fixing intent or effects have evolved. It is essential to determine certain practical aspects about price-fixing apart from deciding whether a particular arrangement is in fact price-fixing.

To what extent does intent play a part?

Clearly if the parties or the monopolist intends to fix prices in the US the violation has occurred though no one takes any action to put the plan in action. Under the Sherman Act an illegal conspiracy[2] would already have taken place (see Chapter 2 on conspiracy). The Common Market authorities have not gone so far; still required is an actual effect on trade or competition (see pages 74–78 where both the Commission and the Europe Court considered this point).

---

2 Obviously not applicable in a monopoly situation where a sole monopolist is involved.

If the parties did not intend to fix prices or even to control them, but the business practice that they did intend had the effect of controlling prices, is that *per se* price-fixing? The *Socony-Vacuum* case discussed above answered this. The court refused to hear evidence about the effect or lack of effect on retail petrol prices, or on tank car prices by the oil companies' simply agreeing to buy distress petrol at fair market prices. The court was not really interested in the purpose of the companies, or that they did not intend to fix prices. The court was satisfied that so long as they had a controlling part in a substantial part of the market, what they actually did would necessarily at least influence prices.

It is not always easy to detect a price-fixing intent or result. One sees already that the court has a task to establish the *per se* illegality of price-fixing—it first has to find that prices have been fixed or were intended to be controlled or fixed. In order to do this the court must go through certain exercises. Was there a purpose to fix or control prices?

Assuming the requisite number of persons are involved and the jurisdictional problem has been solved, how can one know that he is within the proscription of the Sherman Act about price-fixing? Is there some characteristic, some sign, some quality in the plan to condemn it as such? Oppenheim and Weston in their excellent book *Federal Antitrust Laws* list the sort of questions that need to be considered in any price-fixing inquiry. These are:

Is there a purpose to fix or otherwise control prices?
If there is no direct price-fixing through an agreement among competitors as to the market sale price, or resale price, to what extent will the court inquire into the nature of the conduct to ascertain the purpose?
Is the degree of market power possessed by a group of competitors a material factor?
Are distinctions made with respect to whether the arrangement involves control of the market through monopoly power, a substantial share of the market less than monopoly power, power appreciably to affect market price, power merely to influence price?

Or are power and effect irrelevant if the purpose to fix or in any way to affect the market price is found to exist? Is the part or amount of commerce relevant?

Obviously these questions have practical importance to all traders. In a competitive world there is little doubt that competitors will try their best to conduct their affairs in a manner that will not destroy the business or industry on which their livelihood depends. If they do not dare to fix prices as such, they will want to regulate the market so that ruinous competition will not lead to self-destruction. The reader may recognize these words. They appeared in the argument of the defendants in the *Socony-Vacuum* case, the *Chicago Board of Trade* case and in the *Appalachian* case. Where the aim is to regulate trade, but not to fix or influence prices, as in *Board of Trade*, there was neither the intent nor the effect of fixing prices, so that was all right.

In the *Appalachian* case, the coal producers did nothing to affect prices. They used a common selling agency, but the agency sold in open competition without consultation with or influence from the coal producers and, very importantly, failing any evidence of intent or agreement on prices, there had been no evidence that use of the common selling agency resulted in fixing or stabilizing prices. That took the case out of the *per se* category and put it under the rule of reason; that is, the practice of using the common selling agency could become a Sherman Act violation if it was proved that competition in pricing was affected unreasonably. The court did not speculate about when an effect on prices would be unreasonable. Here we must shelter behind the great judicial axiom: it depends on all the facts of the case. In any event we are not concerned with the rule of reason here. It is enough that we learned from the *Appalachian* case that where there was no intent or activity intended to affect prices or any market control over prices, there was no *per se* illegality.

The *Socony-Vacuum* case was quite another matter. There the court found direct evidence of an intent to "stabilize" prices at two levels in the chain of distribution of petrol. First the oil companies agreed to buy tank cars of petrol from the refiners. They did not fix prices, but they agreed to buy the petrol at a fair market price. One would expect that to be all right, but the court felt that even in agreeing only that much, the effect would be at least to stabilize a floor on tank car prices. However noble the intent, it was illegal. Secondly, the court inferred the intent to stabilize retail petrol prices as a necessary result of their concerted actions in tank car purchases. By stabilizing tank car prices, the oil companies were bound to sell to jobbers at a certain price keyed to the price they paid for the tank cars; consequently, the prices charged by jobbers to retailers would also be stabilized. The court found all of that to be wrong. But in declaring its verdict, the court made some useful observations. One of them was "A combination having both the purpose and the power to control the market price of the commodity imposes an unreasonable and unlawful restraint, directly prohibited by the Sherman Act". From this we learn that having the purpose to control the market price and the power to do so is enough for a violation. The purpose can be determined by a court and jury hearing the facts and we have seen how purpose can be inferred from evidence.

But how would a court and jury determine when a party or parties had the power to control the market price? The *Socony-Vacuum* case helps to answer this because in its charge to the jury, the US court which heard the dispute in the first instance said that it was a violation for a group of individuals to act together to raise prices "where they controlled a substantial part of the interstate trade and commerce in that commodity". Accordingly the power to fix prices is presumed when the parties involved control a substantial part of the commerce in the commodity.

Notwithstanding the above judicial pronouncements, the Supreme Court in the Socony case qualified the necessity of controlling commerce in the commodity and said that the power to fix prices might still be found, even in the absence of such control, if the agreed practices and the timing of them in the context of market conditions comprises "effective means" to attain the objective, i.e. fix or stabilize prices. Translating these words, the meaning seems to be that power to fix or affect prices will be inferred from observing some actual influence on prices caused by the practices under inspection, even in the absence of any control of a substantial part of commerce.

It would seem that having the power to fix market prices, and the intent to do so, are two tests for *per se* illegality. In such instances it would make no difference whether the prices were actually fixed, or whether any overt act were done at all.

In the legacy of landmark cases from which the conditions for *per se* illegal price-fixing were designed, perhaps the father of all of them was *U.S. v. Trenton Potteries*, 273 U.S. 392. In one statement the court summed up all of the requisites for price-fixing. The case was decided in 1927 and all subsequent cases virtually concern themselves with analysis of facts only to see if they exhibit the principles proclaimed in *Trenton Potteries*. Where price-fixing is involved there is no defence save to try to prove that price-fixing was neither intended nor effected.

The facts in the *Trenton Potteries* case were simple and uncontested. The case was a test of law, not a quarrel over facts. We discussed *Trenton Potteries* in the earlier explanation of the rule of reason. We discuss it again now for emphasis of its principal importance, the *per se* doctrine. There are few antitrust cases which have only one facet and whose importance is exhausted when that facet has been studied.

The Trenton Potteries decision

It will be remembered that 82% of the market in pottery fixtures was controlled by 23 corporations who had conspired to fix prices. The issue was whether this action by the companies was in itself a violation of the Sherman Act even absent proof of a resulting restraint of competition or whether the effect on the public was good or bad. The Supreme Court held that this was a *per se* violation and went on to say:

> "The aim and result of every price fixing agreement, *if effective*, is the elimination of one form of competition. The power to fix prices, whether reasonably exercised or not, involves power to control the market and to fix arbitrary and unreasonable prices. The reasonable price fixed today made through economic and business changes becomes the unreasonable price of tomorrow. Once it is established, it may be maintained unchanged because of the absence of competition secured by the agreement for a price reasonable when fixed. Agreements which create such potential power may well be held to be in themselves unreasonable or unlawful restraints, without the necessity of *minute* inquiry whether a particular price is reasonable or unreasonable . . ." (our italics).

It is important to observe in these words of the court that the court infers from a power to fix prices that there will be a power to control the market. This might be seen as the converse of the *Socony-Vacuum* principle: the power to control the market implies the power to fix prices; although it must be emphasized that *per se* illegality does not depend on market control. The *Socony-Vacuum* case clearly indicated that it would be sufficient if there was an effect influencing the distortion of natural price movement.

PURPOSE AND/OR EFFECT

There is often some confusion as to the part played by the "character" or "nature" of the practice, and "purpose" or "intent" and, finally, the "effect" of the practice. As a rule of thumb one might say that where the purpose is to fix prices, that is enough for a violation. Where the business conduct is such that it must affect prices, that also is sufficient. Where there is doubt about the legality of the conduct, the actual effect may be decisive. In the instance of the *Trenton Potteries* case clearly the conspiring parties did have the power to fix the market price because of their 82% control of the market.

So much for the major characteristics for *per se* illegality of price-fixing. If there is no purpose or intent, and no market control or power to fix prices, but there is nevertheless a restraining effect on prices and competition because of a particular practice, the rule of reason would come forward as a standard to judge the legality of the practice.

Are the legal principles for establishing per se *illegality in price-fixing unrealistic in their application to the natural adjustments and movement of prices?*

This plea is made whenever businessmen and lawyers meet and the price-fixing issue is discussed. The question is invariably wrongly stated. The principle of price-fixing illegality arose from business realism and the courts do attempt to apply the principle in keeping with the natural movement of prices. The broad base of the principle is simply that competitors cannot intentionally take any steps to make a market price for a product or service which is anything other than what the price would have been if their action had not been taken. There are occasions, of course, when business transactions will affect prices. That is not what the court is seeking. The court is looking first for agreement or concerted actions by competitors which affect prices. Once that symptom is diagnosed the court will search for *per se* elements of illegality.

The real difficulty for a businessman is to determine the limits within which he may adjust pricing policies without stumbling on antitrust irregularities. Market price levels are often set quite naturally by a kind of "consensus" effect that is nevertheless not collusive or illegal. For example, it is common for competitors to adjust their prices in accordance with the price set by a price leader. This often depends on the nature of the products in competition. A standardized product, i.e. a product which does not differ whether supplied by one or another manufacturer, such as lead or salt, will not vary much in price among competitors. If a competitor chooses to fix his price the same as, or more or less than the price fixed by a price leader in the market, that is all right.

This was established in 1927, in *U.S.* v. *International Harvester*, 274 U.S. 693. The court noted that the competitors in following the price leader did so "in the exercise of their own judgment". They did not, therefore, agree among each other to fix a price. One wonders if the answer would have been the same if the competitors *had* agreed among themselves, but not with the price leader, to follow the price leader. The answer is probably that such agreement would be illegal. Such a situation would be similar to the agreement among the oil companies in the *Socony-Vacuum* case to purchase tank car petrol at whatever the fair market price was. That was condemned because the agreement tended to put a floor on the price.

Price-fixing instances seem to arise more frequently, not so much by straightforward agreement but rather when competitors exchange information with each other. We have already been dwelling in this area in the cases discussed. Now we might take a closer look at trade associations, a favourite hunting ground for law enforcement officials.

TRADE ASSOCIATIONS

Trade associations by their nature may spawn every one of the categories of *per se* illegality. They are associations of competitors formed on the basis of at least a kinship in products or services. They can be national or regional. In any event, from an antitrust point of view, there is bound to be danger when competitors bind themselves together however loosely as an association. They may be manufacturers, wholesalers or retailers or any kind of service industry in any level of trade distribution and uses. In some instances businessmen in different levels are formed into a common association. Generally trade associations can take any form. The common characteristic is that the members of every trade association have a business reason to associate, and if they are not already competitors, they should be, or would be.

The antitrust problems arise out of differing opinions about those business reasons for the association and their functions. A principal function of trade associations is the collection and dissemination of information for their members. There would be no associations if the members did not benefit in some way from the membership. The obvious difficulty is that no one can believe that member-competitors will benefit individually from promotion of competition among themselves; and it would be a masterful exercise of rationalization to imagine a trade association purpose other than stabilization and regularization of trading practices. Industry self-regulation for the public good has always been a cardinal purpose of trade association; but this means concerted action among competitors and in that one hears antitrust overtones.

It has been argued that the association is a stimulus to competition because one of its functions is to assist the smaller trader by supplying him statistical information that he could not afford to collect himself alone. It has also been proposed that exchanging information about their industry permits the members to know what the competitors are doing and presumably each is able therefore to return to his company with new ideas for competitive designs and products or services. Undoubtedly there is some truth in these arguments; but it has been the task of the courts to sort out trade association practices that promote competition from those that suppress it. Lurking in the minds of many is the almost irrepressible suspicion that the mere mingling of competitors in a trade association must somehow affect prices and influence competition. Antitrust purists will attack such influences as something not arising from the free interplay of competitive forces.

Yet the trade association cannot be condemned out of hand, that is to say, a trade association is not itself an antitrust illegality. There is no American or Community legislation or judicial determination permitting that kind of flat condemnation. It is therefore the activities of the association that make it vulnerable to antitrust legality.

Trade associations flourish both in the US and in Europe. Indeed, associations go back to the earliest history of

Europe. The guilds could be considered to have been a form of trade association, and, then as now, they performed useful functions within the industry. Trade associations can exert a powerful monitoring influence in their economic sector. Congress cannot delegate to trade associations or to groups of competitors in an industry the congressional duty to formulate codes regulating competition. If congress cannot delegate self-regulating duties to industry, then the courts must take a very suspicious view of trade association activities which tend towards self-regulation. Among the most closely examined activities are those hinting of price-fixing. It is the habit of the court to watch all exchanges of information within an association for their possible effect on market price.

The price-fixing habits of trade associations have a historical basis in the US. In times of war or economic depression, the US government instituted price controls. In this connection the government required the cooperation of the trade associations and encouraged them to regulate their own activities. The result was that after government price controls were abolished the associations continued certain practices which had been engrafted and this led to subsequent antitrust problems. The National Industrial Recovery Act in 1933 permitted certain self-regulation by industry. The Act authorized a committee of the oil companies to take steps to stabilize the industry. What was begun with government blessing ended in condemnation of the oil companies, when the NRA was declared unconstitutional. This historical event helped create the *Socony-Vacuum* case. An example of the inherent contradictions in trade association activities (the promotion of competition by dissemination of information v. collusion to fix prices) was given in 1971 in *American Column and Lumber Co.* v. *U.S.* 257 U.S. 377.

A useful function of trade associations is the dissemination of market information so that their members might have an accurate picture of the market. This would normally be simply a matter of gathering marketing information and distributing statistics to the members. This was the intent of the American Hardwood Association.

There was no allegation of collusion or conspiratorial activity among the association members. The expressed purpose of the members in providing information about their production and market conditions was to permit each member to assess the market intelligently "instead of guessing at it; to make competition open and above board instead of secret and concealed" and, in effect, to counteract the misleading statements by buyers about the market by having the member competitors give the true facts about the market. To achieve this purpose each member supplied certain facts to the secretary of the association. These facts concerned sales, production and stock reports and price lists. Apparently these were simply bits of statistical information, yet the association was attacked by the government as a combination and conspiracy unreasonably restraining trade. (The reader will immediately note that the use of the word "unreasonably" indicates that the court did not entertain *per se* thoughts about price-fixing. The reason for this will soon become apparent.) The government viewed the exchange of information as fertile soil for coordination of the members and "an attractive basis for cooperative, even if unexpressed harmony with respect to future prices". Observe the emphasis on "future" prices. The association during trial had made much of the fact that the reporting of past information could not fix future prices. The court held that the association did somewhat more than exchange information about past events.

The issue, then, was how much and what kind of information was permissible within a trade association? The court did not condemn the objective of passing on information so that members could accurately judge market conditions; but the court thought that the amount and quality of the information supplied went beyond what would have been required to assess the market; and, having gone beyond what would have been sufficient, the arrangement lacked only "a definite agreement as to production and prices". There is the clue for not having brought a *per se* price-fixing charge, i.e. there was no definite agreement about prices, or production.

How much information is all right to exchange before antitrust problems arise? The court gave some generally helpful hints. The court first suggested that there might not be anything wrong in simply supplying information about the amount of stock held, the sales made and the prices received because all of this would only be data to assist judging the market "on the basis of supply and demand and current prices". But, thought the court, the association went further than this. The association also disseminated information about the views of the members as to "market conditions for the next few months" and their production for the next "two months" as well as suggestions for future prices and future meetings.

The court felt that information about the future, as well as the kind of information given, combined with the court's faith in the baser instincts of businessmen to make all the money possible was sufficient for the court to find a kind of argument, albeit not a definite one, to fix prices and control production:

> "by the disposition of men to follow their most intelligent competitor especially when powerful; by the inherent disposition to make all the money possible, joined with the steady cultivation of the value of harmony of action; and by the system of reports, which makes the discovery of price reductions inevitable and immediate. The sanctions of the plan obviously are financial interest, intimate personal contact, and business honour, all operating under the restraint of exposure of what would be deemed bad faith and of trade punishment by powerful rivals."

The only factual point in the court's words is that about the system of reports making knowledge of price reductions inevitable. Accordingly, we might assume that exchanging information about future pricing is evidence of illegal price-fixing. The court also indicated association functions which, in the court's opinion, were not innocent activities of competitors.

> "Genuine competitors do not make daily, weekly, and monthly reports of the minutest details of their business to their rivals,

... they do not contract as was done here to submit their books to the discretionary audit, and their stocks to the discretionary inspection, of their rivals, for the purpose of successfully competing with them; and they do not submit the details of their business to the analysis of an expert, jointly employed and obtain from him a harmonized estimate of the market. . . . This is not the conduct of competitors, but is so clearly that of men united in an agreement, express or implied, to act together and pursue a common purpose under a common guide that, if it did not stand confessed a combination to restrict production and increase prices in interstate commerce, and as, therefore, a direct restraint upon that commerce, as we have seen that it is, the conclusion must inevitably have been inferred from the facts which were proved."

The European Court of Justice, in *Imperial Chemical Industries, Ltd.* v. *Commission,*[1] followed a very similar line of reasoning in finding a concerted practice to fix prices among dyestuff manufacturers on the basis, among other things, of the exchange of price information among the manufacturers. It used the intriguing reasoning that the exchange of information among those competitors was a wrongful concerted practice if only because it eliminated "the risk of not knowing their future market behaviour". The European Court went somewhat further than the US Supreme Court in the *American Column and Lumber* case in that it did not limit the application of its view to exchange of future information. The comparison between the American and European interpretations of association members' exchanging of information reflects a fundamental difference between the two. The emphasis in the American decision was the necessary inference of an agreement, however disguised, among the members to control production and prices. The European Court avoided the necessity of finding any kind of agreement and through inverted reasoning found illegal concerted practices among members because the exchange of information, even if it did not lead to or arise from an agreement among them, contributed to some form of concerted practice because by

---

1 See p. 74.

removing the risk of not knowing what the competition would do, the competitors were that step nearer to acting in concert though short of agreement to do so.

Is the test of illegality in the exchange of information whether such exchange must necessarily lead to the unreasonable restraint?

This was the issue stated by the US Supreme Court in *Maple Flooring Manufacturers Association* v. *United States* 268 U.S. 563. The case was decided in 1925, four years after the *American Column and Lumber* case. In the earlier case, the court seemed to pivot its decision on the conclusion that the exchange of information about future intentions of the members as to pricing and production had the necessary effect of controlling prices and production. Indeed, there was a rise in prices charged by the association members.

In the *Maple Flooring* case the association members exchanged the same kind of information as did the members in *American Column and Lumber*, but there were some differences. For example, although the members supplied information about costs, production and prices to a secretary who then distributed all of the information to the membership, the secretary did not reveal or link the identity of the members with any particular information. In this sense the information was a general compilation of statistical data. There was no agreement of any kind, or evidence suggesting the kind of "gentlemen's agreement" found by the court in *American Column and Lumber*, and the government did not allege any inference of agreement. There was no uniformity of prices, save that the evidence showed that the prices charged by the association members were usually lower than the prices charged by non-members. In view of the absence of direct or indirect evidence of any collusion, the court felt that the issue of antitrust illegality would have to turn on the actual effect of the associations activities in the collection and distribution of information as to the cost of the wood flooring. Only by analysing that effect could the court detect any material bearing on the price levels in the industry. This reasoning took the matter out of the *per se* category.

Apparently there was no evidence even suggesting an illegal *intent* by the members. If there had been, the illegality would have been established, on the ground of conspiracy, irrespective of any proof of a restraining effect. The court went a step further and said that the issue was whether what the association did would *necessarily* have the effect of fixing prices, even if an effect had not yet become noticeable. Another important distinction from *American Column and Lumber* was that the members exchanged no information about *future* prices or production. Evidence was given that the association had been advised by counsel not to discuss future prices at their meetings.

The lower court hearing the case took the view that the association's activities must have had a direct and necessary tendency to destroy competition in that there must have been a controlling influence on the natural working of supply and demand. It is very interesting to sense that here the court was coming perilously close to saying that an association of competitors must itself be illegal because of the necessary controlling tendencies that the court believed most flow from such an organization. Indeed the court said, "in consequence, the actual results flowing from such a plan and the execution of it are secondary importance". The lower court was obviously at odds with the view of the Supreme Court, because the Supreme Court defined the test as being whether there would necessarily be an effect of price-fixing. The court did not assume such an effect merely because of the nature of trade association activities.

The reader may recall the Supreme Court's attitude toward the "stabilizing" effect on prices caused by the oil companies' purchases of tank car petrol in the *Socony-Vacuum* case. The court in that case said that even activities tending to stabilize prices were wrong because they interfered with the natural play of competitive forces. That case was decided in 1940, and did not involve trade associations, and the oil companies were found to intend the result of price stabilization. All of these points distinguish *Socony* from the case at hand, but we think it is of some importance that the Supreme Court in 1925 dealing with trade association activities established that such associations were not illegal simply because their activities might help to stabilize prices. The court's exact words were:

"It is not, we think, open to question that the dissemination of pertinent information concerning any trade or business tends to stabilize that trade or business and to produce uniformity of price and trade practice. Exchange of price quotations of market commodities tends to produce uniformity of prices in the markets of the world. Knowledge of the supplies of available merchandise tends to prevent over-production and to avoid the economic disturbances produced by business crises resulting from over-production. But the natural effect of the acquisition of wider and more scientific knowledge of business conditions, on the minds of the individuals engaged in commerce and its consequential effect in stabilizing production and price, can hardly be deemed a restraint of commerce, or if so, it cannot, we think, be said to be an unreasonable restraint or in any respect unlawful."

On first impression this kind of talk from the Supreme Court may seem heretical, because it rings very much like the argument given by price-fixers, i.e. what they did had a beneficial effect. But it is not heretical and there is an important difference from those cases involving trade associations in which the associations were found guilty. In the *Maple Flooring* case the court clearly stated the principle that merely exchanging information even if it leads to stabilization, is not illegal; indeed, it is beneficial.

The distinguishing factor—the ingredient that could turn association activities into illegal practices—seems to be "conspiracy". That is to say, if the association members exchanged information with the view toward eliminating or somehow distorting competition, even if the result was stabilized prices and production, they would be committing illegal practices. On the other hand, if the natural result of exchanging information leads to such stabilization, that's all right—because the result was not planned or intended. The subtlety of the distinction could easily be missed. It might seem ingenuous to suppose that competitor-members of a trade association exchange information about production, prices and supply *without* assuming or having the thought that perhaps such exchanges might at least influence some kind of stability. That stability does not just happen. It happens because competitors let each other know what they are doing. This is what the government's argument was in *Maple Flooring*, but it failed. The court stated what we think might be considered the saving principle for trade associations,

. "We decide only that trade associations or combinations of persons or corporations which openly and fairly gather and disseminate information as to the cost of their product, the volume of production, the actual price which the product has brought in past transactions, stocks . . . approximate costs of transportation from the principal point of shipment to the points of consumption as did these defendants and who, as they did, meet and discuss such information and statistics *without however reaching or attempting to reach an agreement or any concerted action with respect to prices or production or restraining competition*, do not thereby engage in unlawful restraint of commerce" (our italics).

The answer to the question heading this section is, therefore, no; there is no illegality even though the exchange of information must lead to a form of stabilization.

Yet we have a suspicion that ultimately the question of illegality may depend not only on whether the members of an association reach or attempt to reach an agreement or concerted action, but also on the kind of information and the extent of details of information that is exchanged. Justice Brandeis in the dissenting opinion in the *American Column and Lumber* case indicated this. In that case the court made much of the fact that the information given went beyond what was simply industry-wide information. Justice Brandeis picked up this theme and turned it against the majority opinion suggesting that what the association members did was no more than exchange information that would have been available from government sources if the government had provided for such reports. Justice Brandeis gave the example of the commodities industry, saying that the government provided information about what was going on in grain, cotton, coal and oil. Why could trade associations not do the same? Justice Brandeis was probably correct, but he may have overlooked the point that in his case the members informed each other of their *future* activities.

In any event, it would seem safer

(*a*) to exchange only that information which would be normal in government reports (don't give precise, individual pricing information; keep it general and more statistical, industry-wide rather than particular);

(*b*) to avoid exchanging information about the future; and

(*c*) at all times avoid agreeing on anything.

The Supreme Court in 1936 underlined precisely this last point in *Sugar Institute Inc.* v. *United States*, 297 U.S. 553. Sugar refining companies selling 70–80% of the refined sugar used in the US formed a trade association to remedy abuses in the trade. Among these abuses were indiscriminate and harmful pricing policies. They decided that each member could continue to announce price changes in advance. Each member did this independently. The only feature of the practice they shared in common was that they announced the change in advance and allowed some time for buyers to purchase at the lower price. If they had stopped short of further agreement, they probably would have escaped trouble. They went further and required their members to adhere to the practice and keep to the announced price change. That was what bothered the court: the agreement to adhere to a price. "The unreasonable restraints which defendants imposed lay not in advance announcements, but in the steps taken to secure adherence, without deviation, to prices and terms thus announced."

In the absence of agreement, can an association practice neverthe-less be illegal?

Yes. In *U.S.* v. *Container Corpn. of America*, 393 U.S. 333 paper container manufacturers exchanged prices in order to be able to compete for buyers of their containers. There was no agreement to adhere to prices. There was a notice-able stabilization of prices, but in view of the *Maple Flooring* decision, the effect of stabilization is not itself illegal or indicative of anything illegal. And in view of the Sugar Institute case, as there was no agreement, what was troubl-ing the government and the court? The exchange of price information was, in this standardized industry, a most sensitive piece of information and the refiners "through a combination have become too precise, and that precision inhibits competition". The price stabilization resulted, therefore, not in the normal course of trade but rather through an at least tacit agreement among the sugar refin-ers to exchange precise information about prices among themselves individually. The court felt that even though price competition was not eliminated completely, the limi-tation or reduction of price competition by exchanging such precise information interfered with the setting of prices by free market forces. There was something else about the price-information-exchange system that worked against the refiners. The information which they gave to each other was nowhere else available and, significantly, it was understood that if one member asked another what his prices were, he would give that information, even though he was not required to give it.

Any exchange of price information among competitors within or outside of a trade association is dangerous—but when is it least dangerous?

It is least dangerous when:

(a) the information is not concerned with a standardized industry, i.e. the goods involved are not of a uniform character such as sugar;

(*b*) the competitors are not obliged to exchange such information with each other, e.g. as in the *Container* case;

(*c*) the information is not precise or particular as to what is being charged by whom to whom, in other words, the information is statistical within the industry as a whole;

(*d*) the information is available publicly, such as in governmental surveys and reports; conversely, it is not private and personal and available only to a chosen few.

Despite the above there is a tendency in the courts, perhaps justifiable, to make whatever they wish out of situations in which competitors exchange price information or, indeed, any information that would affect prices and competition. Yet, the Maple Flooring principle (a simple exchange of information without intent to affect prices) is probably still good law, although the effect achieved, i.e. price stabilization could be illegal if the court feels that the stabilization has been brought about because competitors exchanged price information on an individual basis. As mentioned at the beginning of this book, court decisions cannot be relied upon as a guide to action totally clear of antitrust difficulty. Although the *Maple Flooring* case may still be good law, a court can distinguish from it in order to find illegality such as price-fixing. Nevertheless, one needs to have something as an indicator of what is the least risky and we think that the principles stated in this section on exchange of price information are an indication of the lesser-risk area.

Finally, one must observe what actually happens when several competitors supply either their own regular customers, or when the field of customers is vast. When a supplier deals with his own customers, he may want to know what his competitors are charging so that his customers might be able to compete. Accordingly he may ask his competitors about their pricing, not for the purpose or effect of stabilizing prices, but rather to fix his own price to his own regular customers. He is not, in such a situation, indulging in control of competition between himself and his competitors or agreeing prices in any way with competitors. The court has had to face this problem and it made this distinction in *Belliston* v. *Texaco, Inc.*, 455 F.2d 175. If in this case Texaco had not been dealing only with its own dealers, the price-information exchanges with other oil company competitors might have been held to be illegal.

Is the fixing of resale prices illegal?

The answer to this is simple: in the US it is *per se* illegal for a supplier to fix the price at which a purchaser from him may resell the product. The exception to this arises under the Fair Trade laws of the individual states. If a state law provided that a purchaser could be compelled to resell at a certain price, that practice would not violate the federal antitrust laws. But such state laws have been declared illegal. Do not fix or attempt to control or fix resale prices.

In the Common Market, the issue is quite clear: price-fixing is illegal. Indeed, it is expressly condemned in the wording of art. 85. Resale price-fixing (or maintenance) is also illegal. The Community view of the acts of trade associations is perhaps even more severe than that of the US. Accordingly one might follow what has been said about the illegality of price-fixing in America and apply it to Europe, keeping in mind, however, the exemption that may be available under art. 85(3).

In this section we were concerned only with price-fixing agreements among competitors or between a supplier and a distributor (vertical price-fixing) as they might apply to and illustrate the *per se* breach of the antitrust law. Price-fixing abuses by those in positions of power (monopoly) will be dealt with in the later discussion of monopoly and monopolization problems in American and Community law. Price-discrimination is something other than price-fixing and is more properly within the province of the Clayton Act as amended by the Robinson–Patman Act and will be treated in a later discussion of particular business problems under the antitrust laws. Nevertheless, having mentioned price discrimination a few words about it in passing are offered.

Briefly, a seller cannot discriminate among his customers as to the price he charges for the same goods or products or services. The reason is that it places buyers in uncompetitive positions. The prohibition does not cover justified price differences such as reductions based on quantities, trade discounts (price differences between sales to wholesalers and retailers), allowances for lower prices to a buyer because it is less costly to sell to him, e.g. geographical location. Apart from such normal trade pricing practices, the laws expressly permit a seller to discriminate by lowering his price to a customer in order to meet the lower price charged by a competitor. Although the Clayton Act and the Robinson–Patman Acts are more particularly aimed at price discrimination, it does not mean that the Sherman Act is not applicable. The scope of the Sherman Act is sufficient to capture discriminatory pricing practices.

7

Dividing markets

As a matter of business reality, short of control of competition by direct agreements to fix prices, probably the business advantage most devoutly to be desired is a protected, exclusive market. There is no substitute for it, and if a supplier is the sole or principal supplier in a given territory he also enjoys the bliss of non-competitive pricing. This is why market-division among competitors is as much a *per se* Sherman Act violation as is price-fixing. Even governments recognize the enormous trade impact of exclusive territories; hence the General Agreement on Tariffs and Trade (GATT) and the dedication of the Rome Treaty to the removal of customs barriers, and the occupation of both bodies of law in the sanctioning of quantity restrictions on imports. The raising or lowering of prices will always have an effect at least on marginal producers and suppliers, but that is not nearly as effective in controlling a market as restricting the quantity of goods that may be imported because such a restriction operates to limit the number of effective competitors or competitive products in the restricted market. Accordingly the protection of a market either by the government through imports and duties, or by agreement among competitors is commercially extremely effective. In the case of individual competitors making such an agreement, the Sherman Act and art. 85 of the Rome Treaty lie in wait. In the case of governments doing the same, GATT and arts. 5, 9 and 32 of the Rome Treaty are applicable.

The cases concerning division of markets have involved companies of considerable size. One would expect this to be the case because the agreement of one company not to sell into the territory of another would be an ineffective gesture if that company were not sizeable enough to constitute a competitive force. This does not mean that the conspirators need to be sizeable before their agreement to allocate markets becomes illegal. The remark about size is an incidental observation having nothing to do with the lawfulness of the agreement. Agreements to divide markets are *per se* illegal because they can have no objective other than to suppress competition and, as we have noted, the amount of interstate commerce affected is not important in such instances.

The difficulty with division of market cases, as with price-fixing cases, is simply constructing the illegal division out of the facts in hand, because a division of markets can arise other than through straightforward agreement to do so. Regardless of the complexity in uncovering an illegal division of markets, there is a principle underlying every scheme. That principle was first enunciated in *U.S.* v. *Addyston Pipe and Steel Co.*, 8 February, 1898.

As in so many landmark antitrust cases, this one involved a trade association, of cast-iron pipe manufacturers. They agreed to allocate among themselves selected parts of the US into which they might sell without fear of competition from the other members. The importance of the case is not solely due to its historic declaration of the doctrine of *per se* illegality in the territorial division of markets by competitors. The court also gave a remarkable insight into the heart of US antitrust philosophy. In its handling of defendants' objections, the court met the logic of trading tactics with the clearest exposition of the reasons for antitrust law. For example, one hears today the same arguments made in 1898 and earlier. "Competition was not affected by our agreement to allocate markets." "Our agreement is between ourselves so it won't affect competition because we cannot stop other competitors from coming in."

The Addyston court had to consider the support for defendant's argument given by yet another historic English case, *Wickens* v. *Evans*. Three trunk manufacturers in

England agreed to divide England into three districts, one for the exclusive use of each of them. The court held the agreement to be reasonable because it left the trade open to any third party to enter into any one of the districts. The Addyston court had to cope with an analogous situation of another English case, one in which the London beer brewers divided London into exclusive territories for themselves. There, the suggestion that this would lead to abuses of monopoly was met by the argument that outside competition would cure such abuses.

The Addyston court accepted the point that such local monopolies might be short-lived because outside capital would be attracted by the lack of competitors and would come into competition with them. The court said, however, "Public policy ... requires the discouragement of monopolies, however temporary their existence may be. The public interest may suffer severely while new competition is slowly developing". The court thus dismissed the traditional defence that division of markets actually would have the effect of attracting competition, with the obvious inference that what the conspiring competitors did was a matter affecting only themselves and not other competitors or the public at large. The court, being thrust into a closer examination of the agreement among the competitors, probed into the common law to test the narrower, more fundamental issue of whether the division of territory among competitors was not itself illegal, irrespective of the actual effect on third parties and the public at large.

The court had to begin with basics: the simple restraint on a seller of a business not to compete for a period of time with the buyer in the same business which he is selling to the buyer. This seemed fair because the main purpose was the sale of the business and it seemed reasonable that the buyer should be protected against the seller, after the sale, turning round and prejudicing the sale by competing in the same business. The agreement not to compete was not the object of the arrangement; it was only ancillary to it. But how about a division of markets arising otherwise than through such a sale?

The court felt that this was quite another thing. It was not ancillary to a main lawful purpose; indeed its only purpose was the elimination of competition between the parties themselves. Such a restriction of territories had to be wrong because (*a*) it was not a necessary protection of either of the parties ancillary to a principal purpose; and having gone beyond what was necessary, the practice (*b*) went against the public interest in that it tended towards monopoly. A division of territory among competitors is itself the objective and its only effect is to eliminate competition between the parties, tending to create a respective monopoly for each of them.

The evil of market division appears in many forms, e.g. distributorships, joint ventures, mergers and acquisitions and in the uses of statutory industrial property rights such as patents and trademarks—but they are not all *per se* illegalities. The most common *per se* illegalities with which we are now concerned are those in which competitors agree to divide territories, products or customers.

The European Community was concerned with precisely the same practice of division of markets. In fact, the Rome Treaty was far more directly concerned with it because art. 85 expressly names "the limitation or control of production, markets . . ." as a prohibited practice. The Sherman Act does not. The condemnation of it was by judicial declaration in the Addyston case.

VERTICAL DIVISION OF MARKETS—ARE THEY *PER SE* ILLEGAL?

In our era of expanding markets and preserving them for new competition, the task of the courts is to apply the Addyston principle to a vast variety of distribution schemes. The precedent set by the Addyston case involved horizontal agreements to divide territory, i.e. agreements among competing persons in the same level of the distribution chain, e.g. manufacturers. It was not until 1963 that the US Supreme Court was compelled to review whether territorial restrictions in vertical arrangements, i.e. arrangements between manufacturer–distributor–retailer were *per se* Sherman Act violations for the same reasons as were horizontal agreements. The case was *White Motor Co. v. United States* 372 U.S. 253, but, unfortunately, the court avoided the issue, though it nevertheless set the stage for what was to follow, and so a brief look into *White Motor* may be rewarding.

White Motor is a well-known US manufacturer of trucks and lorries which it sells to distributors, dealers and some large users. Both distributors and dealers sell to large users, and resell to other dealers, chosen with White Motor's consent. The arrangements between White Motor and its distributors and dealers involved territorial and customer restrictions which were attacked by the government. Typical territorial and customer restrictions were the following clauses in its agreement with distributors:

> "Distributor is hereby granted the exclusive right, except as hereinafter provided, to sell during the life of this agreement, in the territory described below White and Autocar trucks purchased from Company hereunder.
> STATE OF CALIFORNIA: Territory to consist of all of Sonoma County, south of a line starting at the western boundary, or Pacific Coast, passing through the City of Bodega, and extending due east to the east boundary line of Sonoma County, with the exception of the sale of fire truck chassis to the State of California and all political subdivisions thereof.
> Distributor agrees to develop the aforementioned territory to the satisfaction of Company, and not to sell any trucks purchased hereunder except in accordance with this agreement, and not to sell such trucks except to individuals, firms, or corporations having a place of business and/or purchasing headquarters in said territory.
> Distributor further agrees not to sell nor to authorize his dealers to sell such trucks to any Federal or State government or any department or political subdivision thereof, unless the right to do so is specifically granted by Company in writing."

White Motor's arguments for a trial on the merits (as opposed to being greeted with a *per se* invalidity judgment) was simply that in order for a distributor to compete against the larger companies, its distributors had to be protected against incursions by White Motors' other distributors and dealers. White Motor, in fact, paraphrased in 1963 what others had said about 80 years earlier:

"The plain fact is, as we expect to be able to show . . . at a trial of this case on the merits, that the outlawing of exclusive distributorships and dealerships in specified territories would reduce competition in the sale of motor trucks and not foster such competition."

White Motor defended the customer restriction on the ground that competition for such customers was especially fierce and that White Motor wanted to be sure that they would not be deprived of their appropriate discounts because this would lead them to become discontented with White Motor. Thus White Motor pressed for the chance to submit evidence in support of the rule of reason to absolve the territorial and customer restrictions of any taint of Sherman Act impropriety. On the other hand, the government urged the court to follow the line of decisions finding horizontal arrangements to be *per se* illegal. The court was timid and refused to grant a motion for summary judgment to the government:

"This is the first case involving a territorial restriction in a vertical arrangement; and we know too little of the actual impact of both that restriction and the one respecting customers to reach a conclusion on the bare bones of the documentary evidence before us. . . . Horizontal territorial limitations are naked restraints of trade with no purpose except stifling competition. A vertical territorial limitation may or may not have that purpose or effect. We do not know enough of the economic and business stuff out of which these arrangements emerge to be certain. They may be too dangerous to sanction or they be allowable protections against aggressive competitors or the only practicable means a small company has for breaking into or staying in business . . . and within the rule of reason. We need to know more . . . about the actual impact of these arrangements on competition . . .".

Justice Brennan in a concurring opinion raised a point which we mention now because it is germane to a later Supreme Court case which did not avoid the *per se* issue in vertical territorial restraints. He observed that vertical restrictions of territories into which distributors may resell might reduce competition among sellers of the same brand, i.e. intra-brand competition, but the effect on *inter*-brand competition might be something else, and might actually be increased.

IN EUROPE

When we began discussion of *per se* illegalities, we emphasized the reason they were illegal was that their only purpose and effect would be to restrain competition. Thus where competitors agree to share markets among themselves the only effect is the elimination of competition among themselves in the allocated territories. Accordingly the court as early as 1898 did not hesitate to condemn such arrangements. In Europe, similarly, there was no doubt as to illegality and the Rome Treaty expressly condemned agreements sharing markets in art. 85.

But what is the view when it is not competitors dividing markets, i.e. there is no horizontal division, but only a vertical one like that of a manufacturer limiting a distributor or agent from selling in certain areas or to certain customers? Where was the necessary purpose and result of suppressing or restricting competition? Who were the competitors and how were they being restricted in competing? In the Community there was early doubt as to whether art. 85 applied to vertical agreements but this was soon made clear first in cases 56/64 and 58/64 *Consten and Grundig Verkaufs GmbH* v. *EEC*, [1966] C.M.L.R. 418, 13 July, 1966, and then in case 56/65: *Société Technique Minière* v. *Masehinenbau Ulm GmbH*, [1966] C.M.L.R. 357, 30 June, 1966. They held that art. 85 was applicable to vertical arrangements. But the Community makes a distinction about vertical exclusivity and particularly distributorships and exempts them from the application of art. 85 because after the enactment of the notification procedures under reg. 17 the Commission was swamped with agreements. It was practical to grant exemption to certain kinds of agreements, not only to relieve the Commission but also recognize some valid business reasons for certain arrangements, business realities that are not necessarily anticompetitive.[1]

---

1 The following is quoted from a client's letter to the author. The only change from the original is that there is no such company as Sharp Tooth Brushes or Blunt Tooth Brushes.

"I resided for 10 years in Belgium and Holland establishing Sharp Tooth brushes and other consumer products in Europe, Mid-East, Africa and Asia. In most countries our market share was either number 1 or 2. This was done almost exclusively through sales distributors rather than starting our own sales forces.

I am familiar with the difficulties created by the Treaty of Rome in exclusive versus non-exclusive; however you will find that in dealing with distributors they want to be protected despite what the EEC rules require. This is particularly so around areas where merchandise crosses borders because of price disparities. At the moment I am not referring to high priced brushes but to mass consumer products. In Germany, virtually all mass consumer products go through wholesalers, whereas in Italy merchandise is sold direct to retailers by the use of sales forces of several hundred people.

There is a wide consumer price differential between the two countries not only because of a differing price level but also because of the absence of a wholesaler margin in Italy. Blunt's second most profitable market is Italy and yet despite their huge sales force, it is estimated that 25% of the Blunt tooth brush business in Italy is done by Munich wholesalers who sell to the large accounts in Northern Italy and under-cut price structures.

I have elaborated on this because when you need a distributor to introduce a product and to commit to selling, advertising and other efforts, he is not going to do it if there is the danger of merchandise coming in at lower prices and capitalizing on his advertising and other efforts.

One of my responsibilities with another company, Sharp Inc. (a personal care electric applicance company, not tooth brushes) was handling the distributors in Central and South America. An external problem for me was Sharp merchandise being shipped into countries, most notably Venezuela, from Florida, Texas and the Panama Free Zone. At one point, it was so severe, that one distributor simply gave up the line and the resulting publicity prevented us from getting another worthwhile distributor. This was a classic case of a distributor having the sales ability to cover an entire country and who spent time, money and effort to move a product in the market place being undermined by others. Whenever one does not have to 'launch' the product on a broad country-wide basis he can always sell at a lower price.

There are many examples from my own experience of merchandise crossing borders, even as far as from Germany and Bulgaria to the USA and how disruptive and damaging the consequences often are. In one case in the USA it cost hundreds of thousands of dollars to pick up our own merchandise from certain accounts because other accounts refused to buy from us anymore thinking that we were practicing price discrimination. Actually it was merchandise sold from Europe to the USA by third parties and we were in no way involved. What was done was legal but this will never satisfy someone selling

Continued on next page

On 6 March, 1965 Council reg. 19/65 was passed granting an art. 85(3) exemption to groups of agreements including distributorships in which the distributor might be limited to resale only within a specified part of the Common Market and in which he might be limited to purchasing from only the supplier certain products for that resale and the supplier himself might be limited to supplying those products only to that distributor.

About two years later the Commission having experienced the working of reg. 19/65 passed reg. 67/67 which re-affirmed the group exemption for exclusive distributorships, even as to restricted resale territories, and introduced further permissible restrictions on the distributor. For example it was all right to require him not to deal in competitive products. The Commission gave some practical business reasons to support its decision to grant the group exemption. It announced, in part:

> "In the present status of trade, exclusive distributorship agreements in international trade generally result in an improvement in distribution because an enterprise can concentrate its selling activities, is not obliged to maintain a multiplicity of business ties with a large number of dealers, and, since it deals with only a single distributor, can more easily overcome the marketing difficulties resulting from linguistic, legal, or other

---

your product when the same merchandise is being purchased by potential customers of his at lower prices than what he is selling at ... my only concern is to make certain that merchandise does not flow from there into certain countries in which there is a price disparity and where efforts are being made by a local distributor.

Moreover, because of a new name not being established, any worthwhile distributor will have reservations and concerns. He will exhaustively examine to what extent and how we will support and promote a product.

In regard to your paragraph concerning 'a new product in Europe', with most of the potential distributors I have dealt with for items like tooth brushes, pens, electrical appliances, stereo equipment and medium-priced watches, they have wanted exclusivity. Even in cases where a party indicated he would ultimately accept a non-exclusive arrangement, he wanted exclusivity for the trial period. In the event a party is willing to accept 'non-exclusive' arrangements, then no trial period and no minimum purchase arrangement is required. However, I believe that such parties will be the exception and not the rule. Rare indeed is the party who doesn't want his territory protected for his efforts. He doesn't want competition."

differences. Exclusive distributorship agreements facilitate the sales promotion of a product and make possible a more intensive exploitation of the market and a continuous supply while at the same time rationalizing distribution. Furthermore, the designation of an exclusive distributor or of an exclusive purchaser who assumes the sales promotion and customer service and maintains stocks for the producer is often the only way small and medium-size enterprises can enter the market as competitors. Whether and to what extent they wish to include in their agreements obligations designed to promote sales must be left to the contracting parties. Distribution is improved only when it is not entrusted to a competitor."

Note most importantly that the above exemptions apply only to *vertical* arrangements such as exclusive distributorships. They do not exempt horizontal arrangements or arrangements where competing manufacturers grant each other the exclusive distributorship for their products.

From the point of view of the businessman as expressed in the extract of the letter quoted in the footnote, and of the Commission as expressed in the legislative history of reg. 67/67, vertical territorial restrictions such as exclusive distributorships are legal in the Common Market. As we have seen from the *White Motor* case, the issue was not so clear in America.

Four years after the *White Motor* case and at about the same time the Brussels Commission was stating its reasons for reg. 67/67, the US Supreme Court was handing down its historic decision on the legality of that which the Commission had exempted from illegality. Indeed, the Supreme Court was moving a step further. It was deciding on the *per se* illegality of those distributorship restrictions. The case was *United States* v. *Arnold, Schwinn & Co.*, 388 U.S. 350.

Schwinn was a family-owned business engaged in the manufacture of bicycles. It was a highly competitive industry and Schwinn had to compete with larger producers although it was itself sizeable. Schwinn marketed its cycles through distributors who resold to retailers, direct to retailers, and to franchised retailers. Although no one was forbidden to deal in competitive bicycles, there were territorial and customer restrictions on resale of the cycles. The government did not allege that inter-brand competition was restrained. It wanted the court to face squarely the issue of restraint of intra-brand competition by Schwinn's policy of restricting the territories and customers to whom its distributors and agents might sell. The government wanted the court to apply the same *per se* illegality to this arrangement as it did to horizontal market divisions. The government's contention was that regardless of the techniques used by Schwinn, Schwinn was indulging in illegal division of markets. Schwinn, on its part, wanted the court to examine the reasonableness of its practice rather than condemn it out of hand.

Although Schwinn was neither small nor a newcomer to the bicycle market it had to improve its distribution scheme to enable it and the small, independent merchants making up the distribution chain to compete more effectively. To do this Schwinn franchised retail outlets and required them to buy only from certain distributors in their respective areas. The distributors were required to sell only to such approved retailers (hence the customer restrictions). The lower court marked this scheme as a restriction in competition among the distributors, and thereby identified the market that was restricted, ignoring the intra-brand competition.

The fact that only two enterprises took part (Schwinn and its distributor) and the matter involved only resale into a specified area and that it was merely a better way to distribute the product, "promote sales, increase stability of its distributor and dealer outlets, and augment profits" did not impress the court. It said:

"This argument ... is not enough to avoid the Sherman Act proscription because ... every restrictive practice is designed to augment the profit and competitive position of its participants. ... The antitrust outcome does not turn merely on the presence of sound business reason or motive. Our inquiry is whether, assuming nonpredatory motives and business purposes and the incentive of profit and volume considerations the effect upon competition in the market place is substantially adverse. The promotion of self-interest alone does not invoke the rule of reason to immunize otherwise illegal conduct."

The court then reviewed the *per se* areas of illegality and said that there was nothing wrong in a vertical arrangement where a manufacturer simply appoints certain franchised dealers to whom, alone, he will sell his products, and if competitive products are readily available to others. The effect of this would be to define areas almost of exclusivity, but as yet there was no *agreement* to preserve exclusive territory. The lower court had already approved this practice and the Supreme Court confirmed it.

In its agreement with wholesalers, Schwinn required them to sell only in certain territories and to certain buyers. If the persons with whom Schwinn dealt were only agents, there would not have been the requisite two parties. This would have been considered to be a "single trader" situation. But inasmuch as the dealer-distributor bought the bicycles on his own account, he was acting independently so there were the two parties agreeing to divide a territory; Schwinn and the distributor by agreeing on the resale territory were dividing a market. What competition was automatically thereby restrained? The distributors in the other allocated territories.

"Under the Sherman Act it is unreasonable ... for a manufacturer to seek to restrict and confine areas or persons within which an article may be traded after the manufacturer has parted with dominion over it.... To permit this would sanction franchising and confinement of distribution as the ordinary instead of the unusual method ... since most merchandise is distributed by means of purchase and sale. On the other hand ... we are not prepared to introduce the inflexibility which a *per se* rule might bring if it were applied to prohibit all vertical restrictions of territory and all franchising, in the sense of designating specified distributors and retailers as the chosen instruments through which the manufacturer, retaining ownership of the goods, will distribute them to the public.... But to allow this freedom where the manufacturer has parted with dominion over the goods—the usual marketing situation— would violate the ancient rule against restraints on alienation and open the door to exclusivity of outlets and limitation of territory further than prudence permits."

Thus one sees that division of markets between competitors is *per se* illegal; and that a vertical restriction, i.e. a restriction on the right of a purchaser such as a distributor to resell the purchased product is also *per se* illegal.

Nevertheless the Schwinn court gave a strong indication of one kind of restriction that could be permitted. Schwinn denominated certain "franchised" retailers to sell its bicycles. The bicycles were labelled as a Schwinn product. Schwinn did not sell through private labels. The court said that it would be legal for a manufacturer to franchise certain dealers to whom, alone, he will sell his goods, so long as other brands are readily available.

Since the *Schwinn* case the business community has been under the impression that in all distributorships it would be *per se* illegal to impose territorial or customer restraints on the distributor after he has purchased the products from the supplier. This is probably still the safer rule of thumb; but the courts since Schwinn have found exceptions to the rule. The *Schwinn* case has often been considered to be a bad decision and subsequent decisions have tended to interpret its scope narrowly.

EXCEPTIONS TO THE *PER SE* RULE

On either side of the *Schwinn* decision one finds the extremes in market division situations. On one side is the *per se* illegality of competitors agreeing to allocate markets and customers. On the other side is a manufacturer's right to sell to whom he wishes. Schwinn itself held that where a manufacturer parts with title and liability in a product he cannot limit the territory into which the buyer may sell that product. Clearly the *Schwinn* decision placed a severe burden on manufacturers desirous of distributing their products. Distributors want exclusivity, particularly as they will be buying the product on their own account and reselling it to make their profit. They will normally have to invest in advertising and promotion of the product and would not be happy to have to compete with the same product being sold in its marketplace by someone else. The practicality of the problem has led the courts to find exceptions; indeed, the Schwinn court itself showed the way. We have noted the exception in respect of franchised dealers (with which we will shortly deal more completely). The Schwinn court also opened the door for a kind of exclusivity by affirming the use of "areas of primary responsibility", a concept that was carried forward from the *White Motor* case.

The use of areas of primary responsibility walks that fine line between what has been declared illegal and what is a practical business necessity. The manufacturer knows that he cannot contractually forbid his distributor from selling his product outside the territory of the distributorship. The concept of exclusivity has two important faces.

It operates against the supplier because by granting exclusivity to a distributor in a given territory he forecloses himself from selling there and from appointing another distributor there. If he then grants another exclusive distributorship in another territory for the same product, he has the problem of preserving to each distributor the territory granted to him for resale. How can the supplier do this without violating the Schwinn principle? By denoting each of the distributorship territories as the area of primary responsibility of the distributor for that territory.[2] The supplier does not forbid the dealer from selling outside the territory, but he may provide that the dealer use his best efforts to promote and sell the products first in his market territory; and he reserves the right to terminate the distributorship if the dealer does not honour that undertaking because by selling "abroad" he neglects his area of primary responsibility and consequently falls short of using his best efforts. The courts have approved the reasonableness of this; they find it less onerous than the absolute "closed territory" nature of an outright prohibition on sales outside of the territory. Lest the reader take this to be a magic wand to avoid the Schwinn principle, let us study two unrelated

---

2 The Department of Justice is challenging the validity of "areas of primary responsibility".

cases, filed within two days of each other in different courts in different parts of the US.

Areas of Primary Responsibility and Dealer Location Restrictions—Reed Brothers, Inc. v. Monsanto Co. (US Court of Appeals, Eighth Circuit, No. 74-1695, filed 22 May, 1975)

Monsanto manufactured agricultural herbicides and appointed Reed a distributor of the herbicides and assigned to Reed an "area of primary responsibility" comprised of seven counties in the state of Iowa. In Monsanto's standard contract the following clauses appeared:

> "While nothing in this Agreement shall restrict the territory within which Distributor shall be free to distribute the Goods, Distributors area of primary responsibility for distribution of each of the Goods or groups of Goods shall be as defined in Exhibit A.   ***
> Distributor shall exert its best efforts to exploit fully the potential markets for the Goods in the assigned areas."

Reed, in fact, sold most of the herbicides outside his area of primary responsibility and when Reed's contract with Monsanto expired, Monsanto refused to renew it, thus terminating Reed as a distributor. Monsanto later explained that it did not renew his contract because he had "demonstrated inability or refusal to organize and operate the distributorship in a manner which would enable it to adequately and properly develop and maintain the dealer market potential in its area of responsibility". This reason was important because if Monsanto had terminated because of Reed's extraterritorial sales, the court could have dismissed the area of primary responsibility clause as a ruse covering the real intent of the parties to agree that Reed would not sell outside of its area.

So far as it went the court upheld the legality of the clause and Monsanto's termination of the contract.

> "A manufacturer may certainly choose the customers to whom it wishes to sell so long as its conduct has no monopolistic or market control purpose; furthermore, a manufacturer may properly designate geographic areas in which distributors shall be primarily responsible for distributing its products and may

terminate those who do not adequately represent it or promote the sale of its products in such areas."

The court found no agreement between Monsanto and Reed to restrict Reed's sales. If Monsanto had stopped at that, there would have been nothing further to decide.

But Monsanto went further and from its actions subsequent to the termination, the court inferred that the area of primary responsibility clause was not as innocent as it seemed and that Monsanto had indeed embraced an anticompetitive policy. And that, in fact, Monsanto's similar clauses combined with its activities with its distributors in other areas around Reed's area, convincingly established a policy which had the effect of limiting or restricting the territories within which or the persons to whom Monsanto herbicides could be resold.

Despite the termination Reed continued to sell Monsanto herbicides, simply by purchasing them from other Monsanto dealers and reselling wherever he wished. Reed operated as a discounter; buying at a high-volume discount and then selling by telephone to retailers. His overhead was very low and he earned only between about 2 and 4% profit. Monsanto then made two policy decisions which affected Reed's operation.

Monsanto would accept orders for shipment for prepaid delivery only for destinations within the ordering distributor's area of primary responsibility. Moreover, orders for collection of herbicides would be accepted only at Monsanto warehouses within the ordering distributor's area. Clearly this policy made it financially unattractive for any distributor to sell outside of his territory. Monsanto also instituted a "Dealer Compensation Program" under which rebates were paid to distributors for herbicides sold by a contract distributor to a retail dealer—but there was no rebate to a dealer for sales to a wholesaler. Monsanto also changed the boundaries of the various areas of primary responsibility so that those dealers from whom Reed had been purchasing could no longer sell to him because he was no longer within their area. This, combined with the absence of any rebate for sales to Reed, effectively put Reed out of business. The court was satisfied by the evidence of Monsanto's activities that Monsanto could not shelter behind the area of primary responsibility doctrine.

> "It is true, as Monsanto points out, that the courts have approved a manufacturers' designation of areas of primary responsibility for its distributors without more, but here we have so much more. . . . It is those policies and the agreements between Monsanto and its distributors that the law condemns, not the designation of primary areas."

Another practice accepted by the courts although it has the effect of protecting sales territories is the use of dealer location clauses. A case filed in Pennsylvania within a few days of the *Monsanto* case illustrates this use.

Kaiser v. *General Motors Corpn.* (US District Court, Eastern District of Pennsylvania, No. 71-1242, filed 20 May 1975.) Kaiser was a franchised dealer in Pontiac motor cars. Kaiser was contractually obliged to develop retail sales of the Pontiac in a certain part of Bucks County, Pennsylvania. The significant clause of the agreement read:

> "In order to provide product representation commensurate with the goodwill attached to the name Pontiac and to facilitate the proper sale and servicing . . . Dealer will maintain a place of business satisfactory as to appearance and location. . . . Once Dealer is established in facilities and at a location mutually satisfactory to Dealer and Pontiac, Dealer will not move to or establish a new or different location, branch sales office, branch service station, or place of business including any used car lot or location without the prior written approval of Pontiac."

Kaiser repeatedly sought Pontiac's permission to relocate his dealership and one area he particularly wanted was refused him because it was within the area of responsibility of another dealer. Kaiser eventually brought this suit against General Motors alleging that Pontiac had conspired to protect the competitive position of the dealer into whose area he wanted to move his own dealership and that it was illegal for Pontiac to restrict him from moving his business to another location.

The court found no evidence of a conspiracy, so it was left to decide whether it was *per se* illegal to forbid Kaiser move his business. It said that it was not illegal because it was the act of the company alone, not a conspiracy with another to restrict territories. Moreover, a franchise agreement is not in itself illegal. Illegality will depend on the limits or degree of control over the franchisee's freedom of action. The court referred to the Schwinn court's holding that a manufacturer may select his customers and may franchise certain dealers to whom he chooses to sell his goods exclusively—so long as nothing more is involved and so long as other unfranchised dealers have competitive products readily available to them. On the exact issue of the legality of requiring a franchised dealer to remain in one location, the court relied on *Boro Hall* v. *General Motors*, 317 U.S. 695 and also on *United States* v. *General Motors*, 384 U.S. 127 which, briefly summarized, held that it was not unlawful to enforce a location clause by unilateral action.

Thus, the use of areas of primary responsibility and dealer location clauses are lawful so long as they are not enforced for purposes of territorial restrictions, i.e. they are not simply a mask for illegal allocation of markets. The *effect* may tend to preserve markets, but if there is no express prohibition on the dealer from selling outside his territory and the clauses are not used with other practices (as in the Monsanto case) to force a division of markets, there would seem to be no illegality. Obviously such situations are vulnerable to antitrust attack, and franchise-dealer location schemes will be questioned. Indeed, one such scheme recently was the subject of an appeals court decision. In *GTE Sylvania* v. *Continental TV*, the US Court of Appeals for the 9th Circuit handed down an opinion on 9 April, 1976 which is in point.

The court here gave an explicit explanation of why a dealer location restriction is not *per se* illegal, and in doing so provided a useful exposition of the difference between the Schwinn type of territorial restriction on sales and a dealer location restriction. This case has a special interest because the same court on the same facts first declared dealer location restrictions to be *per se* illegal and then reversed itself. The court wrestled with interpreting and applying the Schwinn doctrine, and with the issue itself, irrespective of Schwinn as a precedent, whether location clauses are *per se* illegal. The core of the difficulty was ascertaining whether competition was inevitably unreasonably affected by a franchisor restricting its franchisee from moving its business from one place to another. Here is a skeleton of the facts which plagued the court.

Sylvania manufactured television sets but was losing its market to the point of having to consider going out of business. In an effort to stimulate dealers it instituted a franchising practice, that is, it selected various dealers in different areas and appointed them authorized dealers in Sylvania TV sets. There was no restriction as to where or to whom the franchisees might sell. There was, however, a restriction that the franchisee should not remove the location of his dealership. This was the only issue on which the court was divided. Continental TV Inc. was the franchised dealer in California. Continental shipped Sylvania sets from its franchised location to Sacramento where it was not franchised. Sylvania enforced the location clause and eventually terminated Continental's franchise whereupon Continental brought this suit.

In its first decision the court agreed that Sylvania had the right to franchise by location because that was simply a matter of Sylvania selecting Continental as a franchisee because of the location of Continental's retail stores. If Sylvania later found Continental's locations unsatisfactory it could just as simply terminate the franchise. The court narrowed the issue and found *per se* illegality "in Sylvania's procuring an agreement that these locations are restricted and in its subsequent attempts to enforce the agreement to dissuade and interfere with Continental's business judgment to open and sell in another store and to thwart that decision".

The first stage of the court's attack, then, was the finding of an *agreement* to restrict. The agreement is necessary, the reader will recall, for the plurality of persons required by s.

1 of the Sherman Act. The second stage of the court's attack was the location restriction and the enforcement of it. The court based its view of this aspect on the Schwinn doctrine, in particular on the fact that Sylvania had parted with dominion and control of the TV sets when it sold them to Continental and, having done that, Sylvania had no legal right to restrict Continental's use of them. The court equated Continental's shifting of the sets to another of its stores with the right, established by Schwinn, of Continental to sell those sets anywhere and to whomever it pleased. The court stated its view clearly:

> "If Continental had sold to an unfranchised retailer in Sacramento any attempt by Sylvania to interfere would be as improper as Schwinn's restrictions on resale to discounters or other unauthorized customers. If the antitrust laws would have protected Continental's transfer to such a retailer without Sylvania's approval, there is no apparent reason why they should not also protect the transfer if Continental itself is the retailer."

There was a vigorous dissent to this decision and the Circuit Court of Appeals in 1976 reviewed the matter *en banc* and completely reversed the earlier decision. Why?

There is no doubt that the court was influenced by Sylvania's imminent disappearance as a competitor in an oligopolistic market, and it has been established that a "failing company" or a company entering a new market may engage in some practices which would otherwise be illegal under the antitrust laws, in order to survive or have a chance of surviving in a new market. In fact, testimony was given by Sylvania that it instituted the dealer location franchises "in order for us to get a foot hold in the market". The court endorsed Sylvania's action even though it recognized that the location practice did have some effect on intrabrand competition. The court said:

> "This was an inevitable incident to Sylvania's attempt to promote and maintain interbrand competition. However, to ignore Sylvania's ultimate purpose, to remain in the market as a viable competitor; thereby fostering interbrand competition and to

consider only the fact that its practice slightly limited intra-brand competition, is to overlook the forest while watching the trees."

The real thrust of the court in its reversal was its attack of the previous application of Schwinn. The court carefully distinguished the use and effect of location restrictions from the restrictions in Schwinn and said that Schwinn was not applicable. Amplifying this point, the court said:

"If we were to adopt the approach of *per se* illegality, the ultimate result might be to undermine franchising as a tool to enable the small, independent businessman to compete with the large vertically integrated giants of many industries . . . a single franchisee, allowed to expand into a chain of stores and sell everywhere over the manufacturer's objection and in violation of the contract, might make it impossible for other small single-outlet franchises of the same manufacturer to compete effectively."

Schwinn restricted its dealers as to customers and territories where they might resell. Sylvania did neither of these. Schwinn restricted "vendees"; Sylvania restricted "permissible locations of 'vendors' ". On this distinction alone, Schwinn could not be used as a precedent to condemn Sylvania. The court also distinguished the commercial effect of the Schwinn and Sylvania restrictions.

In Schwinn intra-brand competition was wholly destroyed because a purchaser could only look to one source for the product: the authorized dealer for his territory. On the other hand Sylvania franchised at least two dealers in the major markets and each Sylvania dealer was free to sell to any buyer he chose thereby preserving intra-brand competition among dealers for customers and, conversely, also allowing buyers a choice between dealers. Delivering the coup de grâce to the use of Schwinn to invalidate Sylvania's location restriction the court said that Schwinn itself *permitted* location clauses and quoted, "nothing . . . shall prevent Schwinn . . . from designating in its retailer franchise agreements the location of the place or places of business for which the franchise is issued".

The attitude of the courts towards the use of areas of primary responsibility and dealer location clauses is uncertain. Generally it seems that in vertical distribution chains the courts are much more concerned about provisions in the agreement by which the dealer or distributor is restricted as to whom or where he may not sell. In the case of both the areas of primary responsibility and dealer locations, the clauses are not worded in a prohibitory fashion, i.e. the dealer is not restricted as to whom or where he may not sell.

It has become apparent that the *Schwinn* case will not be the executioner of all vertical restrictions in the distribution chain. The courts have recognized that some vertical restraints might be justified or at least worthy of reprieve from a *per se* judgment. We have seen this in the Sylvania court's remarks about Sylvania's sorry position in the television set market.

In *Coors Co.* v. *FTC* 497 F.2d 1178, the court said that the Schwinn *per se* rule "should yield to situations where a unique product requires territorial restrictions to remain in business". There, as in the later Sylvania case, the courts were concerned with preserving the viability of a business enterprise.

As a corollary to that concern, *Tripoli* v. *Wella Corpn.* 425 F.2d 932 made another exception from the Schwinn *per se* axe when the public would be injured if territorial or customer restrictions were abolished simply because they were restrictions. It seems the courts have turned away somewhat from the original antitrust philosophy that a good end will not justify otherwise illegal means, hence the public benefit from a price stabilization programme would not save the programme from *per se* illegality. Yet in easing away from Schwinn, the courts have at least used the public good as an excuse to shift the litigated business practice out from under *per se* illegality into inspection under the light of the rule of reason. For example, in the Tripoli case just mentioned, the court permitted a resale restraint because of health hazards if unlimited distribution of a certain kind of cosmetic were permitted. In yet another exception to the

Schwinn *per se* rule, the court permitted a manufacturer to require his wholesalers to sell his product for less if the product were to be put to certain types of uses by the purchasers from the wholesaler.

THE SCHWINN DOCTRINE IN FOREIGN COMMERCE

There are very few cases involving the application of the Schwinn *per se* customer and territorial violations in American foreign commerce. In view of the number of distributors of American products who are located in countries foreign to the US, some discussion of one of the cases might be useful. The US District Court for the Eastern District of Pennsylvania had to deal with the problem in a suit filed on 27 February, 1974. The case is *Todhunter–Mitchell & Co.* v. *Anheuser–Busch Inc.* Todhunter–Mitchell was a wholesale distributor of spirits and beer in the Bahama Islands. Bahama Blenders Ltd. was also a wholesale distributor in the Bahama Islands. Anheuser–Busch is a very large manufacturer of beer in the US and had appointed Bahama Blenders as its distributor in the Bahama Islands. Todhunter–Mitchell was interested in importing certain brands of beer made by Anheuser–Busch but was unsuccessful despite repeated requests of wholesalers of the Anheuser–Busch products who were located in Louisiana and Florida. These wholesalers were the appointed distributors for Anheuser–Busch in those territories. This case arose because in connection with a request by Todhunter–Mitchell for a very large quantity of the Anheuser–Busch beer known as Budweiser, one of the wholesalers telephoned Mr Busch for permission to sell the beer and Mr Busch expressly forbade the distributor from selling the beer to Todhunter–Mitchell. Todhunter–Mitchell brought suit under the Sherman Act alleging that this was an illegal territorial restraint on the wholesaler. Anheuser–Busch argued that the Sherman Act did not apply at all because all that the refusal to deal would do was produce elimination of competition between two foreign corporations—Todhunter–Mitchell and Bahama Blenders. The court agreed with this argument but identified the illegality rather in the ultimate result of the restraint placed on the Florida and Louisiana wholesalers. The territorial restriction placed on the wholesaler by Mr Busch directly affected the flow of commerce in beer out of the US to the Bahama Islands and restraints which do have such a direct effect on foreign commerce are subject to the provisions of s. 1 of the Sherman Act. Accordingly the Schwinn principle did apply. It would seem therefore that it would be illegal for an American manufacturer to forbid any of its wholesalers within the US from exporting to a foreign country.

Another exception from the Schwinn doctrine is really more commonly used in Europe than it is in the US but it is becoming more and more popular in the US. The manufacturer who has appointed two or more distributors in certain territories will not have an express or even tacit agreement with the distributors that they will not resell outside of their respective territories; nevertheless, the manufacturer will require a distributor who sells outside of his territory to pay a certain percentage of the sales price to the distributor into whose territory he is selling. For example, if distributor A in one territory sells a product into distributor B's territory, A will be required to pay, say, 7% of the invoice price to B. This of course has the effect of increasing the price at which A will sell the product into B's territory and should have the ultimate effect of preserving B's territory to B alone. Obviously, such payments are very dangerous but they have been justified. It is the way the amount is calculated that justifies the practice. It is understood that a distributor can make a substantial investment in advertising and premises in order to capture the distributorship for a product and that it would be unfair for a neighbouring distributor to take advantage of all that expenditure and sell into that distributor's territory without compensating him in some way. The amount of money that he pays over to the "invaded" distributor, if it is equal to what would be the various costs incurred by the invaded distributor related to such a sale, would be justified by the courts. We must caution the reader, however, that this is an extremely dangerous practice in the US and that if it is to be used it should be completely arm's length with no ancillary conditions or restrictions. It is easy to understand the interest of governments in distribution arrangements involving territorial restrictions.

TERMINATION OF DISTRIBUTORS

Perhaps even more intense, because it is so personal, is the interest of individuals in the termination of their distributorships by their suppliers. A terminated distributor is a most unhappy person who is not unwilling to seek vengeance on his former supplier. Absent a monopolistic intent, the right of a supplier to terminate a distribution arrangement may be unquestioned. The difficulty arises, and terminated distributors always seek this weakness, when the supplier can be found to be in agreement with third parties to terminate the distributorship. In that event, the supplier's unilateral right to terminate does not exist and he enters into the area of yet another example of *per se* illegality. We have seen examples of this kind of conspiracy against distributors in Chapter 2.

Apart from the relief provided by the laws of the European Community and the Federal Laws of the US, the reader would be well advised to consult the law in the individual European nations because it can be extremely difficult to terminate a distributorship or an agency even according to national law apart from any law of unfair competition or restrictive trade practices or antitrust. This does not mean of course that a supplier cannot terminate a distributor for justifiable reasons, but we do put forward the caution that the terminated distributor will find his relief where he can and one of the fertile fields for such relief is in antitrust if he can find any suspicion of collusion between the terminating supplier and another distributor. Probably the most important theme to be remembered in connection with the termination of any distributorship is that the weapon of termination cannot be used to enforce illegal restrictions in the distributorship agreement, e.g. territorial or customer restrictions. Thus, despite what we have said above about the legality of terminating a distributorship because of failure of the distributor to honour his area of primary responsibility or dealer location clauses, the courts always have the latitude to find illegality in such enforcement if the court finds that the enforcement by termination is simply a mask to preserve territorial restrictions. This is simply a restatement of a basic antitrust principle: one cannot use legal means to obtain an illegal result. Again, as we have often remarked possibly the most important initial situation to be wary of is a conspiracy or an agreement with another party that will have the intended result of injuring competition. In this portion dealing with distribution problems and vertical restrictions in them, the key element was the legality of a supplier unilaterally to terminate or refuse to sell to a wholesaler or retailer. This becomes illegal if the supplier agrees with another party to do so. One of the most recent cases emphasizing this point was *Garrett's Inc.* v. *Farah Manufacturing Co. Inc.* which was decided in the US District Court for South Carolina on 12 April, 1976. Farah discovered that one of its customers, Garrett's (a retail store), was selling its merchandise at a very large discount, far below the retail price suggested by Farah. Farah, totally on its own without discussion with anyone, simply discontinued supplying Garrett's with its merchandise. Garrett's of course took the obvious approach and charged Farah with an illegal refusal to deal with it. The court did not uphold Garrett's view because Garrett's failed to provide convincing evidence that Farah refused to supply Garrett's with merchandise "in furtherance of any agreement or conspiracy . . .".

In so far as the European Community is concerned, we outlined its view at the beginning of this section. Horizontal and vertical agreements are illegal under art. 85(1) if they can affect the flow of trade between member states and, of course, territorial or customer restrictions in this respect can certainly have that effect. On the other hand, and quite different from the view of the US courts, vertical agreements such as exclusive distributorships are expressly exempt from the prohibition of art. 85. Notwithstanding reg. 67/67 vertical agreements such as distributorships which impose a re-export or re-import prohibition of the distributor are not entitled to the exemption provided by that regulation. The regulation should be interpreted very narrowly; the expression "agreements in which only two enterprises take part and in which: (*a*) one of the parties agrees to deliver certain products only to the other party for resale within a specified area in the Common Market" means simply that it is permissible for a manufacturer to appoint an exclusive distributor to distribute his products in a certain area in the Common Market. It does not mean that the distributor can be prohibited from exporting the products to another area of the Common Marker or back into the territory of the manufacturer. This regulation also prohibits the kind of situation that we saw above in connection with the Anheuser–Busch case, involving the Bahamian wholesalers of beer. The regulation does not apply when "the contracting parties make it difficult for middlemen and consumers to obtain the products . . . from other dealers in the Common Market . . .".

A Commission decision of 15 December 1975 which was reported on 3 February 1976 takes a similar line to the US in excepting franchise-type practices from illegality under art. 85. SABA, a German company affiliated with General Telephone and Electronics Corp. of New York, manufactures various consumer electrical applicances such as television receivers, phonographs and tape recorders. It sells in the Community through authorized dealers whom SABA selects on the basis of their qualifications to handle such technical devices, as well as for their locations. The franchised dealers are exclusive in the Community but non-exclusive in Germany. They are required to purchase minimum quantities of SABA products. The restrictive clauses in the distributorship contracts which came under the Commission's investigation for the purpose of deciding whether an exemption should be granted were of two kinds: those which, by virtue of their exclusivity, inhibited

SABA from selling to other than those distributors within its distribution network; and those which restricted the distributors to reselling only to those dealers authorized by SABA. The selection of authorized dealers was analogous to the franchise system referred to as permissible in the American Schwinn decision and in the Sylvania case. The Commission accepted the selected distributorship scheme, but the small distinctions from the American approach and treatment of the problem are interesting.

SABA gave evidence that it would sell to any wholesaler or to any retailer meeting various technical, financial and sales standards. This was the first stage of its distribution system. The second stage of the system is replete with what would clearly be US antitrust difficulties but which the Commission almost totally ignored. The second stage chiefly concerned resale restrictions (condemned by the Schwinn court) as to whom the wholesaler could sell, i.e. only to the franchised dealers. The second stage also included other restrictions which would have been troublesome in the US. The exclusive distributors in Denmark, Belgium, Luxembourg and Holland were required not to manufacture or deal in competitive products or "to seek customers, establish branches or maintain distribution depots outside their allowed territory". (Note the analogy with the American dealer location clauses.)

The Commission said there was no illegality or even the application of art. 85(1) in the first stage. It was lawful for SABA to select dealers and wholesalers according to their ability to provide technical expertise. This was a legitimate discrimination and not the kind of restriction on competition envisaged by art. 85. The selection of dealers on the basis of qualitative criteria provided an adequate distribution system and "all persons who fulfil these requirements are in fact appointed as SABA dealers". The part of stage one that disturbed the Commission was not the selectivity of it but rather the ancillary restrictions such as the franchised dealers being required to purchase minimum quantities, stocking full product ranges and entering into six-monthly supply contracts. The Commission said that these made the wholesalers too dependant on SABA and that they "lead to the exclusion of those undertaking meeting the qualitative criteria of appointment but which are not in a position or not willing to comply with these additional obligations" and that the obligations came within art. 85(1) because they "go beyond technical requirements, impede to an appreciable extent the appointment of undertakings as SABA dealers, and thus restrict access to the trade in SABA products".

Let us pause here. The American view of the same facts in stage one is that such selectivity is not within the antitrust laws at all because the exercise of selection is the inherent right of a manufacturer to choose those with whom he wants to deal. The minimum purchase requirements held by the Commission to be within art. 85(1) would be all right in the US; the stocking of full product lines would be all right in the US if no illegal tie-in would be involved. However, the Commission held that despite their anticompetitive effect such restrictions would be entitled to an art. 85(3) exemption because they benefit the public.

Another variance from US thinking is in the attitude towards the resale restrictions. In the US these are *per se* illegal. In Europe, according to the Commission, they are all right. They fall within art. 85(1) but are exempt because the consumer is assured of good service and continuity of supplies and a broader range of goods from a qualified supplier of technical goods. Nowhere did the Commission entertain doubts of anticompetitiveness in the fact that a restraint on reselling meant that the wholesalers could not compete for customers, although the Commission said that they could compete as to the authorized dealers to whom they sold. The Commission also ignored the presence of an "agreement" between SABA and its wholesalers and authorized dealers that was in restraint of trade. In fact, in what seems to us to be a remarkable statement, the Commission seemed to endorse such cooperative activity: "Thus the SABA wholesalers and exclusive distributors are able to participate in production planning for which, because of their proximity to the market, they are particularly suited." That situation would be dangerous under American antitrust law because it is a relationship ripe for price-fixing, conspiracy and illegal customer selections.

So, whilst both the US and the Community arrived at the same result of permitting franchising, each got there by a different route. In Europe such exclusive selectivity is permitted where the nature of the product requires special handling by trained persons. (See the Third Report on Competition Policy, May 1974, and the Official Journal, L 147, 7 July 1970.) Within limits the American view is quite similar. The reader will recall the justification for tie-in clauses and dealer selectivity in connection with hazardous products and franchised trademarks.

Notwithstanding this similarity there is a fundamental difference between US and Community thinking about exclusive and selective distributorship arrangements. The Commission's view seems firmly fixed not so much on the actual effect on competition but rather on the benefit that is brought to the public: "In the Commission's view any limitation on sales between main distributors and retailers and between retailers and ultimate consumers are justifiable only if they result in a downward alignment of prices in the various Member States."

That would not be acceptable in America. The lowering of prices has never cured the illegality of a practice having the intent or effect of unreasonably interfering with the natural play of competitive forces.

Let us return for a moment to a comparative examination of the first stage of the distribution process, i.e. the right in the first place to select certain franchised wholesale-dealers. In the *Schwinn* case, the Supreme Court said that the manufacturer could select and franchise certain enterprises for the further distribution of its goods so long as there were other competitive products and other dealers available to the community. Moreover the Supreme Court noted that this type of activity by Schwinn was *unilateral* and so was not an "agreement" which could even bring the matter within s. 1 of the Sherman Act.

On the other hand, in the SABA proceedings the Commission not once referred to the absence of any kind of an agreement in the first stage of the selection process. This in itself would have taken the matter away from the authority of the Commission to consider the situation at all. The reader will remember that in the absence of any agreement or concerted practice there is no jurisdiction under art. 85. As SABA had only a relatively small part of the market it could not even have been an art. 86 situation which, in any case, would not be subject to the exemption proceedings. We think therefore that the Commission need never have concerned itself with the fact of SABA's selecting franchised wholesalers and dealers and that it was totally unnecessary for the Commission to have the opinion that a large number of distributors that could have fulfilled the requirements and conditions of SABA were excluded from becoming SABA distributors and from selling SABA's products.

One might conclude from a study of the SABA case that there is little that one can say about the boundaries of legality of distributorship agreements, both horizontal and vertical, in the Common Market. Either they are exempt under the group exemption provided by reg. 67/67 or by a special proceeding before the Commission under art. 85(3) or they are illegal under art. 85(1). Probably much more interesting is the development of various techniques in the vertical distribution of products in the Common Market. When the various enterprises realized that they could not restrict distributors in their resale of products and that they could not maintain their traditional territorial division of markets, they turned to the use of various forms of industrial property rights such as trade marks, patents and copyright in an attempt to preserve those markets but as we shall see in the next part of this book the Commission and the European Court of Justice have taken a very strict and narrow view of what is permissible in this respect. In particular, both the Commission and the European Court have consistently struck down uses of industrial property rights to preserve a particular part of the Common Market as the exclusive domain of any particular manufacturer or distributor; more especially they have strongly and clearly condemned the use of industrial property rights in any one country to prevent parallel imports of competing products from another country. We will deal more fully with this later on in Chapters 14 and 15.

When one proceeds from the permissible unilateral actions and decisions by enterprises to select distributors to the conspiracies and agreements leading to territorial and customer restrictions on sales or purchases, one must eventually meet the next section of Sherman Act *per se* illegalities: the group boycotts.

8

Group boycotts

A group boycott in its simplest definition is the agreement, express or tacit of a group of persons not to deal with a particular third person or persons. The boycott is essentially a customer restriction and its restraint on competition is unquestioned. It eliminates competition among the members of the boycott itself and the competitive capacity of the boycotted third person or persons. The only question is whether a boycott can ever be entitled to a rule of reason analysis or whether it must always be considered to be illegal.

A boycott is really nothing more than a concerted refusal to deal. The individual right well established in the law to refuse to deal with a person (absent any intent to obtain a monopoly) can be transformed into illegality when the decision is mutually agreed with another party. A parallel view is taken in Europe, where under art. 85 an agreement among two or more parties is needed before the violation can occur and under art. 86 an individual refusal to deal with a customer can become a violation if the refusing party is in a dominant position and his refusal in some way imposes injury on competition so that the act of refusing could be labelled as an abuse of the refusing party's dominant position.

This matter of refusing to deal with potential customers has more than ordinary practical interest. All business might be grossly divided into two parts: production and distribution. In the field of antitrust most of the difficulties arise in the distribution half of business and in this half of the business one of the problems faced by manufacturers is establishing an efficient distribution network which will sell their products as widely as possible at the best price possible. The manufacturer-supplier does not always feel that his dealers are adequately representing his merchandise and he may want to terminate the distributorship. The law accepts this fact of business life and also accepts the right of the individual manufacturer to terminate distributorships. We have already dealt with this subject but we think it worthwhile to recollect some concepts about it because the individual right of refusal to deal is a springboard to the illegality of the concerted refusal to deal which is called the boycott.

The danger in the exercise of this individual right is that the termination might be interpreted as a conspiracy or act with another in which case the termination may be illegal or be part of an illegal overall plan. The fundamental caution in any termination is this: beware of any taint, suspicion, implication or inference of an agreement of any kind between oneself and another to terminate a business relationship with a third party.

This warning is somewhat of a reprise of the earlier conspiracy chapter which dealt with the courts' views and conclusions of relationships which they considered to be agreements or concerted practices. The courts instinctively find something repugnant in a supplier terminating a distributorship or refusing to deal with any particular party, so they often search zealously for indications that the termination or refusal to deal was something more than a straightforward unilateral decision by the supplier. The US Supreme Court signalled its tendency to whittle at the broad rule of this unilateral right of the supplier in a landmark case called *U.S.* v. *Parke, Davis and Co.*, 362 U.S. 29. Parke Davis, a pharmaceutical manufacturer, had announced a policy of resale pricing. If a dealer refused to maintain the resale pricing policy it was Parke Davis' privilege to refuse to continue to deal with him. Had the matter stopped there, Parke Davis would probably have been well within the accepted practice; however, Parke Davis did not stop there. It sent representatives to the non-complying dealers and attempted to coerce them into compliance; it discussed the problem with its wholesalers who then agreed with Parke Davis to refuse to sell to retailers who did not keep to the resale price programme. In other words, the court found that there was "something more" than a simple unilateral decision to refuse to deal. Even the use of coercion has been found by the court to be a factor turning a legal refusal to deal into an illegal act. Most cases turn up to be exercises in the court's finding illegal concerted refusals to deal in what apparently had been a valid unilateral refusal to deal. One case which is a refreshing exception from the line of judicial condemnations and which illustrates a perhaps subtle difference between individual and coordinate action is *Instant Delivery Corp.* v. *City Stores Co.*, 284 F.Supp. 941.

In Philadelphia, Pennsylvania one company had been providing a delivery service for four of the city's largest department stores. For various reasons, principally because of labour problems, the delivery company had to stop its service and the department stores were compelled to look for other companies to carry on the delivery of packages from their stores. The four department stores were totally independent of each other. Two of the department stores made their own arrangements with one company and the other two stores with another delivery service company. Shortly after forming these arrangements one of the two delivery companies (who themselves were also independent of each other) informed the two department stores whom it was servicing that it would have to go out of business, thus putting two of the department stores into the position that they were before.

The four department stores, recalling the efficiency in the earlier days when they were all serviced by a single company, asked the two delivery service companies to meet their representatives to compete for a consolidated delivery service. The two largest department stores elected one of the two delivery companies and tried to persuade the other two department stores that it would be better all round to use the same carrier. The argument was simply that the company that they had chosen was more stable financially and enjoyed better labour relations. They were successful in convincing the two other department stores to use the same carrier, whereupon the losing carrier sued everyone on the ground of a concerted refusal to deal.

There was no doubt that four companies had in fact agreed to use one carrier rather than the other but the court made the distinction that "their agreement was limited to the re-establishment of a consolidated delivery service with which they had earlier enjoyed a long and satisfactory experience, and to the selection of one of two competing carriers to perform that service". To put it another way, the court did not find that the agreement was *not* to use one of the carriers but rather to select one of two carriers who had been invited to compete for their business. The court summed it up nicely by describing the plaintiff delivery company as "a disappointed competitor, not the object of an illegal boycott".

Another example where the absence of an agreement among competitors removed the matter from Sherman Act illegality is in the use of common buying agencies by groups of competitors. Where the buying agency is not limited to purchasing from a single source of supply and there is no agreement among the competing buyers that they would use exclusively the common buying agency, there is no illegality.

DEALING IN COMPETING PRODUCTS

Arguably, one of the most frequent causes of concern of the supplier is that his distributor not deal in competing products so long as he also is a distributor of the supplier's product. Invariably the question arises as to the legality of a clause in the distributorship agreement in which the distributor agrees not to deal in competing products. In the Common Market there is no problem because such an arrangement is expressly permitted by reg. 67/67, but the situation in the US is somewhat different.

First of all the law does not condemn exclusive dealing as such (and it is exclusive dealing when the supplier asks the dealer not to handle competing products); however, particularly under s. 3 of the Clayton Act and possibly also under the Sherman Act such a requirement could be declared to be illegal if the granting of the exclusive distributorship is conditioned on the dealer not handling competing products. In this respect the supplier-manufacturer should not coerce or bring pressure to bear on the distributor in such a way that the distributor could later prove that the supplier did in fact condition the grant of the distributorship on the dealer's agreeing not to handle the other products. Under the Clayton Act, there would be little question that the practice would be illegal; but under the Sherman Act unreasonableness of the restriction would have to be found. Accordingly such a clause is not in itself illegal and it would not be unlawful for the suppliers simply to terminate the distributorship if he finds that the distributor has been dealing in competitive products.

But what an individual might legally do alone he may not legally do in concert with others, and this brings us to the application of the *per se* rule to commercial boycotts. There is no difficulty in accepting or understanding the principle that a boycott, agreements to refuse to sell or to purchase or to deal, or agreements where someone is coerced to deal with a particular party, or to follow certain practises, are *per se* illegal under the Sherman Act. The anti-competitive effect is obvious. We will mention only briefly three landmark cases exemplifying the principle.

The opening attack leading to the declaration of *per se* illegality of group boycotts occurred in a US Supreme Court case decided in 1914. This was *Eastern States Retail Lumber Dealers Association* v. *U.S.*, 234 U.S. 600. Retail lumber dealers banded together to defend against those of their wholesale suppliers who by-passed them and sold direct to customers. Their association's secretary circulated a list of those wholesalers among the associations members. The purpose of the "blacklist" was to induce the retailers not to purchase from the listed wholesalers, although there was no agreement among them to do so. The court felt that despite the absence of such an agreement there could have been no other purpose for such lists. It was not a question of only the particular retailer not dealing with the wholesaler (which would have been a lawful unilateral decision by him not to deal) but rather influencing all the other member retailers not to deal with him.

The anticompetitiveness lay in that

"these reports not only tend to directly restrain the freedom of commerce by preventing the listed dealers from entering into competition with retailers . . . but it directly tends to prevent other retailers who have no personal grievance against him, and with whom he might trade, from so doing, they being deterred solely because of the influence of the report circulated among the members of the association".

The court made the following quote from an earlier case which did not reach the point of labelling the offence as being *per se* illegal, but it clearly defined the groundwork for such a declaration by saying:

"when (the members) combine and agree that no one of them will trade with any producer or wholesaler who shall sell to a consumer within the trade range of any of them, quite another case is presented. An act harmless when done by one may become a public wrong when done by many acting in concert . . . *if the result be hurtful to the public or to the individual against whom the concerted action is directed*".

We have italicized a portion which indicates the possibility of justification through the rule of reason. Here is where the earlier court fell short of establishing the boycott as a *per se* violation because it seemed to require evidence of injury before declaring illegality. The Eastern States court cured the defect:

"When the retailer goes beyond his personal right, and, conspiring and combining with others . . . seeks to obstruct the free course of interstate trade and commerce and to unduly suppress competition by placing obnoxious wholesale dealers under the coercive influence of a condemnatory report circulated among others . . . he exceeds his lawful rights, and such action brings him and those acting with him within the condemnation of the act of Congress . . .".

The *per se* illegality of boycotts was confirmed 27 years later in *Fashion Originators Guild of America Inc.* v. *Federal Trade Commission*, 312 U.S. 457. The Guild was a powerful combination of textile manufacturers and dress designers and manufacturers who sought to protect themselves against the unfair practice of non-members pirating their designs. They agreed not to sell to those retailers who dealt with dresses embodying their designs pirated from them and manufactured by others. They defended their boycott on the ground that there was no legal protection of their original designs available to them and that pirating was unfair competition.

The Federal Trade Commission, the body who first heard the dispute, refused to listen to evidence that the pirating was unfair and that the Guild's actions were reasonable and necessary to protect the members. It was enough that the boycotting policy "narrows the outlets to which garment and textile manufacturers can sell and the sources from which retailers can buy . . . and has both as its necessary tendency and as its purpose and effect the direct suppression of competition from the sale of unregistered textiles and copied designs . . .".

The Fashion Originators case involved an organization which controlled the market. Is it necessary that the boycotters have such power? The question was answered 18 years later in *Klor's Inc.* v. *Broadway–Hale Stores, Inc.*, 359 U.S. 207. The only facts important to our purpose are these: Klor's and Broadway–Hale are competing department stores. Broadway–Hale is bigger than Klor's and conspired with its suppliers of major appliances either not to sell to Klor's or to sell to Klor's at discriminatory prices. These facts were not disputed. Broadway–Hale defended simply that there are "hundreds of other household appliance retailers . . ." and that the controversy was purely personal between the parties which did not amount to a "public wrong proscribed by the Sherman Act". The Supreme Court thought otherwise and in doing so established that the boycott was wrong and

> "is not to be tolerated merely because the victim is just one merchant whose business is so small that his destruction makes little difference to the economy. Monopoly can as surely thrive by the elimination of such small businessmen, one at a time, as it can by driving them out in large groups. In recognition of this fact the Sherman Act has consistently been read to forbid all contracts and combinations which tend to create a monopoly, whether the tendency is a creeping one or one that proceeds at full gallop."

The last few phrases were quoted by the court from the International Salt case with which we shall deal in Chapter 9 on tying illegality.

Notwithstanding the abuses by boycott illustrated in the above three cases, there is the equal burden of the courts to preserve the right of an industry to regulate its activity in the public interest, a right which need not cross into the area of *per se* illegal boycotting. For example, industrial groups may lawfully enact rules and regulations which, if suspect under the antitrust laws, at least deserve the hearing of evidence under the rule of reason to ascertain whether any anticompetitive effect is an unreasonable and unnecessary restraint. In this regard the test seems to be whether the association's rules and regulations are directed against and intended to exclude competition, with the added ingredient of coercion upon outsiders. In such cases, the courts would probably find a *per se* violation. But where such factors do not exist and especially in the absence of economic pressure or coercion to bring about compliance, the courts would retreat from a *per se* attitude and accept evidence of reasonableness of the rules.

Secondary boycotts

The characteristic of a "secondary" boycott is the introduction of coercion on customers to influence them to stop dealing with a particular party. The "primary" boycott would be the agreement among a group not to deal with that particular party. To strengthen the effect of the primary boycott, the boycotters will then through coercion or even peaceful means try to influence the customers of the boycotted person not to deal with him. A secondary boycott is as unlawful as the primary one.

9

Tying arrangements

If one understands the inherent repugnance of any anti-trust law to the commercial effects of "exclusivity", one will understand why "tying" arrangements have always been condemned. They are a kind of exclusivity, or bring about effects similar to those of exclusivity because they restrain the freedom of a person to act commercially, and unnecessarily affect competition in products that are secondary to the main subject matter of an agreement. The Sherman Act does not define a tying arrangement but s. 3 of the Clayton Act does. In general terms it is the leasing or selling of "goods, wares, merchandise, machinery, supplies or other commodities, whether patented or unpatented" for use or resale within the US on condition that the lessee or purchaser of the products will not use or deal in the products of a competitor of the lessor or seller. The full definition is more sophisticated and detailed but we are being intentionally brief to illustrate more clearly the precise nature of the illegality in tying arrangements.

Tying arrangements take their most common form in sales or licences where the buyer or the licensee (lessee) must accept from the seller something other than the products for which he has contracted. Accordingly, the principal product being sold or leased is called the "tying" product and the other products which the buyer or lessee must take are called the "tied" products. In these kinds of arrangements the seller is using the tying product as a lever to compel the buyer to take other lines of products, sometimes called "full-line forcing". If he is going to be successful in doing this the seller clearly must have control over the tying product. For example, a seller of sugar would not be very convincing in selling the sugar to a buyer if he said, "I will sell you the sugar if you will also buy 100 lb of potatoes". This would be an ineffective tying arrangement because the intended buyer could easily refuse the offer and buy his sugar elsewhere. Such an attempted tying contract even if completed would not be subject to the Sherman Act, or indeed, to the Clayton Act. That is precisely what the US Supreme Court established in *Northern Pacific Railway Co.* v. *U.S.*, 356 U.S. 1. Moreover, the court in that case went a step further and said that a "not insubstantial" amount of commerce must be affected in the tying practice.

In a tying arrangement, where is the restraint on competition that is the illegal effect? Although tying arrangements have always been disapproved as legitimate and lawful business practices it is not as apparent as one might suspect exactly why and how (and if) competition is restrained. One of the members of the Attorney General's Committee that studied the US Antitrust laws in 1955 said:

> "both the Congress and the courts have for many years disapproved tying arrangements. Such contracts have been almost universally regarded as monopolistic devices. Upon analysis, however, the matter becomes far from obvious and perhaps should rather be termed mysterious. Whether prohibition of tying improves the allocation of resources is open to question".

The illegal effect must relate to competition for the tied product because the presumption is that the seller has such control and dominance over the tying product that there is no effective competition in it but is sufficient to bring about the tying-in of a product over which the seller does not enjoy such control. In the simple illustration just given, the competition that the court would be concerned about would be in the potatoes if, that is, the seller had an effective monopoly in sugar. The Supreme Court in the Northern Pacific case, in explaining the evil of tying arrangements, said that they serve hardly any purpose except to suppress competition because they deny competitors "free access to the market for the tied product, not because the party imposing the tying requirements has a better product or a lower price but because of his power or leverage in another market". Then the court gave a definitive statement of when a tying arrangement would be considered to be *per se* unreasonable:

> "They are unreasonable in and of themselves whenever a party has sufficient economic power with respect to the tying product to appreciably restrain free competition in the market for the tied product and a not insubstantial amount of inter-state commerce is affected".

In our introductory comments about *per se* violations we said that it was not important how much competition or interstate commerce had to be affected before the matter was serious enough to amount to Sherman Act *per se* unlawfulness. Now we see the Supreme Court stating that in so far as tying arrangements are concerned free competition in the tied product must be "appreciably" restrained and "a not insubstantial amount of inter-state commerce" must be affected. This is unlike the *per se* categories discussed in the preceding chapters. In price-fixing cases, for example, no such measure of the effect on competition or commerce was necessary.

Apparently in building an argument for *per se* unlawfulness of "tying" or "tie-in" practices the necessary restraint on competition is not presumed to be inevitable in every case. There must be an actual appreciable restraint on competition and an effect on a "not insubstantial amount of inter-state commerce". If the defendant is all-powerful in the market for the tied product, and has the required control in the tying product, the court would infer the necessary effects on competition and commerce, so the *per se* judgment would follow from a showing of that control and power in both the tying and tied products.

The *Northern Pacific* case illustrates the need for these prerequisites to a *per se* ruling, and the reader's attention is called to the dissent of Justices Harlan, Frankfurter and Whittaker. The facts are as follows. In 1864 and 1870 the Northern Pacific Railway Company was granted about forty million acres of land in the northwest of what is now the US. It was to use the land to build a railroad. The company sold most of the land but reserved mineral rights in 6,500,000 of the sold acres. It then leased most of the unsold land. The land which it sold and leased was rich in timber, iron ore, oil and gas and various mineral deposits. This case arose because the company inserted in its sales and leasing agreements a clause requiring the buyer or lessee to use the seller's railroad to transport the commodities produced or manufactured on the sold or leased land. Obviously the amount of interstate commerce concerned was substantial. There were other means of transportation for a large portion of the commodities.

In 1949 the government attacked this practice (which they called "preferential routing") as an unreasonable restraint of trade under the Sherman Act, and, in its discussion of tying conditions, made the bold statement, "Where such conditions are successfully exacted competition on the merits with respect to the tied product is inevitably curbed". Indeed, "tying agreements serve hardly any purpose beyond the suppression of competition". (Observe that there is no qualification of "appreciable" or "not insubstantial" effects.) The court explained more precisely the anticompetitive nature of tying clauses: "They deny competitors free access to the market for a tied product" because the party imposing the tying requirements has power or leverage in another market.

There is a wealth of material in just these few words of the court. For example note the flat conclusion that (*a*) competition in the tied product must be curbed; (*b*) the party is *imposing* the requirement (implying the agreement was not freely entered into by both parties); and (*c*) the party imposing the requirements is able to impose them because he has certain and sufficient power in another area which he uses to compel the other party to accept the conditions. The court then had to find the facts to fit into the three conditions, as well as the "appreciable" effect on competition in the tied product and the effect on interstate commerce. As to the power in the tying product, the court saw this in the Northern Pacific's extensive landholding. The tied "product" was the railroad.

There was no doubt as to the effect on interstate commerce. Northern Pacific, however, did introduce evidence to weaken the government's argument in respect of the compulsion to use its railroad. The parties buying or leasing the land from Northern Pacific at all times had the option to use competing railroads if their charges were lower than Northern's or if they provided better service. For reasons which are unclear the court did not give much weight to this evidence and commented only "however that may be, the essential fact remains that these agreements are binding obligations held over the heads of the vendees which deny defendant's competitors access to the fenced-off market on the same terms as the defendant". Presumably the court meant that despite the fact that Northern's customers could use a competitor's railroad, the customers and competitors were nonetheless restrained because the customers could not exercise their option unless and until the competition lowered their price or improved their service, and even then, if Northern met that lowered price or equalled the improved service, the customers would have to stay with Northern. One wonders why there should be any legal objection to such tying clauses if they could have the apparent effect of actually promoting competition, e.g. between Northern and its competitors.

We think that probably the basic feature of tying, as seen by the court in the *Northern Pacific* case, despite the "escape" clause for its customers, is that Northern always has the power to keep the customers to itself and this power is effected by contractual obligations rather than by its merits as a railroad carrier. We mentioned the dissent of Justices Harlan, Frankfurter and Whittaker. It is, in our opinion, the most pointed and clear analysis of the illegality of tying clauses. The Justices first objected that an important prerequisite for *per se* illegality was not proved. This was whether Northern's landholdings did, in fact, give them sufficient control over the relevant market for land to afford Northern the "lever" to compel customers to use its railroad. "Because the Government necessarily based its complaint on s. 1 of the Sherman Act rather than on s. 3 of the Clayton Act[1] it was required to show that the challenged tying clauses constituted *unreasonable* restraints of trade."[2]

To that end, the government had to prove Northern's dominance over the market for the tying product, i.e. the landholdings with their timber, oil, gas, minerals etc., *and* that an appreciable volume of business in the tied product, i.e. railroad transport was restrained. Such requirements are necessary, argued the dissenters, because the real evil in tying arrangements is the use of "monopolistic leverage" in one market to expand into another. The *per se* nature of the illegality does not arise simply because the clause is a "tying" clause, but rather "from its use by virtue of a vendor's dominance over the tying interest to foreclose competitors from a substantial market in the tied interest".

THE RELEVANT MARKET OVER WHICH A DEFENDANT MUST HAVE DOMINANCE IN A TYING ARRANGEMENT

In the *Northern* case, was the relevant market only the *kind* of land held by Northern or was it the *particular tracts* of land that it held? The answer is critical to a verdict on tying illegality. If the relevant market was the *particular* tracts,

---

1 The Clayton Act relates only to goods, wares, merchandise, machinery, supplies or other commodities. Accordingly it does not cover railway services. The Sherman Act is not so limited.

2 The Clayton Act has its own "rule of reason" or standard to measure a violation, built into s. 3. By doing this, the legislators made it much easier for the court to decide when a violation occurred and the court did not have to go into all of the wide-ranging details of economic effects to decide whether a particular practice was undue in its restraint on trade. For example, the pertinent part of s. 3 of the Clayton Act condemns exclusive dealing (such as would be found in a tying contract) if the effect of the exclusive dealing is "to substantially lessen competition or tend to create a monopoly in any line of commerce". The simplifying effect of these words is that so long as the stated conditions are met the violation is deemed to exist; no evidence of justification or beneficial effects—characteristics typically argued in Sherman Act "rule of reason" defences are permitted.

then the government's case is easily made, because obviously Northern had control and dominion over them and *could*, therefore, coerce a buyer who wanted those tracts to accept a "tied" condition. On the other hand if the relevant market was only the same *kind* of land held by Northern, the government's case is not so easily made. It would have to be shown that only Northern had that *kind* of land, or that for some reason, the customers could not without unreasonable effort, find the same kind of land elsewhere. The dissenters felt that the relevant market was wider than the particular land owned by Northern.

> "The District Court should have taken evidence of the relative strength of (Northern's) landholdings *vis-à-vis* that of others in the appropriate market for land of the types now or formerly possessed by (Northern), of the uniqueness of (Northern's) landholdings in terms of quality or use to which they may have been put, and of the extent to which the location of the lands on or near the Northern Pacific's railroad line, or any other circumstances, put (Northern) in a strategic position as against other sellers and lessors of land. Short of such an enquiry I do not see how it can be determined whether Northern occupied such a dominant position in the relevant land market."

COERCION AS A FACTOR IN ANTITRUST ILLEGALITY

The dissenting Justices introduced a concept, irrespective of the existence of a relevant market and its dominance, which, we think, represented a new breach in business practices making them vulnerable to antitrust attack: coercion of the other party to do something. Mr. Justice Harlan said:

> "I do not deny that there may be instances where *economic coercion* by a vendor may be inferred, without any direct showing of market dominance from the mere existence of the tying arrangements themselves, as where the vendee is apt to suffer economic detriment from the tying clause because precluded from purchasing a tied product at better terms or of a better quality elsewhere. But the tying clauses here are not cast in such absolute terms" (our italics).

The coercion referred to was not present in the *Northern* case because Northern's customers had the option to use other railroads to transport the products obtained from the land purchased or leased from Northern.

WHEN IS A TYING ARRANGEMENT *PER SE* UNLAWFUL?

After studying the *Northern Pacific* case one might be excused for being unclear as to when the three elements (tying product, coercion, and tied product) are deemed by a court to combine into *per se* unlawfulness. The dissent in the *Northern* case accents the somewhat blurred reasoning of the majority as to why tying clauses are illegal (is it the clause itself or the actual effect brought by the tying arrangement on competition in the tied product?) and what is it in the tying arrangement that dooms it to illegality (sufficient control over the tying product to compel the other party to accept the tied product?).

The court in the *Northern Pacific* case refers to *International Salt Co.* v. *U.S.* 332 U.S. 392 and if we trace the development of judicial thinking from the *International Salt* case and perhaps one or two others a picture may develop allowing us a firmer grasp of exactly what it is about tying clauses that is wrong. It will be seen that the struggle has been, on the side of industry, the appeal for assessment of the reasonableness of the tying scheme; and on the side of the government, the desire to use a broad brush to paint *per se* illegality on all tie-in arrangements. The courts have been caught in between as arbiters and in their desire to achieve fairness and justice have woven the three elements of a tying arrangement into a Gordian knot.

There is no particular problem in understanding the theory of tying illegality—the *Northern Pacific* case clearly established that tying arrangements are "unreasonable in and of themselves whenever a party has *sufficient economic power with respect to the tying product to appreciably restrain free competition in the market for the tied product and a not insubstantial amount of interstate commerce is affected*" (our italics). This was the test for illegality under the Sherman Act. The

Clayton Act identifies the standards in its s. 3 to be "when the seller enjoys a monopolistic position in the market for the tying product *or* if a substantial volume of commerce in the tied product is restrained". The Sherman Act is not quite so stringent in requiring a monopoly-type power over the tying product. All that is required is a sufficient amount of economic power so that the seller can impose the sale of the tied product. The problem arises when each of the three elements of a tying arrangement needs to be analysed to see how it may be applied to the Sherman or Clayton Act standards. It is in this respect that the courts created the Gordian knot.

In the *International Salt* case the defendant International Salt Co. owned two patented machines which were used to process salt into commercial products. It leased these machines and in the leases required the lessee to use only the salt manufactured and sold by International Salt in the machines. The defendant had asked that the legality of their practice should be judged after investigation of the actual proportion of commerce in salt affected by the leases; whether the restraint of trade and commerce was unreasonable; and whether competition in salt had been substantially lessened. The government argued that the amount of commerce affected was immaterial; that no investigation of reasonableness was required because agreements that compelled the purchase of other products (in this case they would be the unpatented salt) are *per se* unreasonable restraints of trade. The government's view was that the exclusion of competitors by the use of the tie-in was a wrong sufficient unto itself.

The facts reveal that International Salt Co. was by far the largest supplier of salt and salt products in the US but the leases in question provided that the lessee could purchase salt from any other source if they could get it at a better price and if International Salt Co. could not provide the same grade of salt at that competitive price. Thus far, of the three elements of tying that were mentioned above, one may see that the first element (the dominion and control over the tying product) was present and that the third element (the restraint of competition in the tied product) was very probably present. International Salt owned patents covering the two machines but in the US the ownership of patents does not confer any right on the patentee to compel the use or purchase of patented or unpatented materials to be used with the patent. We would point out that the view in Europe is somewhat different and we shall deal with that point presently.

International Salt argued that it was necessary for the lessee to purchase salt from them because only salt of a certain degree of purity could be used in the patented machines without disturbing their function. (In *International Business Machines Corpn. v. United States*, 298 U.S. 131 IBM used the same argument in defending against a tying case in which they compelled lessees of their computers to use punched cards obtained only from IBM. The IBM punched cards were the only ones that would ensure satisfactory performance of the IBM machines.) The court rejected this argument quite easily by saying that as the requirement was only the use of salt meeting a certain specification of quality, then the remedy should have been simply to require the lessees to use salt of such quality—not that the salt should be purchased only from International Salt. (The court in the IBM case rejected IBM's argument on exactly the same ground.) The only significance of the patents is that they actually worked against the interests of International Salt because the court took the existence of the patents as conclusive proof of International Salt's control over the tying product.

As regards the second essential (the coercion), International Salt had argued that the tying clause had not always been insisted upon nor had it always been enforced when it was included. The court, however, ignored the argument by saying that it did not justify the general use of the restriction. The court apparently found *per se* illegality simply in the use of a tying arrangement "to foreclose competitors from any substantial market". Although the court accepted the necessity that the volume of business being affected by the tying arrangements should not be insignificant or insubstantial, it did not seem to put as much quantitative weight on this factor as one might expect. It seemed to be more impressed with the foothold obtained by a tie-in in the market of the tied product. After commenting on the fact that the volume of business affected was neither insignificant nor insubstantial the court went on to say "and the tendency of the arrangement to accomplishment of monopoly seems obvious". It then continued with what has become one of the most well-known phrases in antitrust law "under the law, agreements are forbidden which tend to create a monopoly, and it is immaterial that the tendency is a creeping one rather than one that proceeds at full gallop; nor does the law await arrival at the goal before condemning the direction of the movement". Despite the apparent clarity and conviction of the courts both in the *International Salt* case and in the *Northern Pacific* case, one feels a vague dissatisfaction in either decision as a guide for business planning.

A PURELY BUSINESS VIEW OF TYING ARRANGEMENTS

We feel that a pause in the legal consideration of *per se* violations is necessary because the courts seem to have become entangled in the niceties of legal dissection of tying arrangements and perhaps have lost the essence of the business reasons why they might be wrong and whether the legal arguments to condemn tying arrangements stand investigation in the light of business reality. Let us first observe the first essential of a tying arrangement, i.e. the control over the tying product, and the second essential that goes along with it, i.e. the use of that control as a coercive lever in convincing the potential customer to take the tied product.

It seldom, if ever, happens that any company has such a hold on a particular product that it can exert force based only on that control on a potential customer. We say this is seldom or rare because the potential customer, if he finds the terms too onerous may well turn elsewhere for the equivalent of the product. For example, no one doubts the extraordinary position of Kodak in the photographic market; yet, it is doubtful that the Kodak company could impose or compel a potential customer to accept its cameras, for example, only if that customer will accept also only Kodak film for use in the camera. If the customer feels that the business terms are not bearable he will turn to another camera. Indeed the reader will recall that the dissenting Justices in the *Northern Pacific* case found this weakness in the majority opinion when it faulted the opinion because the court had not entertained evidence as to whether there were other landholdings like those of Northern Pacific which could have been just as easily available to the purchasers and lessees from Northern Pacific, the inference being that Northern Pacific's control over the landholdings might not have been such as to be sufficiently effective as a lever to compel the purchasers and lessees to ship the products of those lands over the railroads owned by Northern Pacific. In the *International Salt* case, it is interesting that at no time was the question raised whether there were any other machines, not owned by the International Salt Co., which the potential customers of International Salt could have purchased or leased. If such other machines had been available, the potential customers could easily have purchased salt from other suppliers and the entire tying situation would have disintegrated. The obvious weakness in both of these famous cases suggests subsequent developments in legal thinking concerning the concept of economic power over the tying product. Indeed, the decisions since the *Northern Pacific* case have been a metamorphosis from actual economic power to simply the appeal or attractiveness of the tying product. In other words it could be sufficient to have a tying situation if a company merely possesses something which is wanted by someone else, irrespective of the fact that equivalent things are available elsewhere. Of course the customer has the choice of purchasing the item desired from that company or going elsewhere for it; and, conversely, the company has the right to sell that item to that customer or not to sell it to him. Once, however, the two parties come together to arrange a purchase and sale, it would be illegal for the seller to condition the sale of that item on the purchase of unrelated items which the purchaser might not want to have. The coercion arises simply from the conditioning of the sale on the purchase of these other items, not on the measure of economic power held by the seller over the desired item. Evidence of such "coercion" is not difficult to find and in the cases in which this has been an issue, the plaintiff has been able to present memoranda and various correspondence indicating that he, as a customer, had in some form or other objected to the inclusion in the contract of the requirement that he purchase the other undesired items. An example of the new thinking about the kind of economic power needed over the tying product may be found in *Fortner Enterprises Inc.* v. *U.S. Steel Corpn.*, 394 U.S. 495.

Tie-ins are undoubtedly commercially very attractive for the seller and tie-in practices take on innumerable disguises but the courts have consistently struck them down. Retreating into a narrower field, companies found themselves employing industrial property rights such as patents and trademarks with the sometimes mistaken notion that their possession would give them firmer ground to include a tied product. As we have seen in the *International Salt* case, this was not true. In Europe it is permitted to condition the licensing of a patent on the licensees purchasing his requirements for use in the patented subject matter, from the patentee. The justification for this, in Europe at least, is to preserve the patentee's right to have his process or his patented product used to the best technical advantage. The same kind of argument presented in the *International Salt* case and an analogous argument used in the *IBM* case briefly mentioned above was struck down and the court in rebuttal said that if it was necessary to have special material used in a leased or a patented machine, the lessor or the licensor could simply require the lessor or the licensee to use a material meeting a certain specification. This would be quite different from requiring the lessee or the licensee to purchase the material only from the lessor or the licensor.

When it comes to trademarks, however, we have an anomalous situation. The tie-in problem appears in the use of trademarks most typically in franchising operations. In view of the popularity of franchising, this particular form of doing business has rapidly been taking its own shape and giving rise to new legislation and new judicial decisions, but basically a franchise is built around a trademark. The owner of the trademark licenses the use of the trademark in return for royalty payments and other fee arrangements normally or usually calculated on the basis of the turnover in the business conducted under the trademark. In recent years the franchise system has rooted firmly in "fast food" enterprises. These are most elaborate schemes but the part which is of interest to us at this time is the tying arrangements which accompany a large number of the franchise agreements. It is the concern of the owner of the trademark that the use of the trademark be such that the goodwill in it is protected. To this end, the franchisor might require the franchisee to purchase certain materials or equipment from him in connection with the franchised business. One sees immediately the classic ingredients for an illegal tying arrangement. Sometimes, however, the tie-in is perfectly legal and other times it is not. Where is the distinction?

Antitrust law comes to a confrontation with trademark law in this respect. Whereas antitrust law abhors tie-ins, trademark law actually requires that the owner of a trademark

"in order to retain his right to his mark, when he elects to license others to use his mark, *retain sufficient control* over his licensee's dealings in the end product to ensure that they will apply the mark to either the same product or to one of substantially the same quality with which the public in the past has associated the product" (our italics).

So spoke Commissioner Jones of the Federal Trade Commission in commenting on Carvel Corporation's franchise agreement. Commissioner Jones continued:

"in general, the most usual means employed by trademark owners to maintain the necessary quality control over their licensee . . . sellers insisted on requirements that the licensees manufacture in accordance with actual samples submitted . . . that licensee dance studios, for example, employ instructors trained by the licensor and follow only dance procedures laid down by the licensor . . . or that licensee bakeries be required to purchase the batter mix exclusively from the licensor . . .".

The reason for this obligation of the owner of the trademark to take care of the quality of the product covered by the trademark is inherent in the nature of the trademark itself. Unlike the device covered by a patent, the product covered by a trademark is intimately and inherently bound with the trademark itself. One might, for example, have a patent covering a razor blade and the scope of the patent would cover razor blades regardless of what trademark or name is used on the razor blade. On the other hand the name "Gillette" or "Wilkinson" or "Schick" when used on a razor blade is intimately bound with that particular razor blade. Therefore when the owner of any of these trademarks licenses their use the owner must be concerned with the quality of the razor blade because that razor blade carries the goodwill in the trademark itself. In the case of Carvel Corporation about which we quoted Commissioner Jones' remarks, it was Carvel's practice in its franchise agreements to require the franchisee to purchase from Carvel or from sources designated by Carvel all of the ingredients for the mix, toppings, flavours and other ingredients and cones which are used in the ice-cream which is eventually sold under the Carvel label. This unique characteristic of trademarks was mentioned in an earlier court decision involving the Carvel Corporation. This was the case *Susser* v. *Carvel Corp.*, 332 F.2d 505. Apart from remarking about the necessity of the trademark owner to exercise control to protect its goodwill, the court added that "something so insusceptible of precise verbalisation as the desired texture and taste of an ice-cream cone or sundae" might be difficult to control unless the formula or the ingredients were purchased from the owner of the trademark himself; moreover, apart from matters of textures and taste, there was also the risk of injury to the goodwill of the trademark if a foreign substance were found in the ice-cream mix. The trademark owner could assure himself of this kind of control for the safety of the public, if one wishes to put the point that way, by himself selling the ice-cream mix to his franchisee.

One steps outside the protective screen of the trademark when one compels the trademark licensee or franchisee to purchase products which are not related to the trademark goods themselves. For example in *Siegel* v. *Chicken Delight*, 307 F.Supp. 1491 a fast food franchisor required his franchisee to purchase certain packaging items, cookers and friers as well as mixers for food. This was condemned because the scope of the required purchases was wider than what was covered by the trademark itself.

OTHER EXCEPTIONS TO *PER SE* ILLEGALITY OF TYING CLAUSES

Generally where the nature of the business is so technical that it requires control by a seller, a tie-in will be permitted, at least in the beginning and particularly if the business is a new industry. This was illustrated in *U.S.* v. *Jerrold Electronics Corp.*, 187 F.Supp. 545. A community television and antenna system required certain components as well as special servicing. The tie-in of the components and the service contract was permitted because it was a new industry and the use of such sensitive equipment by untrained personnel would probably have caused the new industry not to succeed.

Similar reasoning would permit a tie-in where, for example, the manufacturer of gigantic earth-moving equipment such as walking draglines might require the purchaser of such equipment also to purchase special services for training personnel to use the walking dragline or even to purchase ancillary equipment for use with the walking draglines so that it might be used without danger of injuring the public. In other words where there is justified concern not for the profit of the seller but rather for the protection of goodwill for the public or the introduction of a new item or a new industry, a tie-in would likely be permitted, certainly in the early stages of the new business.

IN EUROPE

To begin with there is no difficulty in the legality or illegality of such clauses. Unlike the development in the US, tying clauses in Europe did not need a judicial declaration (as for the Sherman Act) to establish their illegality. Article 85(1) (*e*) expressly condemns them. It says that it is illegal to make "the conclusion of a contract subject to the acceptance by the other party to the contract of additional obligations, which, by their nature or according to commercial practice, have no connection with the subject of such contract." Inherent in that description are the essentials of the American-type of tying agreement: there is the tying product and control over it to an extent sufficient to make the conclusion of the agreement "subject to the acceptance by the other party", i.e. there is the necessary coercion, and the tied product being the "additional obligations". The interesting aspect of the European definition is the qualification that the tied products have "no connection with the subject of such contract". In America it made no difference whether the tied product had such a connection, the inference being in Europe that if there is a connection with the subject of the contract, the tying arrangement might be all right.

Tying arrangements have always been illegal as such in Europe and there are specific clauses in the German law on unfair competition dealing with it. Under Common Market law there simply have not been enough cases for any one to distinguish a developing pattern of the Commission's or the European Court's view of tying arrangements.

Regulation 17, art. 4(2) provides that where only two enterprises are involved in the agreement and the sole effect of the agreement is "to impose restraint on the exercise of the rights of any person acquiring or using industrial property rights—particularly patents . . . or trademarks—and their sole object is the development or uniform application of standards and types", those agreements need not be notified to the Commission. The meaning of this is that in so far as patents and trademarks are concerned, the licensor may condition the grant of the license on the licensees purchasing from the licensor or from some party designated by the licensor such materials or products or equipment as the licensor may deem to be necessary for the proper technical utilization of the subject matter of the licence. This view has traditionally been accepted by the national courts and presumably it will be accepted by the Commission and European Court of Justice (particularly in view of the express exemption from the need to notify agreements containing such tie-ins). Nevertheless, tie-in clauses as mentioned before are expressly prohibited by art. 85 and their illegality would be reprieved only by the exemption from notification under reg. 17, art. 4.

In view of this attitude in the Community, one might expect that the *International Salt* case and the *IBM* case referred to above would have been decided differently in Europe. If we might carry our analogy a bit further involving the *International Salt* case, and also add a particular consideration of the *Northern Pacific* case, we might expect another interesting and different result in the Community. In each of those cases the defendant argued that the tie-in was not effective because the other party could have either bought their salt (in the case of the *International Salt* case) or transported their commodities over another railroad (in the case of Northern Pacific). This provision gave the other party a kind of "escape" mechanism and it could be that such an escape clause in Europe would save an otherwise illegal tie-in arrangement. We caution the reader that this is pure speculation and no case has yet been decided testing this particular principle. In the UK there is an express provision excluding tie-in clauses from illegality if the party obliged to purchase a particular product is given the alternative of purchasing it elsewhere. Notwithstanding this kind of "escape" one might still query whether an English

court or the European court would come to different conclusion from that in the *International Salt* case and in the
Northern Pacific case because in both of those cases the end
result was that the party who was tied had no option but to
purchase from the seller, albeit at a lower and more competitive price. As lower prices seem to form a basic part of
the Commission's and Court's thinking about what is good
or bad in the Common Market, it could also be that if a
defendant to a charge of illegal tying could show that the
public benefited because a lower price evolved from the
terms of the agreement the tying arrangement might well
be excluded under the exemption provided by art. 85(3).

In other respects there is a similarity between the European and American views. The Americans required that
competition be appreciably restrained and that a not insubstantial volume of commerce in the tied product be
involved. There is no particular quantitative measure of the
effect on competition or inter-state trade in Community law
but if there is or if there is likely to be a *noticeable* effect, then
presumably the tying clause would come within art. 85. A
notable difference from the US view, however, is that
concerning the conditioning of licensing of a patent or a
trademark on the licensee taking certain products from the
licensor. This is simply not acceptable in the US unless it is
essential to protect the goodwill of a trademark.

Despite the European allowance of tie-ins in industrial
property licensing, there has always been a question among
many learned authors on community law as to whether art.
85(1) does in fact apply to all tie-in clauses or only to those
which are part of horizontal cartel agreements. If that is the
case, then one would be driven into consideration of art. 86
in connection with vertical tie-ins and look at tie-ins as an
abuse of a dominant position. Article 86(*d*) repeats the
language of art. 85(1)(*e*) and condemns, as an abuse of a
dominant position, "making the conclusion of contracts
subject to acceptance by the other parties of supplementary
obligations which, by their nature or according to commercial usage, have no connection with the subject of such
contracts".

Probably one reason for the view that the evil of vertical tie-ins arises only under art. 86 is that unless one of the parties is in a dominant position there would not be the necessary "leverage" obtained from dominance over a product to compel the buyer to purchase other items. Moreover, in the absence of a dominant position, there would hardly be any effect on competition or inter-state trade in a "one-off" transaction, that is a transaction in which the seller requires the buyer to purchase other goods at the same time. It would be a different matter if this were to be a continuing obligation on the buyer because in that case unless the tie-in comes within the purview of reg. 17, the inter-state effect would be much more likely and the agreement invalid under art. 85.

10

Monopolization and abuses of a dominant position

In the US one is in a monopolistic position when he has the power and the intent, in a particular market, to control prices or to exclude competition. His actions are covered by s. 2 of the Sherman Act:

"2. Every person who shall monopolize, or attempt to monopolize, or combine or conspire with any other person or persons, to monopolize any part of the trade or commerce among the several states, or with foreign nations, shall be deemed guilty of a misdemeanor."

In the Common Market a dominant position has not yet been clearly defined. Probably the best one can accept at the moment is that given by the Court of Justice in the *Continental Can* case:

"Undertakings are in a dominant position when they have the power to behave independently . . . without taking into account their competitors, purchasers or suppliers . . . the position when, because of their share of the market . . . they have the power to determine prices or to control production or distribution for a significant part of the products in question . . .".

In so far as the effect on competition is concerned, the Commission said:

"If an enterprise is able, at its pleasure, to oust a competing enterprise from the market it might already occupy a dominant position and exert a controlling influence upon the practices of other enterprises even if its own share of the market is still relatively small".

The European equivalent of illegal monopolization is covered in art. 86 of the Rome Treaty, and nowhere else:

"Any abuse by one or more undertakings of a dominant position within the Common Market or in a substantial part of it shall be prohibited as incompatible with the Common Market in so far as it may affect trade between Member States. Such abuse may, in particular, consist in:

(a) directly or indirectly imposing unfair purchase or selling prices or other unfair trading conditions;

(b) limiting Production, Distribution or Technical Development to the Prejudice of Consumers;

(c) applying Unequal Conditions to other parties in respect of equivalent goods or services, thereby placing such other parties at a competitive disadvantage;

(d) making the conclusion of a contract subject to the conditions that the other party to the contract accept additional goods or services which are not related to the subject of the contract either by their nature or by commercial custom".

It is intriguing to consider that each of the four examples of abusive practice given in art. 86 would be a Sherman Act s. 1 or a Clayton Act s. 3 or 7 violation in the US regardless whether one or both of the parties was in a dominant or monopolistic position if only because each of them would *tend toward monopoly*—an equally bad result. In the European Community it is similarly correct that each of these four abusive practices could also qualify for a prohibition under art. 85 if done in combination with another, but if any one of the four practices were done by an individual who was not in a monopolistic or dominant position, the practice would not be a violation of the Treaty of Rome at all because it would escape art. 85 (only one party involved) and art. 86 because not in a dominant position. Obviously the failure of art. 86 to cover the use of mergers to obtain a dominant position will attract much attention of the Commission and also judicial interpretation by the European Court of Justice. In the meantime, following on the Continental Can decision in which the Commission strove mightily in the European court to have Continental Can's attempted acquisition of a Dutch company declared to be a violation of art. 86 in itself, a member of the European Parliament put a question to the Commission: would it be a violation of art. 86 for a company to strengthen a dominant position by means of internal growth? Under the rules of the Common Market, the Commission must answer questions put to it by the European Parliament and the Commission answered in this case that it would not be an abuse of art. 86 if a company strengthened its dominant position purely by means of internal growth. While such pronouncement is extremely important in principle, in practice it is seldom difficult for a court to find some kind of activity which is not "purely internal" in order to arrest the growth of a company into a monopolistic position. The Parliamentary Question was not about achieving a dominant position, but rather strengthening one already obtained.

The US view of monopolization was given relatively early and well in *Standard Oil Co. of New Jersey* v. *U.S.*, 221 U.S.1, mentioned above at page 87. This case is important for several reasons among which are its discussion of the legislative history of the Sherman Act; that it was enacted because of the power that was an attribute of size. The aim of the law and even of the early common law in England was to protect the public against the exercise of that power not only by dissolving existing power structures but also by arresting any practice that could lead to the acquisition of that power. Initially the particular evil of size was "the power which the monopoly gave to fix the price and thereby to injure the public". The Standard Oil Company did not grow to its size purely by internal exertion. It arose from the formation of many trusts and corporations through which Standard Oil acted and by which Standard Oil eventually owned the stocks of 37 corporations. The evil of this concentration of power was the "inevitable result" in establishing Standard's power over the market in petroleum. Despite the fact that there was no clear holding by the court that such a powerful market position in itself was bad the court said that such a position of power "gives rise in and of itself ... to the prima facie presumption of intent and purpose to maintain the dominancy over the oil industry" and a necessary corollary of this was the exclusion of others from the trade.

The issue here was the fact of the acquisition of all of the competitive corporations in the petroleum trade and not any specific act done by Standard Oil once it had been established.

If it is rare today to find any single cartel or company so powerful as to completely dominate an entire industry, although Xerox, Kodak and IBM have been challenged by the US government as being just that powerful, it is not so rare to find instances in a competitive society where one company grows stronger whilst another grows weaker; where a smaller company in the course of competitive struggle becomes bigger; or where a company having attained a certain position of power seeks to maintain that position. In all of these examples one sees the indicia of monopolization, attempts to monopolize, and the maintenance of a monopolistic position. All three of these characteristics are the targets of s. 2 of the Sherman Act.

THE DISTINCTION BETWEEN SS. 1 AND 2 OF THE SHERMAN ACT

Section 1 prohibits contracts, combinations or conspiracies in restraint of trade. Section 2 prohibits monopolization or attempts to monopolize or combinations or conspiracies to monopolize any part of interstate trade or commerce or the foreign commerce of the US. There is an overlap between the two sections and combinations or agreements or conspiracies to monopolize would also likely infringe s. 1 but it is possible to have a s. 1 offence which does not amount to the monopolization condemned in s. 2. The essence of monopolization or, to be more precise *unlawful* monopolization, is the possession of monopoly power (meaning, in the economic sense, the capacity to control market prices or exclude competition) coupled with deliberateness or the intent or purpose to use or maintain that power; or, failing possession of that power, the intent or purpose to acquire it.

An infringement of s. 2 of the Sherman Act has another rather important attribute which is not enjoyed by s. 1; it is a crime and the guilty party can be imprisoned. The element of "power" is not essential in a s. 1 violation but it is in s. 2 although it is not necessary actually to show the use of that power in action, e.g. one need not give evidence that prices have been raised or that there has actually been an exclusion of competitors from a particular market.

"Monopolizing" or "monopolization" need no qualifying words to explain when they become illegal. They are illegal acts because "monopolizing" and "monopolization" in s. 2 of the Sherman Act mean sufficient power to control and dominate trade to exclude competitors and the accompanying intent and purpose to exercise that power. Yet another peculiar feature of s. 2 is that the attempts to obtain that kind of power, even when done unilaterally with no suggestion of collusion or agreement such as that under s. 1 of the Sherman Act, is illegal.

The latest landmark case paraphrasing the classic definition of monopolization is *U.S.* v. *Grinnel Corp.*, 384 U.S. 563. Grinnel manufactured plumbing supplies and fire sprinkler systems and over the years acquired stock in other corporations in the same business. It was also very heavily involved in burglary protection services and eventually controlled about 87% of the business. Under these circumstances the Supreme Court simply confirmed the offence under s. 2 of the Sherman Act saying that the offence "has two elements: (1) the possession of monopoly power in the relevant market and (2) the willful acquisition or maintenance of that power as distinguished from growth or development as a consequence of a superior product, business acumen, or historic accident".

The Federal Courts examined the business practices, policies and the actual transactions themselves in a charge involving s. 2 of the Sherman Act as evidence to assist the court to determine whether the defendant so charged was guilty of any of the three offences of s. 2, i.e. monopolization, attempts to monopolize or a combination or conspiracy to monopolize. Any one of the *per se* illegalities or the conspiracies discussed earlier could be evidence of any one of the s. 2 offences. Moreover, the acquisition or merger of competitors could be evidence of an attempt to monopolize although it is not necessary that an actual exclusion of competitors or a variation in price be shown to result from it.

THE DIFFERENCE BETWEEN OFFENCES IN SS. 1 AND 2 OF THE SHERMAN ACT

In s. 1 the offence is causing the restraint of trade and commerce by means of combined action of two or more persons. If there is no overt act but only an intent to cause the restraint, the offence is still present in the form of a conspiracy. In s. 2, the offence is monopolization and attempts to monopolize. The offence is not in itself the restraint on trade and commerce. Section 2 is aimed directly at the monopolization and attempts to monopolize. Restraint of trade is not mentioned in s. 2 because once acts of monopolization or attempts to monopolize have been proved, the necessary presumption is either a *de facto* restraint of trade and competition or the power to restrain them; because monopolization means having sufficient economic power in a particular market to control the price of the market and to exclude competitors. Accordingly one finds in every aspect of s. 2 the two elements of the possession of monopoly power in a relevant market and the wilful acquisition or maintenance of that power as distinguished from natural growth or development. It is essential to note that the mere possession of monopoly power is not in itself an offence. Something more is needed. The spectre of illegality looms in the way that the monopolistic position has been obtained or attempted to be obtained or the way in which that position is being maintained.

In *American Tobacco Co.* v. *United States*, 328 U.S. 781, the Supreme Court was asked whether an actual exclusion of competitors was necessary to establish monopolization as a crime under s. 2 of the Sherman Act. The court immediately excluded from consideration the situation in which a single company finds itself in a monopolistic position because of a discovery or entering a new field of trade in which it happens to be the only participant. The court said that it was not necessary to show the power and intent to exclude *all* competitors. All that is required by the Sherman Act is monopolization of "*any part* of the trade or commerce". The issue arose because the earlier American Tobacco case decided in 1911 dealt with monopolistic power in the tobacco industry obtained through the purchase or control of competitors. The later court again facing monopolization in the tobacco industry was asked to judge on the basis of the earlier case, namely whether there had actually been exclusion of competitors. But there were new factors. The monopolization charge occupying the court's attention involved the power over purchases of raw material and sales of the finished product in the form of cigarettes, a more sophisticated exercise of monopoly than in the earlier days when growth and power was achieved through straightforward acquisition of competitors. In this later American Tobacco case, growth and power over the market was obtained by the competitors maintaining their independent identities but combining either in the form of holding companies or through agreements with each other to dominate the market and exclude competitors. The evidence showed that the American Tobacco Company, Liggett, and Reynolds companies controlled 68% of the market in 1939 falling from 90% in 1931, but that there was also a decrease in the market share of the six other competitors of this "big three". In its decision the court commented on the sums of money spent by the "big three" for advertising. The court did not condemn advertising as such because obviously extensive advertising of cigarettes was bound to have, in the opinion of the court, some benefit indirectly for the competitors of the "big three" in that it would induce the public at large to take up cigarette smoking. The point was, however, that this enormous expenditure on advertising illustrated the use of a very powerful weapon which could discourage the entry into the market of a new competitor unless that competitor had the conomic resources to establish advertising for itself. It was found that the "big three" tobacco manufacturers had conspired to fix prices and to exclude competition in the purchase of two kinds of tobacco, a domestic type of flue-cured tobacco and burley tobacco. In fact, they had purchased a combined total of between 50 and 80% of the flue-cured tobacco and between 60 and 80% of burley. The evidence showed generally a combined attitude toward many different aspects of the tobacco business including appearances at tobacco auctions and in the distribution and sale of their products. But there was no evidence showing any actual exclusion of competition and this was the issue to which the Supreme Court confined its deliberation. As mentioned above, they decided that it was not necessary to prove this exclusion and that it was sufficient simply to show that the power and the intent to do so existed: "the authorities support the view that the material consideration in determining whether a monopoly exists is not that prices are raised and that competition is actually excluded but that power exists to raise prices or exclude competition when it is desired to do so."

The view in Europe is totally contrary to the American view in that art. 86 requires an actual abuse to take place while in the US all that is required is the power to do so.

Having established the necessity of power to affect a market, one must understand what is the relevant market. This is of fundamental importance both in the US and in Europe and is underlined by what happened in the European Continental Can case, Case 6/72: *Europemballage Cn. and Continental Can Co.* v. *E.C. Commission,* [1973] E.C.R. 215.

Continental Can Company was an American company which already held a dominant position in a substantial part of the Common Market in the market of light containers for canned meats, meat products, fish and shell fish, as well as in the market for metal covers for glass jars. It attempted to acquire about 80% of the stock of a Dutch company called Thomassen and Drijver–Verblifa. The Commission attacked the proposed acquisition on the grounds that the result would be the virtual elimination of competition in the market of packaging products in a substantial part of the Common Market. The importance of the case was that it was the striving by the Commission to extend the application of art. 86 to acquisitions and mergers despite the fact that the article itself said that the infringement would be the abuse of a dominant position and not the obtaining of one. The Commission's view was that the attempt to acquire shares in the Dutch company was itself an abuse of the dominant position that Continental Can already had. Unfortunately the court avoided a clear decision on that particular issue but nevertheless it provided a valuable expression of principle in the meaning and importance of what constitutes a relative market in which one holds the dominant position. The Commission had alleged that Continental Can through a German subsidiary had between 70 and 80% of the market for cans for meats and that as regards the market for cans for fish products, glass jars and plastic containers about 30% of the entire market. In an attempt to expand the relevant market Continental Can argued that the glass jars and plastic containers were in fact competitive with the metal containers that were used for meats. The Commission on the other hand attempted to segment the relevant market and argued that the glass jars and plastic containers and canned fish could not be on one side as competitors with metal containers on the other side. Continental Can injected the argument that light metal containers are not *interchangeable* with other containers, thus introducing another consideration for fractionating a market into as many component parts as possible and blurring the outline of the relevant market so as to make the issue of dominance even more difficult to determine or establish. Clearly if the market is widened by the concept of substitute or interchangeable products the possibility of dominance becomes weaker.

Avoiding having to decide clearly if the acquisition of one company by another would itself be an abuse under art. 86, the court nevertheless began its decision by suggesting that it might be an abuse. It said that the spirit of the Rome Treaty in respect of competition would not permit a presumption that art. 86 would permit enterprises "through a merger into an organic unity, to attain a position of such dominance as to virtually remove any serious possibility of competition". Obviously the court was not clear as to whether it was a violation of art. 86 for Continental Can to go through with the acquisition of the Dutch company but it did suggest that a merger that would "virtually remove any serious possibility of competition" could be a violation of art. 86. The implication contained in this suggestion, however, is that substantially all of the competition would have to be eliminated by virtue of the merger before a violation of art. 86 could take place. Moreover the court simply ignored Continental Can's argument that if there was to be an abuse at all there had to be a causal connection between the use of its dominant market position as a kind of lever and the acquisition of the Dutch company; that is, the abuse of the dominant position would be the use of the dominance of the position to make the acquisition. The court dismissed this and said that it made no difference what the means were to attain the ultimate dominant position resulting from the merger and that the abuse condition would be satisfied in the strengthening, itself, of the position held by Continental Can by the acquisition of the Dutch company.[1] The court then came to the nub of the matter: the definition of the relevant market dominated by the entity resulting from acquisition and the court decided against the Commission's position on the ground that the Commission had failed to define it. The court saw the market as divisible into three parts: a market for light containers for canned meat; a market for light containers for canned fish; and a market for metal lids for the canning industry. The court criticized the Commission for not adequately explaining the distinction of these three markets from the general market for light metal containers such as those metal containers which

---

1 See pages 190 and 191 for Parliamentary question about internal growth.

are used for canned fruits and vegetables, condensed milk, olive oil, fruit juices and industrial products.

> "It can be assumed that these products have a separate market only if they are distinguishable from others not just by the mere fact that they are used for packing certain products, but also because of special production features that make them specifically suited for that purpose. On this basis a dominant position on the market for light metal containers for canned meats and fish is not shown so long as it has not been proved that competitors in other areas of the market for light metal containers can not, by making a simple adjustment, step into that market with sufficient strength to provide a serious counter balance."

In 1956 the US Supreme Court in *U.S.* v. *E. I. Dupont de Nemours*, 351 U.S. 377 expressed much the same view of the relevant market. In that case Dupont was accused by the government of having an illegal monopoly in cellophane (polythene). Dupont produced almost 75% of the cellophane sold in the US and the cellophane constituted less than 20% of all flexible packaging material sales. The Supreme Court said that the monopolization charge had not been established because there were other competitive flexible packaging materials available to the public. It said "every manufacturer is the sole producer of the particular commodity it makes but its control ... of the relevant market depends upon the availability of alternative commodities for buyers ...". The court continued "moreover it may be practically impossible to commence manufacturing cellophane without full access to Dupont's technique. However, Dupont has no power to prevent competition from other wrapping materials". The suggestion of the court in that statement is that even though the competition is totally eliminated in respect of that one product there still would be no illegal monopolization so long as a competitive product was available. We have seen this kind of reasoning earlier in connection with the justification of exclusive distributorships and selective distribution networks. The reader will recall, for example in connection with franchising, that the exclusive franchise system was declared to be legal if there were other dealers, i.e. non-franchised independent dealers having competitive products readily available to the public.

Having established this kind of measure of the relevant market one will quickly appreciate that the conflict in many such cases will usually resolve itself into argument as to whether the product over which the defendant is charged to have monopoly power is in fact interchangeable with other available products. Once having identified the market, however, one must still ascertain whether the defendant has the power required by law. Ordinarily such power may be inferred from the predominant share of the market—so said the Supreme Court in *U.S.* v. *Grinnell*, 384 U.S. 571.

One needs to dig a bit deeper because clearly it seldom happens that any particular product can be said to have an exact competitive equivalent in all respects and uses. The moment one produces a non-standardized product one will be able to find distinction from competitive products. The court in the Dupont case recognized the absurdity of seeing monopoly power in a product simply because it was different. In this respect it said:

"determination of the competitive market for commodities depends upon how different from one another are the offered commodities in character or use, how far buyers will go to substitute one commodity for another. For example, one can think of building materials as in commodity competition but one could hardly say that brick competed with steel or wood or cement or stone in the meaning of the Sherman Act litigation; the products are too different".

Since 1956 there has been virtually no change in the legal view of the relative market, save for increased sophistication in detecting submarkets within a larger market.

Apart from the market in the product, there is significance in the relevant geographic market. This is somewhat easier to determine and can be broadly described as the area in which the sellers sell and in which the purchasers purchase. It might be national and it might be portions of the US. The same concept exists in the Common Market, i.e. the relevant geographic market could be any substantial part of the Common Market.

Monopolization cases are, happily, firmly rooted in business reality. Any legal theorization must yield to the same kind of hard facts that a businessman must face in corporate planning. For example, a corporate planner must assess whether there is a consumer market for his product; the size and location of the market; what products are in competition with his product; who is the competition and how strong it is and what it will cost to enter into the market.

If a company finds itself in a position of having lawful monopoly power in the economic sense, that position which was lawful can become unlawful if the existence of the power is linked with a purpose or intent to exercise that power. The *American Tobacco* case discussed above made this clear. This should not be misunderstood to mean that a company in a monopolistic position cannot function normally as a company in the sense of setting its prices or refusing to deal or choosing to deal with suppliers or customers. These acts of course are simply normal business functions but they can become illegal in the hands of a monopolist if the acts can be shown to be exercised with the purpose or intent of controlling market prices or excluding competition. Obviously one cannot go further than state the legal principle. It must be left to time and events to serve up individual fact situations to be measured against that principle. Even in the absence of monopoly stature, the same kind of purpose and intent is necessary as a foundation for the offence of attempting to monopolize. The only difference is the added ingredient that there also must be a "dangerous probability" that the attempt will be successful. In the case of attempting to monopolize, however, there has been some question of whether proof of a specific relevant market is necessary to establish the illegality; the theory being that an intent to monopolize any significant part of interstate commerce is sufficient in itself to be a violation, something analogous to a conspiracy charge in the sense that the conspiracy itself is the offence without the necessity of showing any actual effect of the conspiracy. The distinction from the conspiracy illegality under s. 1 of the Sherman Act is, in s. 2, the necessity of the defender having the power or apparent power to attain monopolization. No "power" is necessary to create the conspiracy offence under s. 1.

SUMMARY

Evaluation of the past and present and a somewhat cautious look into the future compel the following thoughts about monopolization. Under s. 1 of the Sherman Act, the ultimate villain of all illegality is the resulting tendency towards monopoly, even if it is not intended. Under s. 2, attempts to monopolize and acts of monopolization are themselves the intended villains. All antitrust roads lead to illegal monopoly. In the US the wrongfulness lies in the way one achieves or attempts to achieve monopoly power. In Europe wrongfulness is in acts which abuse the monopoly position already achieved. There is a trend towards attacking size itself as a symbol of monopoly power.

Whilst not so obvious or explicit, the signs are there also in Europe, save those pragmatic instances when monopolies under the guise of "rationalization" of small entities into a big one are encouraged, indeed instigated and supported by governments in the name of the public benefit. Notwithstanding these bits of evidence of the state controlling the private sector by the creation of large economic entities, we are in danger of equating sheer size with unlawful monopoly. At the same time that governments are creating "size" and monopolies they are considering destroying or at least fragmenting the large companies (e.g. the US Oil Companies, International Business Machines Corporation) simply because they are big, i.e. they are monopolies. We question the economic or legal justification for this tendency. The courts themselves have shown the error of measuring economic markets in terms of how many corporations control how much of a nation's corporate wealth or total corporate assets. General Electric Company (both in the UK and in the US), Westinghouse and Phillips are very large companies indeed and yet they are in fierce competition with each other. The same is true of Exxon, Shell and British Petroleum. Yet, it is possible for a much smaller business entity to enjoy and exercise absolute monopolistic power in a given market. If this is so, why then is there this movement toward the reduction of size? We may not be far from the declaration of *per se* illegality when a company reaches a certain size for then it may be unlawful monopoly itself. Abuses of a dominant position or monopolization or attempts to monopolize will be joined by a new villain, bigness—if not on economic or legal grounds then simply because "bigness" is socially unacceptable.

Part II
Trading practices

Trading practices

In this part we will discuss some business practices which seem to be most prone to antitrust attack both in the US and in Europe. The examples will necessarily involve one or more of the essentials discussed in Part I and there will be a certain amount of cross-referencing because rarely will a given set of facts of business behaviour avoid touching more than one kind of antitrust violation.

For example, illegal division of markets will almost always involve some charge of price-fixing and may even go as far as to bring in suggestions of illegal boycotts. Certain particular kinds of businesses, for example, the production and distribution of spirits and alcoholic beverages; advertising and advertising practices; tobacco and tobacco products and petroleum and petroleum products have always been popular fields for such offences.

Pharmaceutical manufacture and distribution and licensing, as well as franchising are equally popular areas for antitrust violations involving the use of industrial property rights such as patents and trademarks. During times of a scarcity of commodities, there is antitrust activity attacking joint ventures and mergers in those industries. For example, this happened in the early days in the US (the *Appalachian Co.* case) and has happened recently within the copper industry. Most recently banks and banking have been receiving enormous press coverage and there has been considerable antitrust activity in respect of the control of bank acquisitions and mergers as well as joint ventures and syndication of banks. But it is not so much the particular nature of the business with which we will now concern ourselves because obviously it would be impossible to cover them in any way adequately. We think it would be more helpful to take examples illustrating the kind of business practice (rather than the nature of the business itself) which is most sensitive to antitrust law.

To begin with, mergers, acquisitions and joint ventures are arguably in this category of sensitivity. One might equally argue that the uses of industrial property rights have been so attacked recently, particularly in the Common Market, that research and development planning and, indeed, the use of licensing as a means of distribution of products resulting from research and development have been made so unclear that serious uncertainty exists. As each of these kinds of business practices covers a wide variety of the kinds of business in which companies and persons are engaged, we think that a careful discussion of each of them, with the use of examples, might lead the reader engaged in other businesses to apply parallel anti-trust planning and thinking.

II

Mergers and acquisitions

SOME BUSINESS REASONS WHY COMPANIES MERGE OR
ACQUIRE OR ARE ACQUIRED

The history of mergers is very well documented and is usually divided into three phases. Although there is a minor dispute about the exact span of each phase, they divide roughly as follows: the first phase of mergers in the US can be said to be from 1890 to 1904, the second phase from about 1920 to 1929 and the third phase is that beginning after the second world war and continuing to the present day. More interesting in merger history is not so much the phases in which they occurred but in what was merged. In the first phase the great combines in the oil, steel, railroad and meat packing businesses were formed. It was at about this time too (1911) that the *American Tobacco Co.* case was decided (see pages 194–197 and that giant company became the separate and independent corporations R. J. Reynolds Tobacco Co., Liggett and Meyers Tobacco Co., P. Lorillard Co. and United Cigar Stores Co. One of the characteristic features of the second phase of merger history was the extreme activity in the stock exchange in New York. Within the short span of 1925–1931 the General Foods Co., Owens-Illinois Glass, and United Aircraft were formed. It was during this period too that the Public Utility Holding Companies Act was passed because an important characteristic of this particular phase was the formation of large holding companies. Since the second world war merger activity has been intense and in tracing its pattern one finds oneself in the great miasma of the conglomerates.

Why do companies merge?

For the purposes of this book let us at once dismiss tax considerations. Although they may be valid considerations to justify a merger, it would be more reasonable to suppose that corporate mergers occur for business trading reasons and not tax reasons. Regardless of the business reasons, an acquisition or merger becomes unlawful where the effect of the acquisition or merger may be substantially to lessen competition or to tend to create a monopoly in any line of commerce in any section of the country. That, in a nutshell, is the prohibition in s. 7 of the Clayton Act. Mergers and acquisitions come within the Sherman Act just as any other business transaction but the Clayton Act is the principle law covering mergers and acquisitions. The philosophy dictating the legality of mergers is that competition is more intense when there are more competitors in a given market, so market concentration becomes a factor as well as the relative size of the competitors. General principles such as those just stated are not very helpful in determining any particular situation or in determining whether your company should acquire or be acquired by another company but it should be helpful to be conscious of the general attitude of the government and of the courts in cases of acquisitions and mergers. Unfortunately there is a built-in problem with almost all acquisitions and mergers. Their purpose must be to expand, never to contract; and the method of doing so always involves some form of reduction of competitors in a given market or even the elimination of a potential entrant into the market. Where either party has any significant size or power in the market, that merger or acquisition will be vulnerable to antitrust attack. As a result, those cases decided by the courts or investigated by the Federal Trade Commission or the Department of Justice resolve themselves chiefly into defensive arguments that the merger or acquisition was necessary in order that one of the two parties survive, or that the relevant market in which competition would be reduced is something other than that defined by the plaintiff. The result is that the defending corporation much more often than not loses its case.

The government through the Department of Justice and the Federal Trade Commission, and private persons or corporations may challenge acquisitions or mergers and apply for temporary injunctive relief, i.e. an order from court temporarily stopping the acquisition or merger from going through.

If the acquisition and the merger has already been completed, relief may be obtained by an order to the acquirer (or surviving company) to divest itself of the stocks or the assets acquired. In view of the enormous difficulties that would attend either kind of relief, but particularly being required to divest oneself of the stock or assets already acquired, one should consider the available channels for preliminary advice about the legality of the merger or acquisition. The government realized the disruption that would be caused by its taking action for a temporary injunction or ordering divestiture after the event, so it provided guidelines and policy on anti-merger enforcement. The Department of Justice or the Federal Trade Commission may be consulted prior to the merger or acquisition of stock or assets of a corporation. Although each government bureau has its own procedure (Business Review Procedure) for obtaining its respective opinion, substantially their advice is aimed at doing the same thing, that is, advising the corporation consulting it whether it intends to take action against the merger or the acquisition if it is consummated. Except for certain kinds of transactions, there is no general obligation for any corporation to notify the Department of Justice or the Federal Trade Commission in advance of a merger or acquisition which it intends to consummate.[1] The Federal Trade Commission's policies are more specific to particular industries, e.g. food, than those of the Department of Justice and they particularly identify those transactions which the FTC would more closely consider with a view toward enforcement.

Under the circumstances one would expect that it would be prudent to obtain advance clearance and notification.

---

1 At the time of going to press the US Congress had enacted a law requiring prenotification of intended mergers of a certain size.

The usefulness of the guidelines is somewhat limited because, for one thing, there is no guarantee that if the corporation follows the guidelines it will be safe from antitrust attack. The guidelines can be varied from time to time and the Department of Justice or the Federal Trade Commission may take action even before the guidelines are amended and a merging company may find itself under attack in a merger or acquisition because of a change in thinking by the Department of Justice or the FTC. Nevertheless the guidelines may have some value. By way of introduction to a brief survey of the merger guidelines of the Department of Justice, we think that the following quoted discourse from the dissent in *U.S.* v. *Columbia Steel Co.*, 334 U.S. 495 in 1948 dramatically illustrates the trend then and the continuing attitude today against the general principle of mergers and acquisitions:

"We have here the problem of bigness ... the Curse of Bigness shows how size can become a menace—both industrial and social. It can be an industrial menace because it creates gross inequalities against existing or putative competitors. It can be a social menace—because of its control of prices. Control of prices in the steel industry is powerful leverage on our economy ... our price level determines in large measure whether we have prosperity or depression—an economy of abundance or scarcity. Size in steel should therefore be jealously watched. In final analysis, size in steel is the measure of the power of a handful of men over our economy. That power can be utilized with lightning speed. It can be benign or it can be dangerous. The philosophy of the Sherman Act is that it should not exist. For all power tends to develop into a government itself. Power that controls the economy should be in the hands of elected representatives of the people, not in the hands of an industrial oligarchy. Industrial power should be decentralized. It should be scattered into many hands so that the fortunes of the people will not be dependent on the whim or caprice, the political prejudices, the emotional stability of a few self-appointed men. ... Competition is never more irrevocably eliminated than by buying the customer for whose business the industry has been competing ...".

MERGER GUIDELINES OF THE DEPARTMENT OF JUSTICE

The competitive effects of a merger cannot be measured unless one first defines the relevant market in which competition is supposed to have been affected. The relevant market is defined as "any grouping of sales (or other commercial transactions) in which each of the firms whose sales are included enjoys some advantage in competing with those firms whose sales are not included". The market is then defined in terms of product ("line of commerce") and geography ("section of the country"). Despite the fact that other products might be interchangeable with a product in terms of price, quality and use, the line of commerce is defined to be "any product or service which is distinguishable as a matter of commercial practice from other products or services . . .". Where two products are reasonably interchangeable and are sold to a group of purchasers, they may be grouped together to constitute a single market.

Section 7 of the Clayton Act requires that there be a substantial lessening of competition or restraint of commerce "in any section of the country". The Department of Justice defined "section of the country" in connection with its definition of the market as follows:

> "the total sales of a product or service in any commercially significant section of the country (even as small as the single community), or aggregate of such sections, will ordinarily constitute a geographic market if firms engaged in selling the product make significant sales of the product to purchasers in the section or sections".

1. *Horizontal mergers*

These are mergers between direct competitors, that is, competitors in the same level of the business trading ladder. The Department of Justice is principally concerned with the prevention of concentration in any given market, the elimination of any company which would likely have been a substantial competitor in the market, and also with preventing any company or small group of companies from obtaining a dominant position in the given market. The

Department gives its view of what it considers to be a highly or a less highly concentrated market but this is not really very helpful because the dispute is almost always a definition of the market itself in a merger. Nevertheless, this is what the Department of Justice suggests: in a market in which the shares of the four largest firms amount to at least about 75% it will ordinarily challenge the mergers where the acquiring firm and the acquired firm have 4% of the market each; or where the acquiring firm has 10% and the acquired firm has 2% or more; or where the acquiring firm has 15% or more and the acquired firm has 1% or more.

A less highly concentrated market in which the four largest firms have less than about 75% of the market will attract the Department of Justice's attention if the acquiring and the acquired firm have 5% of the market each; or where the acquiring firm has 10, 15, 20, or 25% or more of the market and the acquired firm, respectively, has 4, 3, 2, or 1% or more of the market.

The Department of Justice recognises that not every merger of competitors will be illegal. One might have the impression that because every merger will reduce the number of competitors at least by one and will concentrate a market at least by one, the merging parties are at least headed in the wrong direction from an antitrust point of view. There are however justified mergers and the guidelines mentioned two of them.

"Failing Company" The Department of Justice will not ordinarily challenge a merger if the resources of one of the merging firms are so depleted and its prospects for rehabilitation so remote that the firm faces the clear probability of a business failure, and good faith efforts by the failing firm have failed to elicit a reasonable offer to acquire it from a firm which intends to keep the failing firm in the market. The Department of Justice takes a very strict view of what is considers to be a failing company. For example it does not regard a firm as failing "merely because the firm has been unprofitable for a period of time, has lost market position or failed to maintain its competitive position in some other

respect, has poor management, or has not fully explored the possibility of overcoming its difficulties through self-help". It is not considered to be a justification for an acquisition, that the merger will produce economies such as improvements in efficiency.

2. *Vertical mergers*

This concerns acquisitions of a supplier by its customer or vice versa. Anticompetitive effects are likely to occur "whenever a particular vertical acquisition or series of acquisitions . . . tend significantly to raise barriers to entry into either market (supplying or purchasing market) or to disadvantage existing nonintegrated or partly integrated firms in either market in ways unrelated to economic efficiency". A merger in which the supplying firm accounts for about at least 10% or more of the sales in its market and one or more purchasing firms which account in all for about at least 6% of the total purchases in that market will attract the Department of Justice's attention, unless it clearly appears that there are no significant barriers to entry into the business of the purchasing firm or firms.

Taking a view of a vertical merger from the side of the purchasing firm, the Department of Justice will ordinarily challenge a merger between a supplying firm which accounts for 20% or more of the sales in its market and a purchasing firm or firms accounting in all for at least about 10% of the sales in the market in which it sells the produce whose manufacture required the supplying firm's product.

3. *Conglomerate mergers*

These are mergers that are neither horizontal nor vertical. In these mergers the Department of Justice does not look for similarity of product or interests but rather simply in the likely effect on market structure from the merger of perhaps totally unrelated companies. The department has grouped conglomerate mergers into those involving potential entrants into a market and those creating a danger of reciprocal buying. The Department of Justice will ordinarily challenge any merger between one of the most likely entrants into the market and any firm with at least 25% of the market; or one of the two largest firms in a market in which the shares of the two largest firms amount to at least 50%; or one of the four largest firms in a market in which the shares of the eight largest firms amount to at least 75%, provided the merging firm's share of the market amounts to at least 10%; or one of the eight largest firms in a market in which the shares of these firms amount to at least 75% but in this instance either the merging firm's share of the market is not insubstantial and there are no more than one or two likely entrants or the merging firm is a rapidly growing one. Reciprocal buying is simply a "you scratch my back and I will scratch your back" kind of situation. This is not looked upon favourably because it does give a competitive advantage which is unrelated to the merits of the product so any merger which has a significant danger of reciprocal buying will be challenged by the Department of Justice. The Department measures a significant danger being present whenever about at least 15% of the total purchases in a market in which the selling firm sells is accounted for by firms which also make substantial sales in markets where the buying firm is both a substantial buyer and a more substantial buyer than all or most of the competitors of the selling firm.

The above is a very sketchy paraphrase of the Department of Justice's guidelines. Obviously, they are only guidelines and in view of the many possibilities for differing opinions, for example, of the relevant market and of who would be a potential new competitor, the safest course in any merger or acquisition is to take advantage of the advance clearance and notification provisions of the Department of Justice or the Federal Trade Commission. Of course, there could be good commercial reasons not to bring such matters to the attention of government agencies but if advance clearance has not been obtained and the merger goes through only to be attacked successfully later on, the normal remedy is to compel divestiture of the assets or the shares of stock acquired, and this could be an extremely unprofitable task.

EXAMPLES

It would not require a great deal of legal sophistication to suspect that the horizontal merger of two healthy and influential companies might be attacked as a violation of s. 7 of the Clayton Act and even, perhaps, of s. 2 of the Sherman Act. It would be more profitable to discuss more practical aspects of problems in mergers and acquisitions. For example, it is not unusual for a manufacturer to entertain thoughts of acquiring its distributor because the distributor has a very efficient and widespread distribution network. If the manufacturer does not want to acquire all of the share capital of the distributor it may at least want to have an option to buy up to, say, 49% of the share capital of its distributor, and it may provide for such option in the distributorship agreement. There is nothing illegal in simply having such an option. Any Clayton Act difficulties would arise if the option were exercised. Corporations have different philosophies about their acquisition programmes. One company will not acquire another unless it can obtain control of all of the share capital of the other company or at least a majority shareholding in it. Other companies have a policy of taking only minority shareholding positions in another. Either view makes no difference to s. 7 of the Clayton Act; the violation can occur whether "the whole or any part of the stock or other share capital" is acquired "directly or indirectly" and the effect of such acquisition may be "substantially to lessen competition, or to tend to create a monopoly . . . in any line of commerce in any section of the country".

In our case of the manufacturer considering the acquisition of his distributor, the questions to be searched are whether as a result of the acquisition the manufacturers' competitors are foreclosed from using the distributor for their own products, and whether competitors of the acquired distributor are themselves foreclosed from the source of supply provided by the manufacturer.

One might puzzle over the distinction from an ordinary, straightforward exclusive distributorship agreement. Those agreements are legal and competitors of the distributor would be foreclosed from obtaining the products from the supplier who has made the distributor exclusive, meaning that the supplier himself cannot sell to anyone save the distributor. "An exclusive agency or dealership necessarily involves a limited monopoly to sell the product of the manufacturer in the area covered by the exclusive agreement. Such limited monopolies are not invalid . . .". Note the distinction from an acquisition in that the exclusive distributorship is a limited arrangement in a limited area. The acquisition would place the acquirer in a position unlimited as to time or geography. Furthermore, it would be wrong to assume that all exclusive distributorships are lawful. "They may not be used to extend the producer's monopoly into other fields" and they may not be "used to establish market dominance and drive out the products of competitors".

Our manufacturer, before he proceeds with the acquisition of the distributor, must determine the relevant market and the effect that his acquisition might have on competition within that market in a way peculiar to the business he is in and which, therefore, might be different from the way a court would label the market. Certainly important both to a legal analysis as well as business evaluation, the manufacturer would want to know the location of each of the distributor's stores and the areas into which it sells. He would also presumably know who and where not only his own competitors but the distributor's competitors are. These considerations would relate to the geographic market.

Similarly, the manufacturer would want to know the other products that the distributor was selling and what competitive products would be available from other dealers. (Note, in this respect, the analogy with the tests for justifying the exclusive franchise system whereby a supplier appoints certain franchises, i.e. selective distribution schemes. These have been declared to be legal where there are other dealers providing readily available competitive products. The same sort of consideration might be used by a court in deciding whether a merger was legal or not, i.e.

the availability of competitive products from other companies.) This was in fact a decision in the Southern District Court of New York which reached the Supreme Court that illustrates the importance of not foreclosing competitors from their selling outlets. This was *U.S.* v. *Bausch and Lomb Optical Co.*, 321 U.S. 707. Bausch and Lomb manufactured a certain kind of pink-tinted lens exclusively for Soft-Lite Lens Co. who then distributed the lens through wholesalers and retailers under the trade name "Soft-Lite". Bausch and Lomb manufactured only for Soft-Lite, thus assuring Soft-Lite of a product of uniformly good quality and assured Bausch and Lomb of a good outlet for its pink lenses. Soft-Lite purchased these lenses only from Bausch and Lomb. The agreement was not limited to any territory; it was nationwide. The government contended that the exclusive arrangement was unlawful. The court held that the arrangement was legal. It said:

> "nothing in the evidence indicates that Bausch and Lomb enjoyed a monopoly in the manufacture of glasses for lenses, whether pink or otherwise. On the contrary the evidence is clear that *other manufacturers of lenses have had access to pink glass* from other sources and that the success of Soft-Lite has stimulated emulation and competition" (our italics).

That case was decided in 1942 and later in 1955 in the Report of the Attorney General's Antitrust Committee, the committee commented about the theory suggested in the Bausch and Lomb case that all exclusive dealing arrangements are illegal *per se*. The committee said:

> "It is of course true that a manufacturer ownership of a processing or distributive outlet is more permanent than exclusive dealership established by contract . . . exclusive dealings . . . achieved by ownership or otherwise, are not illegal until the effect of such control is to unreasonably restrict the opportunities of competitors to market their product".

The Clayton Act does not apply to companies purchasing stock only as an investment. In the case of our manufacturer, of course, he is not purchasing his distributor solely as an investment. He wants to use his stockholding at least to ensure or secure the benefits of having the distributor distribute his products.

A latent danger in the Clayton Act is that it applies not only to the initial merger or acquisition of a company but also to shareholdings which though at the time they were acquired may have been lawful have, after a number of years, become unlawful. Taking the example of our manufacturer once more, assume that he goes forward and acquires only 26% of the shares of his distributor and that the acquisition at the time it is made is completely lawful. In the course of time the antitrust importance of that shareholding may be promoted by the increased economic importance of the distributor. The distributor may have increased his share of the market by his own diligence and talent. The number of competitors may have decreased for whatever reason so that the market for distributors and the particular competitive products became more concentrated. At that point the government may take the view that, because of that shareholding, competition in the distribution of competitive products has been substantially lessened. The manufacturer could then be required to divest itself of its shares. This illustration is a clumsy imitation of a more explicit and very important Supreme Court decision, *U.S.* v. *E. I. Du Pont de Nemours & Co.*, 353 U.S. 586.

Du Pont and General Motors were and are giant companies who do not compete with each other. Du Pont supplied automobile finishes and fabrics to General Motors and in 1947 purchased 71% of the output of the Du Pont Finishes Division. General Motors was also the largest purchaser of automobile fabrics from Du Pont's Fabrics Division. Du Pont supplied about 68% of General Motors' requirements for finishes and, in 1947, 38.5% of its requirements for fabrics. There was little doubt that Du Pont had a substantial share of the relevant market in these materials. The government felt the same way and brought an action under s. 7 of the Clayton Act. Du Pont defended that the Clayton Act was not applicable to shareholdings that were already well established. Du Pont had purchased a very large block of General Motors' stock in 1917 when General

Motors produced only about 11% of the US automobile production. There was clear evidence that Du Pont had not purchased the General Motors' shares only for investment and that Du Pont wanted to secure General Motors as a good customer for its paints and varnishes. The Supreme Court rejected Du Pont's defence and said that the Clayton Act applied:

> "any time when the acquisition threatens to ripen into a prohibited effect.... To accomplish the congressional aim, the government may proceed at any time that an acquisition may be said with reasonable probability to contain a threat that it may lead to a restraint of commerce or tend to create a monopoly of a line of commerce. Even when the purchase is solely for investment, the plain language of s. 7 contemplates an action at any time the stock is used to bring about or in attempting to bring about the substantial lessening of competition".[1]

An essential issue in cases challenging the acquisition is the effect of the acquisition on competition. The lessening of competition or the tendency to create a monopoly in any line of commerce must be as a result of the acquisition. Accordingly, if our manufacturer is going to buy into his distributor, he should take care to maintain a minority position and not insist on being represented on the Board of Distributor Company. In short, he should eschew any taint of control or influence. His posture should be that of a portfolio investor. (Be aware also of the danger of a "conspiracy" charge under ss. 1 or 2 of the Sherman Act in the event that the manufacturer might be accused of conspiring with its distributor to the detriment of the public. If the manufacturer has only a minority holding in the distributorship, he cannot defend on the basis of a "single trader" or "intra-corporate doctrine".)[2] On the other hand, if he takes a majority position in the distributor company, he may escape the Sherman Act ss. 1 and 2 conspiracy

---

1 Note the basis has been established here for the present attempts by the government to break up the large oil companies and International Business Machines Corporation.
2 See pages 33–78..

charges but find himself in a monopoly situation under s.2 or even under attack through s. 7 of the Clayton Act.

Geographic market

The Clayton Act's application to mergers and acquisitions reaches internationally in the requirement that both the acquirer and acquired corporations be "in commerce". Foreign commerce is included in the definition of "engaged in commerce". It is local to the US only in that "any section of the country" be the place where a substantial anticompetitive effect occurs or is likely to occur. Accordingly a foreign corporation even though it is not doing business within the US would be subject to s. 7 of the Clayton Act if it is at all engaged in the foreign commerce of the US, so any attempt by a foreign corporation to acquire or merge with an American corporation could come within the scope of the Clayton Act. Similarly an attempt by an American company to acquire or merge with a foreign company could come within the Act. The principle requirement in either situation is that the *effect* of the acquisition must be "in any line of commerce in any section of the country".

The second paragraph of s. 7 of the Clayton Act, however, does not require the acquiring corporation to be engaged in commerce. The second paragraph reads simply

> "no corporation shall acquire, directly or indirectly, the whole or any part of the stock or other share capital . . . of one or more corporations engaged in commerce, where in any line of commerce in any section of the country, the effect . . . may be substantially to lessen competition, or to tend to create a monopoly".

Only the *acquired* corporation needs to be engaged in commerce. The paragraph is silent about this attribute for the *acquiring* corporation. This second paragraph was intended to cover the actions of holding companies. As there is no requirement that the corporation must be one organized within any one of the US presumably the second paragraph would also cover foreign holding companies. In view of the above, if we return to our example of the manufacturer contemplating the acquisition of his distributor (although the same reasoning would apply to an acquisition of its supplier by the same manufacturer) we see that if the manufacturer is located in a country foreign to the US and his distributor is within the US, he would come within the Clayton Act. He is "engaged in commerce" in that he had been selling to the distributor, and the effect, if any, would be within the US. There are some interesting variations of structural corporate relationships involving, for example, a foreign company with subsidiaries in the US and an independent US company which come within the Clayton Act. Perhaps this would be a good time to deal with them. However, before taking up the matter of the Clayton Act's applicability to foreign business, we would like to dispel certain notions that the US government is against acquisition of American companies by foreign companies.

FOREIGN COMPANIES

There have been very few cases involving US antitrust enforcement against acquisitions, mergers and joint ventures in foreign commerce. On the contrary, a substantial number of foreign corporations have shareholdings in a substantial number of American corporations, and many of those shareholdings are more than portfolio investments. The facts speak for themselves; there is no evidence that there is any discrimination against foreign companies.

What would be the view of US antitrust enforcement officials of a merger of two *foreign* firms? Mr Douglas E. Rosenthal, Assistant Chief of the Foreign Commerce Section emphasized, whilst answering this question, that the US government had never challenged a merger of two foreign firms.[3] He went on to say "though I believe such a

---

3 Although this may be technically correct, the US expressed its displeasure against just such a merger in another way. See below page 229 about the Ciba–Ceigy merger.

suit could be brought where a substantial percentage of their foreign production was exported to US markets, where they were large firms in an industry with a tendency toward concentration and where they were subject to the jurisdiction of US courts".

FOREIGN ENTRY INTO THE US BY WAY OF ACQUISITION

Some foreign corporations would ignore the US market. Many of them are content to sell direct from abroad into the US. Others, however, may decide that it is better to locate physically within the US in order to compete more effectively there. Some of those corporations having made that decision then feel that it would be cheaper and faster to acquire an American corporation rather than commit what could be substantial capital expenditure in what would virtually be a "start-up" operation.

The law has recognized this difficulty and has permitted so-called "toe-hold" acquisitions in order to enter the market. This method of entering the market, however, needs to be exercised with caution. It may be acceptable where the newcomer into the market acquires a small company; but when the acquiring company is itself a major *potential* entrant into the market, there is serious doubt whether the acquisition will pass inspection by the Federal Trade Commission or the Department of Justice (if the result would be at least a tendency toward monopoly). The success of such an acquisition becomes all the more doubtful when the company which is acquired is not a small company but rather a leading company in the market. The essence of the government objection to such an acquisition for entering into a market is that the acquirer itself would have entered the market and would have been an additional competitor in that market; whereas, by virtue of the acquisition it eliminates the competition between itself and the acquired company.

This was illustrated in one of the first landmark cases in the US, *U.S.* v. *El Paso Natural Gas Co.*, 376 U.S. 651. The facts in the case are rather complicated but for our purposes we can simplify them to the following: the state of California was an expanding market for the use of natural gas. The El Paso Co., at the time, was the only out-of-state supplier into California. The Pacific Northwest Pipeline Corporation had received approval from the Federal Power Commission to build a pipeline to supply the Pacific Northwest area of the US with natural gas. It had acquired natural gas reservoirs in the Rocky Mountain area of the United States and had also received large quantities of natural gas from Canada. Southern California Edison Co. used natural gas in southern California. Pacific Northwest wanted to enter the California market. The Edison Co. began negotiations with Pacific Northwest to obtain natural gas from Pacific Northwest because it could not conclude satisfactory arrangements to obtain it from El Paso. El Paso had been interested in acquiring Pacific Northwest for some time and by May 1957, probably spurred by Edison's approaches toward Pacific Northwest, El Paso had acquired almost 100% of Pacific Northwest's outstanding stock. Shortly thereafter the US Department of Justice brought an action charging that the acquisition was unlawful under s. 7 of the Clayton Act. The issue was whether the acquisition had a sufficient tendency to lessen competition. The Supreme Court held that the acquisition was unlawful because "Pacific Northwest, though it had no pipeline into California is shown . . . to have been a substantial factor in the California market at the time it was acquired by El Paso". The court noted that Pacific Northwest had not been successful in entering the California market in spite of the fact that it had been approached by Edison as a firm purchaser of natural gas, not only because Pacific Northwest at that time had no pipeline to service the Edison Co., but also because El Paso had offered a better deal for the supply of natural gas to the Edison Co. Under the circumstances there would seem to have been no rational objection to El Paso's acquisition of the Pacific Northwest Co. because they were not in fact in competition. Notwithstanding this, the court felt that "we would have to wear blinders not to see that the mere efforts of Pacific Northwest to get into the California market, though unsuccessful, had a powerful influence on El Paso's business attitude within the state. We repeat that one purpose of s. 7 was to arrest the trend toward concentration, the tendency to monopoly, before the consumer's alternatives disappeared through merger . . .". In other words, the court believed that Pacific Northwest could have become a competitor in California and that the acquisition of it by El Paso removed Pacific Northwest as that competitor.

A FOREIGN ACQUIRER

A recent Federal Trade Commission decision affords another illustration of the principle that acquisition can be unlawful because it removes a potential competitor from entering the market. This was the Federal Trade Commission docket no. 8955 involving the British Oxygen Co. Ltd. and some of its American subsidiaries as the acquiring company and Airco Incorporated an American company, which was the target company for the acquisition. In 1973 British Oxygen acquired 35% of the common stock of Airco by means of a public tender offer. The Federal Trade Commission obtained a court injunction requiring British Oxygen to maintain Airco as an independent company and restraining British Oxygen from voting the Airco stock which it had acquired.

The FTC's complaint was that the acquisition "may substantially lessen competition in industrial gases, inhalation therapy equipment, and inhalation anesthetic devices". More particularly the FTC was concerned that British Oxygen's acquisition eliminated British Oxygen itself as the most likely potential entrant into that market in the US, i.e. the industrial gases industry; and that actual competition between Airco and the American subsidiaries of British Oxygen in the inhalation anesthetic equipment and therapy equipment was eliminated. British Oxygen is a well-known publicly-held British company and a large part of its business is the production and sale of industrial gases. At the time that it acquired Airco it was the second largest industrial gases firm in the world. Airco is a publicly-owned New

York corporation and manufactures industrial gases as well as medical products. The principal issue that we will concentrate on is the role of British Oxygen as a potential entrant into the market for industrial gases. Its subsidiary companies were not involved in this particular market. British Oxygen disagreed with the finding that the US as a whole was the appropriate geographic market in which to measure any anti-competitive effects.

British Oxygen had argued that the proper geographic market to measure such effects would be the regional markets themselves. The evidence shows that British Oxygen had shown some interest in regional firms but this was for the purpose of evaluating whether they would constitute feasible footholds for a subsequent national company. In any event, Airco was itself engaged nationally in the industrial gases business. The industrial gases industry in the US is highly concentrated. All the parties agreed that there were substantial areas for entry into the industrial gases business in the US. Substantial capital investment would be needed for production plants and a new entrant would suffer a cost disadvantage in trying to compete in areas supplied by established plants. Except for a toe-hold acquisition entry in 1968, there had been no significant entry into the US market. This market had been dominated by three firms and Airco was one of them.

The facts also show that as to possible future entry, there were only two possibilities: either there would be no further substantial entry into the American market or there would be entry by British Oxygen or possibly two or three other large international firms. All of the industrial executives who gave evidence on the possible future entry into the US market agreed that British Oxygen was the most likely of the small group of three international firms to enter the market.

The crucial question from an antitrust point of view was how British Oxygen would expand into the American market. The company itself did not dispute that it had the financial, technological and business ability to expand there. In fact it had already gained some American business experience through a joint venture with Airco in the manufacture and sale of air separation plants in the US. British Oxygen said that it had made a study of the US industrial gases market in 1969 and that its management was convinced that there was no feasible means of entering it and that it would not in fact have entered the US market but for the opportunity provided by Airco. The Federal Trade Commission itself was not convinced that this was so. It found evidence that this was not a final decision by British Oxygen management because in a report it was written that the "generally negative conclusion is in relation to the forseeable future and should not be considered final. Opportunities could rise in the future and a periodic view of the situation is recommended". British Oxygen said that it could never and would never have entered the US market save on a national scale and that it would cost about 240 million dollars for it to do so. Against this view, the Federal Trade Commission took the example of L'Air Liquide, a leading French firm who successfully entered the American market by purchasing a small regional firm. Thereafter, it continued to purchase small regional companies. The Commission felt that if L'Air Liquide could have entered on a modest scale, so could have British Oxygen.

The real difficulty with the case was that the industrial gases market in the US was highly concentrated and that Airco was too large a company in this field nationally in America for its acquisition to be considered merely a "toehold" into the market. In short, the Commission found that British Oxygen was a potential entrant into the American market and that by acquiring a leading American firm already in the market, it eliminated the beneficial effects that would result from its own competitive entry into the market.

US SUBSIDIARIES HAVING FOREIGN PARENTS

Contrary to Mr Rosenthal's suggestion above,[4] the merger of two foreign companies was challenged by the government in 1970. The US involvement occurred because each of

4 Page 223.

two diversified Swiss chemical companies had a large subsidiary in New York and New Jersey respectively. One Swiss
firm was Ciba and the other was Geigy and the matter
involved the merger of the two companies into what is now
known as Ciba–Geigy. The two companies merged in Switzerland and the US government feared that because of the
merger there would be a substantial lessening of competition between their subsidiaries in the US. Accordingly, the
merger was challenged by the antitrust division of the
Department of Justice in the US District Court for the
Southern District of New York and both of the Swiss
companies consented to the government's requirements
that the merged Swiss company should form a new company to whom it would transfer certain assets. The government required certain other complicated transactions
between the merged company and the new company but
the gist of the matter was that after a certain time the new
company would be sold. This was the US government's way
of remedying the anticompetitive effect because, certainly,
the US government could not impose its law in Switzerland
to compel the merged company to divest itself. In fact it
obtained jurisdiction over the Swiss only because they consented to a strictly limited consideration of the conditions
relating to the formation of the new company. No challenge
of the merger itself was possible.

AMERICAN FIRM ACQUIRING A FOREIGN COMPANY

A foreign corporation needs to be wary of possible Clayton
Act implications whenever it is approached by an
American company who desires to acquire a shareholding
in the foreign company. The foreign company should
carefully examine all of its contractual relations with any
other American company because any one of those relationships could act as a bar to the American company's
proposed acquisition. This happened to the American Gillette Co. It wanted to acquire Braun, a German electric
razor manufacturer. Braun itself was prevented from
entering the US market under the terms of a licensing

agreement it had with another American company. The government objected to the proposed acquisition because had it been consummated competition would have been eliminated between Gillette and the American licensee licensed by Braun.

The government had a similar concern in *U.S.* v. *Joseph Schlitz Brewing Co.*, 253 F.Supp. 129. Schlitz wanted to acquire a Canadian brewer but the stumbling block was the fact that the Canadian had a subsidiary which operated a brewery in California. The government attacked the acquisition because if Schlitz had acquired the Canadian company it would also thereby have acquired the California subsidiary and this would have had the ultimate effect of eliminating the Canadian company as a potential competitor in the California market.

FAILING COMPANY

If a company is in such a state that it faces the "grave probability of a business failure" and there is "no other prospective purchaser" (other than the company interested in acquiring the failing company) the acquisition would obviously not create anticompetitive effects. The courts and the government have taken a very strict view of what constitutes a "failing company" and as a practical matter this needs very close examination should such a situation arise. We mention it only to make the reader aware of the presence of this doctrine.

RECIPROCITY

This means simply "if you purchase from me I will purchase from you". It is not at all uncommon, particularly in Europe, but also in the US, for one company to purchase its requirements in a particular product or commodity from the other whilst the other company purchases its requirements from the company to whom it sells. The antitrust danger in this should be clear—it is a fairly old thought in US antitrust law that it is illegal to use purchasing power to coerce or encourage suppliers to make purchases. Where there is no such compulsion or use of power and the two companies simply purchase from each other as a matter of convenience, and there is no unreasonable or substantial adverse effect on competition, the practice is probably all right. If we translate the concept into the field of mergers and acquisitions, the result can be different. When one company acquires shares in another company the necessary ingredient of "compulsion" or at least "influence" on the acquired party to purchase from the acquirer is obvious; but this does not mean that every acquisition will result in illegal reciprocity in trading. The Supreme Court itself stated that "we do not go so far as to say that any acquisition no matter how small, violates s. 7 if there is a probability of reciprocal buying . . . but where the acquisition is of a company that commands a substantial share of a market, a finding of probability of reciprocal buying . . . should be honoured, if there is substantial evidence to support it". The reader will recall the discussion above in connection with the Du Pont shareholding in General Motors, that this was part of the consideration of the court in compelling Du Pont to divest itself of the shares that it held in General Motors. Du Pont supplied a substantial portion of General Motors' needs in varnish and paint finishes. Although there was no reciprocal buying involved i.e. that Du Pont had to purchase from General Motors, the relationship of Du Pont's behaviour to the reciprocal buying with which we are now concerned is obvious. If it was illegal for Du Pont to have a shareholding in a company to whom it sold then logic dictates that it would be no less illegal for Du Pont to be influenced to purchase from General Motors. The reciprocity effect is a timely concern because of the recent trend toward conglomerate mergers. Although the acquired companies within the conglomerate may be in diversified products, they may be engaged in reciprocal buying among themselves. Indeed, this may well be one of the reasons why the conglomerate was formed. John Mitchell, then Attorney General, said as much in an address on 6 June 1969. He said "one of the most easily understandable dangers posed by the conglomerate merger is reciprocity—

when a diversified corporation favours with purchases firms which purchase from it. We know reciprocity is widely practiced".

This does not mean that two companies cannot purchase from each other. The key elements for unlawfulness under the Clayton Act (and possibly also the Sherman Act s. 1) are the concept of coercion or undue influence resulting from the acquisition and the concurrent lessening of competition in the given market. This danger is present more frequently in highly concentrated or oligopolistic markets.

Unrelated to the problem of reciprocity except perhaps at a distance, is the interesting view taken by the US where two companies exchange stock interests. This occurred when the American company General Cable Corporation and British Insulated Callender's Cables Limited exchanged 20% minority shareholdings in each other. The American corporation, American Smelting and Refining Co. owned the General Cable stock. The government consented to the share transaction on condition that General Cable and British Insulated Callender's Cables would not use their shareholdings as leverage to fix prices or to prevent mutual competition anywhere in the world. A further interesting point is that the government also required that neither company have an officer, director or employee sitting on the other's board of directors.

A few final words about mergers in general and conglomerate mergers in particular. The commercial reasons for mergers are many and varied and the US government has been troubled by the merger movement, seeing in it a tendency toward concentration of power in fewer firms becoming larger and larger. A contribution to the merger movement is that a takeover offer itself can instigate a defensive merger by the target company. This occurred when, for example, Gulf and Western made a public offer for the shares of the Sinclair Oil Co. In response Sinclair arranged a merger with Atlantic Richfield whereupon the government brought an action against the latter merger. In 1969 the then Chief of the Antitrust Division of the Department of Justice, Mr Richard W. McLaren bluntly warned businessmen and lawyers "that they cannot rely on the Merger Guidelines issued by my predecessors in this area (conglomerates)—that we may sue even though particular mergers appear to satisfy those Guidelines—and that, to be safe, firms desiring to merge should learn our enforcement intentions by applying for a Business Review letter".

The European Community and elsewhere

There is little to add in connection with mergers and acquisitions that has not already been said in the *Continental Can* case discussed above, in so far as the Community is concerned. It seems strange that the provisions of art. 85 have not been applied to mergers and that art. 86 has been the basis for the only actions taken by the Commission against mergers. Article 85 could, in theory, be applicable because there must have been an agreement between the acquiring company and the target company being merged. Possibly mergers have escaped the umbrella of art. 85 because art. 85 requires that the agreement itself be likely to affect trade whereas in a merger situation, the anticompetitive effect does not arise from the agreement but rather from the existence of the merged company itself. In any case no action has been brought against acquisitions or mergers under art. 85. Notwithstanding the slightly ambiguous stand taken by the Court of Justice in the *Continental Can* case, the safer view would be to assume that one way or another the Court of Justice will apply art. 86 to mergers. There was indication of this in the European Parliament when a question was posed to the Commission concerning a proposed merger in the automobile tyre industry in Europe. The commission answered "in the absence of any precise information on a specific merger, it cannot say whether such an operation would fall within the provisions of art. 86 of the Treaty". The only inference from this is that mergers do come within art. 86. Apart from this view, there have been some tactical measures to control the development of multi-national enterprises through acquisition and merger that do not challenge the merger itself. There was a proposed European Council resolution expressing the intention to propose measures to protect the rights of workers in cases of merger, concentration or rationalization of enterprises.

The ambivalence of the Commission as to whether art. 86 covers mergers and its attitude toward mergers was nowhere better expressed than in its own words in 1974:

> "Many mergers, as a result of the structure of the markets in which they occur, *in no way lessen competition* but on the contrary can *increase* it. However, the Commission can not overlook that the EEC Treaty, in making it responsible for applying the rules of competition, requires it to preserve the unity of the Common Market, to ensure that the market remains open and ensure effective competition. Excessive concentration is likely to obstruct these aims".

Up to this point one notes clearly that the Commission recognizes that not all mergers are bad and that in some cases can actually promote competition. The Commission revealed its uncertainty about the application of art. 86 when it said:

> "the legal instruments in the field of competition law currently available do not give adequate means of dealing effectively with the dangers arising from excessive concentration . . . Concentrations . . . are covered by Community rules on competition only if they constitute abuses of dominant positions within the meaning of Article 86 . . .".

The Commission is aiming at those mergers where neither party is in a dominant position (such as Continental Can) so that the merger of one by the other would be or could be considered an *abuse* of the dominant position. In its prelude to a proposed regulation to control mergers, the Commission talked about what concerned it most in the effect on competition. In the end, the Commission is concerned that the merger will achieve a dominant position. The Commission is not as concerned as the US with the fact that the merging parties no longer compete with each other. The Commission said:

> "Through mergers, firms can reach a market position where they can avoid the pressure of competition. They no longer

need to adjust the price, quantity or quality of their products to demand. The market position of such firms allows them to adopt a price strategy which is largely independent of economic developments . . .".

Accordingly the thrust of the Commission's proposals is toward preventing such concentrations through merger as would hinder effective competition within the Common Market. Concentrations involving firms with aggregate sales of 1,000 million units of account would be subject to prior notification. Final action on these proposals or even amendments to them have not yet been taken but obviously one must be watchful and at least aware that the Commission is taking steps to obtain regulations controlling the merger movement within the Common Market.

CANADA

Canada has had a law relating to mergers and combines since 1889 but it was virtually a criminal law and was somewhat commercially unrealistic. Historically Canadian merger law was also weak in that it required almost a total elimination of competition before the criminal law standard of proof could be met. The US and Canada have agreed to exchange information and to consult with each other in connection with the enforcement of their respective antitrust and anti-combines laws. Canada has enacted a law under which foreign investment in Canada may be prevented if it is not to the "benefit" of Canada. "Benefit" is not defined.

We cannot leave the subject of mergers and acquisitions without some reference to the Sherman Act, because the Sherman Act is applicable to them on the same principles that were discussed at length in Part I.

SHERMAN ACT AND MERGERS AND ACQUISITIONS

Suppose that company A and company B, competitors with each other, form a holding company for their capital shares? At once there is the problem that the act of forming the holding company could be a conspiracy to restrain trade because it would be tantamount to an agreement between the competitors not to compete with each other. If the formation of the holding company passes this obstacle, what would be the view if the holding company then begins purchasing controlling interests in other companies? Under the Sherman Act the activity of the holding company (and the two shareholders) could be an illegal attempt to form a monopoly.

12

Joint ventures

We have separated discussions of joint ventures from their normal inclusion in a section on monopolies and acquisitions because they are not quite the same as a merger or acquisition. A merger occurs where two or more companies transfer their share ownership and only one company survives. An acquisition is where the company simply purchases a portion or all of the shares or assets of another company but both companies retain their identities. These are simplistic definitions but they are given here only to distinguish from the joint venture.

The joint venture in its widest sense is two or more separate and independent entities acting together to achieve a common objective which may be narrowly "one-off" in nature or a continuing programme. In the context of the line of development of the legality of mergers and acquisitions under the antitrust laws, the joint venture with which we will now be concerned is the formation of a third corporation by two or more separate and independent companies to achieve a common objective which is normally longer-lived than a "one-off" transaction.[1] Typically the joint venture third company is formed and owned by the others to do something that neither company alone wants to do. The government may leap at this on the grounds that it eliminates competition between the joint venturers in the sense that they would have entered into the

---

1 The expression "joint venture" also means the joint activity of two or more independent companies, usually in research and development technology, which does not involve the formation of a third company commonly owned by all of them. In that case, the antitrust problems reside in the terms and conditions of the operation of the joint venture.

new field as competitors but for the formation of the joint
venture company. That is the core of the government's
objection to such joint ventures. The government will
attack such joint ventures under the Clayton Act although
there was always a question (at least originally) whether the
Clayton Act would apply at all. Note that in a joint venture
no corporation in existence is being acquired and because
the joint venture company has not yet been formed, it
cannot be engaged in commerce at the pertinent time.
Nevertheless, these questions were quickly swept away and
one should accept the fact that the Clayton Act will apply to
joint ventures. That was purely the legal problem with joint
ventures. The business problem is something else and it is
in joint ventures that one sees the muddle of the government zealously pursuing legal theory about potential competition, the business reality which may not at all be
anticompetitive in intent or effect, and the middleground
that sometimes the reason for the joint venture is, in fact, to
avoid wasteful competition. In the following example one
may see an expression of the chief antitrust danger in joint
ventures and, at the same time, the failure of the government's legal theory in the face of business reality.

Company A for many years has been a producer of a
chemical compound (let us call it sodium chlorate). Company A also manufactures other chemicals. It produces the
chemicals including the sodium chlorate and sells them
throughout the US. It is not the largest producer of sodium
chlorate and there are two other producer-competitors of
company A. Company A accounts for about 14% of the
production of the chemical in the US. It produces the
sodium chlorate in the Northwest portion of the US. Its two
competitors have manufacturing facilities scattered
throughout the US including the Southeast portion. Company A sold into the Southeast at a non-competitive price
because of the substantial transportation costs from the
Northwest portion of the US.

Company B is a large diversified corporation which
among other things also produces chemicals and chemical
products, but not sodium chlorate. Company A had always

used company B as its sales agent for sodium chlorate. In an effort to improve its competitive position in the Southeast, company A had undertaken several cost and market studies to build a plant in the Southeast to manufacture and sell the sodium chlorate there. Company A is a profitable corporation with earnings of several million dollars annually but its feasibility study for the building of a plant in the Southeast indicated that the cost would be so great that the rate of return on investment made the project unlikely. Company A then heard that its principal competitor in the Southeast was going to increase its capacity for the production of sodium chlorate. Company A, having decided that it would not be reasonable to commit so great an investment for the building of a plant in the Southeast, approached company B with a view toward combining forces to build a jointly owned plant in the Southeast. Company B, though never having produced sodium chlorate, did account for considerable use of it because it owned and licensed a patented process for bleaching paper, and the process used sodium chlorate. In view of company B's interest in sodium chlorate, and the fact that company B was not a competitor of company A, the idea seemed to be a good one. Indeed, company B had itself looked into the possibility of producing sodium chlorate but for various technical and financial reasons company B's management did not feel that such a project would be worthwhile. The chairman of company B, having been approached by his opposite number in company A reviewed the situation with his advisors and the decision by both boards was that while the project was not feasible for either of them alone it would be viable with the risk of loss divided between the two.

Accordingly companies A and B formed a jointly owned subsidiary in the Southeast of the US to build a plant to produce sodium chlorate. Under the joint venture agreement company A would operate the plant and company B would use its expertise to sell the plant's production in the Southeast. The joint venture proved successful and after about two years it accounted for 27% of the sodium chlorate sales in the Southeast.

Companies A and B as well as the joint venture company were served with complaints by the US government under s. 7 of the Clayton Act charging that the formation of the joint venture company substantially lessened competition in the production and sale of sodium chlorate in the Southeastern portion of the US. Companies A and B answered as their first line of defence that the Clayton Act does not apply to an acquired company because it is not engaged in commerce at the time that it is formed. The government won this issue, with the court dismissing the defence on the ground that the test of the application of the Clayton Act is the *effect* of the acquisition; the formation of the joint venture being comparable to an acquisition because the purchase of its corporate shares by companies A and B would substantially lessen competition between companies A and B. The court avoided any further debate on the issue by taking the stand that the joint venture was engaged in commerce at the time the complaint was filed and the economic effect of the formation of the joint venture should be measured at that time rather than at the time of its formation.

Companies A and B argued that a joint venture is not the same as a merger or acquisition and that the court cannot measure the legality of a joint venture the way it would a merger or acquisition. The court answered that company A and company B each had the resources and general capability to build and operate a sodium chlorate plant without the help of the other. Because of this the formation of the joint venture was simply another form of acquisition whereby A and B mutually excluded themselves as competitors, certainly as potential competitors.

Company A argued that if only one of them would have entered the Southeast, the government's case would founder anyway because such entry would still not have created competition; B would have remained the non-competitor it had always been. In other words both A and B would have had to make independent decisions to enter the market before they could be considered to be in competition with each other there. This argument won in a lower court but the government appealed to the Supreme Court.

The court reviewed A's proof that it had already made its decision not to "go it alone", and there was no proof that B would "go it alone". The court, however, on the issue of whether it would have been necessary for both to have entered the market, raised the intriguing theory of the competitive value of "threatening". The court said that even if only one of the two had entered the Southeast market, there would have been competitive value in having the other one remaining on the edge of the market "threatening" to enter it. But the existence of the joint venture totally eliminated this threat because it would be unrealistic to believe that A or B would compete with their own subsidiary. As for the realistic appraisal of the value of the "threat", there is, said the court, something in it. The threat of entry would keep the one in the market from overcharging or failing to give good service. So the court remanded the case to the lower court to look into the point about one of them entering the market and whether the other would be a "threat".

And, again, the lower court reviewed the evidence and found that neither company would have entered the market alone. The government had argued that either A or B *could* have entered the market. A and B argued that that is not the question; the fact is that neither of them *would* have entered it alone. The court agreed with A and B. The above example is a paraphrase of an actual case, *U.S.* v. *Penn–Olin*, 378 U.S. 158.

What can be got out of the case as a guide for future joint venture considerations in the US? Certainly, it helps to show that the market is not such as to justify the risk of one party committing investment capital to build plant and equipment. The test is not that a company has the means to enter a market, but rather whether it would enter it alone. Then, one would have to assess the competitive value of the threat of the proposed joint venturer as a potential competitor. That would be a realistic appraisal. But realism is needed all along the line of enquiry. Competitors are shrewd judges of the market. They know fairly well how much business is there and how quickly it might be saturated. If a company is diversified, it is unlikely to risk substantial capital in a new venture on its own, particularly as it does not need to do so.

Antitrust enforcement agencies sometimes seem to be consumed with suspicion that all joint ventures are open to suspicion because they eliminate competition between the joint venturers and also between the joint venturers and the joint venture itself. Any joint venture should be entered into keeping in mind that particular concern of the government. Sometimes the suspicion is justified. But there are many times when it is not.

In recent years there has been important activity in bank joint ventures: different banks syndicating, or forming a joint venture bank. The purpose is to provide a bigger source of funds. When a loan prospect appears, the normal procedure is for the syndicated bank to make the loan, with each of its shareholders taking its proportionate part of the risk—and the profit. It is not always a non-competitive kind of operation. Not all bank syndications have been happy joint ventures. It has happened that one of the shareholders wanted to handle the deal alone, and there you have the seed of competition between one of the joint venturers and the joint venture company. This inner conflict between the individual's interest and that of the joint venture has led to the failure of a number of bank joint ventures.

Professor Pitofsky, in his fine article on the *Penn–Olin* case in the *Harvard Law Review* (vol. 82: 1007, 1969) says that "The effect of a joint venture between parent companies that compete horizontally usually is to eliminate competition . . . A common example is a joint sales agency which eliminates price competition between manufacturing parents in the products sold by the agency". That is too broad a statement. The joint selling agency in the *Appalachian Coal* case discussed above was approved by the court.

FOREIGN JOINT VENTURES

There is not much to be said on this because most of these joint ventures successfully attacked by US courts were done so because the joint venture was part of a larger illegal scheme. The Department of Justice gave the best guide for action in this respect (in the absence of any other useful guide):

> "In general joint ventures abroad by American companies in cooperation with foreign companies present no antitrust problems unless (1) participation in the joint venture is a prerequisite to competition and some American firms are arbitrarily excluded or (2) the activities of the joint-venturers has some substantial impact on the domestic commerce of the United States, in which case the venture will be judged by rules applying domestically."

This statement by the Department of Justice does not indicate a strong antipathy against Americans forming joint ventures abroad. In so far as the Clayton Act is concerned, a violation would be somewhat remote because although the "engaged in commerce" requirement would be met (because the joint venturers would be engaged in foreign commerce, and certainly in the internal commerce of the US), there is a question whether the second requirement of an effect on commerce within the US could be satisfied. Far more likely would action be taken against the joint venture under s. 1 of the Sherman Act, and even in this respect such action would not be primarily against the joint venture as such but rather because of the activities of the joint venture or of the use made of it. We saw this in the *Timken* case discussed above where the American Timken Company was involved with joint ventures in France and in Britain and was found to have violated the Sherman Act because of using the subsidiaries to divide territorial markets.

In *U.S.* v. *Minnesota Mining and Manufacturing Co.*, 92 F.Supp. 947 a similar situation arose, but in that case all of the joint venturers were major US competitors. They combined to form a Webb-Pomerene Export Association[2] and then formed joint ventures abroad to produce products outside of the US. The essence of the objection was simply that the government felt that foreign joint ventures by major US competitors unreasonably blocked their exports from the US. Apart from this restraint on American foreign commerce provided by the major US joint venturers themselves, the presence and function of their foreign joint venture plants had the coincidental effect of inhibiting their formerly competing US producers from exporting to the markets being supplied by the jointly owned foreign plants. The court saw anticompetitive ripples reaching even further and felt that the mere formation of anything as intimate as a joint venture among competitors would inevitably cause the joint venturers to be less enthusiastic to compete with each other in the US market.

The antitrust lesson to be learned from this is that a foreign company entering into a joint venture outside of the US with an American corporation should be aware not only of the possible effects within the US arising because of the formation of the joint venture itself, but also of the subsequent actions of the joint venture. Although the US courts might not obtain jurisdiction over the foreign joint venturer, it certainly would have jurisdiction over the American joint venturer and the consequences of an unfavourable decision could be disastrous to the joint venture itself.

Where the joint venturers themselves are both foreign, Clayton Act concern may arise only remotely and, perhaps, as in the *Ciba–Geigy* case discussed above, if each of the foreign joint venturers has a subsidiary within the US. At present, pending the Brussels Commission obtaining the regulation which they seek for the control of mergers, there is no effective Common Market law to prevent the formation of joint ventures. This has always been true of Europe generally and the formation of transnational European

---

2 The Webb-Pomerene Export Act of 1918 was enacted to permit American companies to engage in export trade without fear of violating US antitrust law. There are certain conditions attached to this exemption.

joint ventures has been common for many years. Indeed some of the most famous are Royal Dutch–Shell, Agfa–Gevaert, Dunlop–Pirelli, and General Electric–Honeywell, although some of these are more properly called some form of merger.

In more recent times the reasons for the formation of joint ventures have passed from the earlier primary objective of improving distribution and product rationalization to solving the simple problem of rising costs in research and development. It has become impractical or even impossible for individual companies to undertake research development on their own and the result of this is that more joint ventures have been formed, and the result of that has been increased interest by the US government antitrust authorities. Of course, one solution is for the corporation to cut their own research and development budgets and purchase outsiders' ideas. Indeed, in 1968 Radio Corporation of America employed a well-paid full-time professional resident in London for the sole purpose of looking for new products. According to the National Science Foundation between 1969 and 1976 the number of scientists and engineers doing research in 8,000 US companies declined 8%. In addition it seems that an inordinately large number of researchers are spending more time substantiating advertising claims and coping with federal regulations than they do in inventing and developing new products. As the market becomes more filled with products, it becomes more competitive, and as it becomes more competitive more new products are fed into the market place. Patrick McGuire, Project Director at the Conference Board, a non-profit New York organization involved in business research said, "The new-product rat race is analogous to the arms race. Companies have to run harder just to stay in the same spot. If they put 50 raw ideas in at the top and get one good one out at the bottom they are doing all right. But they aren't putting in enough at the top". From an antitrust point of view, the US government should be more sympathetic to stimulating research and development than to the purchasing of new products, because there would be increased competition in research and development, a substantially more productive field for the public benefit than the crass purchase of products from other sources. Unfortunately in many cases the only practical way in which research and development can be carried out is through a joint venture because the soaring costs of research and development programmes, as already mentioned, prevent many companies from attempting it. It is not a question of whether any single company could afford to carry out research and development. The risks are so great in developing a new product that many boards of directors will not commit that kind of expenditure to something which is new and untried. If we might borrow from the principle stated in the *Penn–Olin* case, the argument that a company *would* not enter a market is legally more persuasive and justified than government insistence that a company would be a potential competitor because it *could* be one. But old habits die hard, as they say, and in early 1976 we saw a proposed joint venture in the extremely difficult and expensive aircraft engine industry arrested by the US government. Because of the importance of the project and the attitude of the US Department of Justice we will give the facts of the proposed joint venture, and the statement of the Justice Department, and then make a couple of observations that may be useful for planning future joint ventures.

THE ROLLS ROYCE AND PRATT AND WHITNEY JET ENGINE DEVELOPMENT PROGRAMME

Pratt and Whitney began design work on a new jet engine having about 25,000 pounds of thrust to power the 1980s generation of aircraft. After having begun the work, it announced in May 1973 that it was going to continue the collaboration on the engine with a German firm and with the Italian firm, Fiat. While Pratt and Whitney was working on the new engine, Rolls Royce was investigating the market for a new jet engine for the 1980s generation aeroplane to follow its RB211 engine which is used to power the Lockheed L-1011 aeroplane known as the Tristar.

At the same time, General Electric Company of America was progressing in partnership with France's SNECMA in the development of an engine similar to the Pratt and Whitney JT10D. The GE/SNECMA engine was called the CFM56. Rolls Royce and Pratt and Whitney saw that there might be three engines in the market: the JT10D from Pratt and Whitney, the contemplated engine from Rolls Royce, and the CFM56 from GE/SNECMA. Rolls Royce and Pratt and Whitney each claimed that neither of them could afford to develop the engine in isolation. Mr Mulready, Pratt and Whitney's New Business Development Manager said "When you are faced with the magnitude of investment, it is increasingly hard to do it yourself. It's not a prudent commercial risk". Rolls Royce could only agree with such a statement, in view of its near-disaster in connection with the RB211 engine development for the Lockheed Tristar. It is well known that high-technology research and development in the production of something like a new jet engine is extremely hazardous and the cost estimates could very easily be exceeded by a factor of three or more. The cost estimate for the development of the JT10D was 500 million dollars over four years to obtaining an airworthiness certificate; and then more funds would be needed for development and production. Under the circumstances talks began between Pratt and Whitney and Rolls Royce towards collaboration on the project.

Quite possibly Pratt and Whitney in conjunction with Fiat and the German company could have moved ahead with the project without Rolls Royce's help; however Pratt and Whitney had learned from experience with its larger JT9D engine, used for the wide-bodied Boeing 747 and the McDonnell Douglas DC10 aeroplanes that its profitability was impaired because of strong competition with the Rolls Royce RB211. Accordingly, Pratt and Whitney would welcome the partnership of Rolls Royce in the group because by reducing a market of three competitors down to two competitors, its chances of profitability would be increased.

From Rolls Royce's point of view, since it could not possibly develop such an engine on its own, the alliance with

Pratt and Whitney was essential. If Rolls Royce could not develop such an engine it would have to get out of the jet engine industry altogether because it could not rely on only the RB211. In the partnership with Pratt and Whitney and the German and Italian firms, Rolls Royce's share would be 34%, the German and Italian firms together would account for 12% and Pratt and Whitney would have the remaining 54%. This would mean that Rolls Royce's commitment would be at least 170 million dollars. Rolls Royce did not have this money and would need UK government funds.

Whilst the primary objective of the joint programme was the production of the JT10D, included in the collaboration was the development of a second engine, a smaller, 6,000 pounds thrust jet engine, the RB401, designed for a totally different market: the smaller executive jet aircraft. This particular project was already well under way. It was designed by Rolls Royce and the first engine was expected in 1976.

Clearly, Rolls Royce would need to obtain the funds for its share of the joint venture with Pratt and Whitney from the UK government because private funds would not likely find their way into the project since return on the investment was not expected until at least 1986. The *Wall Street Journal* in reporting on the joint venture said "For financially-strapped Rolls Royce, the arrangement seems to assure a continued place in the commercial aircraft engine market, a place it otherwise might not be able to afford on its own". The joint venture was made subject to approval from the US Department of Justice, who on 13 January swiftly gave its opinion.

The US Justice Department opposed the joint venture on antitrust grounds. It said that the collaboration on the engine would present serious competitive problems. It did not oppose the cooperative effort on the larger JT10D, and the Department seemed to understand that this engine was probably too expensive for only one manufacturer to develop on its own. But it was concerned about the smaller engine, the RB401 executive jet engine which was included in the package. The Justice Department felt that either of the companies could afford to move ahead on this one on its own and "Not to do so would deter competition".

Note that the Justice Department's view had nothing to do with the creation of a third company as such but rather in the substantive nature of the collaboration itself, regardless of the form which it would take. Nor did the Justice Department object to any particular terms in the proposed collaboration. The essence of its objection, was that no joint venture was necessary to develop the small engine because either company could do so on its own. If the two companies together agreed to build the smaller engine one of them would be effectively eliminated as a potential competitor.

We think that the government may have put forward the wrong objection and omitted the point made in the *Penn–Olin* case. The issue was not whether either company *could* have developed and produced the smaller engine on its own. The correct issue, in accordance with the *Penn–Olin* case was whether either company *would* proceed on its own with the smaller engine. Rolls Royce was already well under way in the development and production of the smaller engine, the RB401, so the question should have been put: would Pratt and Whitney have gone forward on its own in the development and production of a smaller executive jet engine that would have been competitive with the Rolls Royce RB401?

This poses a difficult subject for antitrust analysis because it is highly likely that the entire joint venture has to be seen as a package deal. It is possible that Pratt and Whitney did not need Rolls Royce's assistance in the development of the JT10D; after all, it had already begun the programme on it. It is undoubtedly correct that Pratt and Whitney would not be dissatisfied with the infusion of British government money, but it probably was not necessary to obtain those funds. It is equally realistic to suppose that Pratt and Whitney would not expect Rolls Royce to enter the race on its own. The memories of the RB211 must still be fresh in British minds. Accordingly, Pratt and Whitney probably did not have any serious concern of a third Rolls Royce engine in competition with the JT10D and the GE/SNECMA CFM56. If these assumptions are reasonably correct, one might suppose that the "sweetener" was Rolls Royce's progress with its own RB401, the smaller executive jet engine that the US Department of Justice said that Pratt and Whitney would have competed with on its own. It could be just as well argued that Pratt and Whitney would not have competed in that smaller engine market. At any rate, it would be the burden of the Department of Justice to prove such willingness on the part of Pratt and Whitney rather than the capability of Pratt and Whitney to do so.

MARINER INTERNATIONAL CORPORATION

Another joint venture agreement between a US manufacturer and a foreign firm which was challenged by the Federal Trade Commission was that between the Brunswick Corporation and Yamaha Motor Corporation Limited. These two companies formed Mariner International Corporation. Brunswick was to purchase some newly issued shares of a Yamaha subsidiary which produced outboard motors. These shares were then to be transferred to Mariner and Mariner was to be the exclusive marketing arm in North America for the motors produced by the Yamaha subsidiary. The Brunswick Corporation produced a well-known outboard in the US called the "Mercury". Under the terms of the agreement forming the joint venture, Yamaha would not make any outboard engines similar to the Mercury. Apart from the very probable antitrust problems in the terms and conditions of the agreement itself, which formed the joint venture, the Federal Trade Commission alleged that s. 7 of the Clayton Act was infringed because potential competition was eliminated among Brunswick, Yamaha, and the joint venture Mariner. In particular, Yamaha would be eliminated as one of the few likely potential entrants into the American market for outboard motors.

SUMMARY

Although a joint venture company formed by two or more companies not already in the particular market in which the joint venture company will become involved is itself a fresh competitor in the field, the test to win acceptability for it would be to blunt either of two government arguments: The likely government argument that both of the joint venturers would have entered the market if the joint venture itself had not been formed, or the argument that even if only one of them had entered the market, the mere presence of the non-entrant on the sidelines as a threatening potential entrant would serve to promote competition. But there is an important distinction where the two joint venturers are already in the market. The well known case *U.S.* v. *Imperial Chemical Industries, Ltd.*, 100 F.Supp. 504 illustrates this. There we had an American company and a British company both already established in a foreign local market. The Supreme Court said:

> "...there is nothing *per se* unlawful in the association or combination of a single American enterprise with a single concern of a foreign country in a jointly owned manufacturing or commercial company to develop a foreign local market. But the proof here shows an American concern, already established in a foreign local market, and a British concern, which has a foothold in the same foreign local market, combining to form a jointly owned company to the end that the same foreign market may be developed for their mutual benefit and profit divided on an agreed basis".

It is obviously important, indeed, essential, to identify and outline the boundaries of the relevant market in which competition is affected in all cases of mergers, acquisitions and joint ventures. It is more often than not an extremely difficult task. It sometimes helps simply to look around to see who gets hurt. That uncomplicated view of the field can sometimes surprisingly clarify the market.

When we began this discussion of joint ventures we suggested another kind of joint venture which did not involve the creation of a third company but simply contractual relations between two or more corporations in connection with, say, a research and development project. No discussion of that aspect of a joint venture can avoid careful and deep consideration of the use of industrial property rights. This will be the subject of the next chapter.

13
Uses of patents and trademarks

To begin with it will be helpful to remember that in the US there is only one national patent and only one national trademark, in the sense that the government is concerned with only one patent or one trademark to cover the entire national area. In the Common Market the Commission is concerned with ten individual national patents and ten individual national trademarks. We think that this distinction has had more than a little influence in the development of antitrust thinking of the US government and the Commission and the European Court of Justice in respect of the use of patents and trademarks, particularly in the licensing of them.

The US government is therefore more understandably concerned with the existence of the patent itself and its use *vis-à-vis* the licensee. In the Common Market, on the other hand, the Commission has not centred its attacks so much on the rights of the licensee for the sake of preserving the licensee's rights, as it has on the use of national patents themselves to prevent or impede imports and exports of the patented products and competing products. Accordingly, one finds the Commission and the Court of Justice becoming progressively more antipathetic towards *exclusivity* of the patent licence and the effects of it, rather than restric-· tions on the licensee himself. In Europe, the Commission is troubled by the chequerboard of individual nations, each with its own patent system and the exploitation of national patents to frustrate one of the major objectives of the

Common Market—the freeflow of goods and services between member nations.

AREAS OF PATENT LICENSING VIOLATIONS IN THE US

1. It is unlawful to require a licensee to purchase unpatented materials from the licensor.
2. It is unlawful for a patentee to require licensee to assign to the patentee any patent which may be issued to the licensee after the licensing arrangement is executed.
3. It is unlawful to attempt to restrict a purchaser of a patented product in the resale of that product.
4. A patentee may not restrict his licensee's freedom to deal in the products or services not within the scope of the patent.
5. It is unlawful for a patentee to agree with his licensee that he will not, without the licensee's consent, grant further licenses to any other persons.
6. Mandatory package licensing is an unlawful extension of the patent grant.
7. It is unlawful for a patentee to insist, as a *condition* of the licence, that his licensee pay royalties in an amount not reasonably related to the licensee's sales of products covered by the patent, e.g. royalties on the total sales of products of the general type covered by the licensed patent.
8. It is unlawful for the owner of a processed patent to attempt to place restrictions on his licensee's sales of products made by the use of the patented process.
9. It is unlawful for a patentee to require a licensee to adhere to any specified or minimum price with respect to the licensee's sale of the licensed products.

AREAS OF ANTITRUST VULNERABILITY IN THE COMMON MARKET UNDER ART. 85

1. Restricting manufacture or sale under licence to a specific territory, or to certain methods, or restricting

the use of the product. Such clauses in both trademark and patent licences are generally safe, by express declaration by the Commission, but can become violations if pursued as a general plan to divide markets.

2. Exclusive licensing by which only one party is granted the right to manufacture or sell in a specific territory, or is granted the right to use a certain method or is granted the right to use a product for a particular purpose. This is the most sensitive and vulnerable clause in any patent or trademark or technical knowhow licence because exclusivity necessarily implies that even the licensor may not use in the licensed territory the rights which he has granted to the licensee, and, moreover, may not grant those rights to any third party so long as the licence is in force. In the US, the Patent Law itself expressly permits the granting of exclusive licenses.[1] On the other hand, there is nothing at all expressed about this anywhere in the Treaty of Rome but the Commission, in the same declaration in which it said that it was all right to include the restrictions mentioned in preceding para. 1 declared that the granting of exclusive rights may constitute a violation of art. 85(1). Since that declaration in 1962[2] decisions by the Commission and by the European Court have come closer and closer to outlawing exclusive licenses altogether. We shall discuss this point below.

3. Restricting the licensee to a particular sales territory, i.e. prohibiting him from exporting from the licensed territory. These provisions in licensing agreements are more susceptible to illegality then the exclusivity mentioned in para. 2. Indeed such limitations would run totally contrary to the purpose of the Common Market and must in themselves constitute

---

1 35 U.S.C. § 261: "The applicant, patentee, or his assigns or legal representatives may . . . grant and convey an exclusive right . . . to the whole or any specified part of the United States".

2 Official Notice on Patent Licensing Agreements, 24 December 1962.

violations of art. 85. This type of clause as well as the exclusivity clauses will be discussed and illustrated by examples.

4. Clauses regulating the relationship between the licensor and the licensee are generally safe, save for two types of clauses which are also disfavoured in the US, the difference being that in the Common Market the reasons for their disfavour are different from those in America. There are no objections to granting licences for the life of a patent. For the same reason that exclusivity may be unlawful, covenants by the licensor not to compete with the licensee by exploiting the licensed subject matter in the licensed territory may also run into problems with art. 85. It is proper to demand royalty payments for the licence and even if the licensed patents expire or are declared invalid, or even if the patentee fails to have any patents or patent applications remaining in a licensed agreement, the licensee can still be required to pay royalties although at a reduced rate. In the US it would be unlawful to require the payment of royalties under a licence when there are no longer any patents. The rationale for such illegality is self-evident. If there are no longer any patents, there is no longer any need for a licence and there is no longer a basis for the licensor to collect royalties. It is lawful to require a licensee to inform the licensor of any new information it may have gained in connection with the licensed subject matter but it can be unlawful to compel the licensee to assign back to a licensor the right obtained on improvements developed by the licensee himself. It is also unlawful to require the licensee to undertake not to challenge the validity of the patents. Both of these last two issues are also illegal in the US but the interesting aspect is that the reason for illegality in the US is totally different from the reason for their illegality in the Common Market. This will be discussed later on as well.

5. In Europe one finds much more often than in the US that the licensor desires to control the pricing of the

products which are the subject matter of the licence. In the US this was, at the beginning, permitted under a narrow doctrine which came to be called the "General Electric Doctrine" but in the years since that decision, the doctrine has been so narrowly construed as to be non-existent. In the Common Market there have been no decisions on the point but theoretically such a clause fixing the price of the licensed product could come within art. 85, although we think that this is only a remote possibility if only because it would be difficult to judge how the fixing of the price would affect trade between member states. Even if it did affect that trade, there would be the possibility of an exemption under art. 85(3).

6. Clauses limiting the quantity of the licensed product being produced are lawful but there has been no decision on the point. We think that these clauses could become unlawful if they are part of a plan to maintain high prices of a licensed product by control of the quantity of the product being produced.

7. It is lawful to require the licensee to purchase other materials from the licensor or a source specified by the licensor if this is necessary "for a technically proper utilization of the patent". Such clauses have been traditionally allowed in European licence agreements although they are straightforward tying clauses. Recently, however, there is a tendency developing within the Common Market that such clauses will be permitted only if that is the only way that the licensor can be sure that his licensed patent is being properly employed; otherwise a definition of the quality standards and specifications of the required materials should be sufficient for the patent to be properly utilized. The licensee would then be free to purchase materials meeting those standards and specifications from any source he wished, thereby dissolving the tying characteristics of the arrangement.

8. It is lawful to require the licensee to mark the product with the number of the licensed patent or the

indication that the trademark on the product is a registered trademark. The Commission's 1962 announcement specifically emphasized that such marking was not prohibited. One wonders why such an announcement was necessary at all. In most countries not only is such marking permissible, it is absolutely required. If, for example, a product is patented but is not marked as being patented, the patentee would not be able to claim damages for infringement, on the ground that the infringing party had no way of knowing that the product in which he was dealing was patented. A requirement to affix a trademark has a somewhat different standing. It is not a question of the public knowing when anyone is infringing the trademark because the only way the trademark could be infringed is by using it. Presumably the Commission suspects that there may be ways of restricting competition by requiring licensees to mark the products with the licensed trademark. Be that as it may, clauses requiring marking are permissible.

9. Clauses requiring the licensee not to deal in competing products, processes or trademarks are obviously likely to affect trade between member states. As such they would be illegal, but there is a possibility of an exemption under art. 85(3). There have been no decisions or announcements on this point from the Commission although such a clause might be all right if one were to follow and draw an analogy with the Commission reg. 67/67. In that regulation relating to exclusive distributorships, one of the restrictions that is declared to be permissible is that requiring the exclusive distributor not to deal in competing products during the term of the agreement.

The above listings and comments fairly summarize the essential antitrust views of licensing, especially of patents but applicable as well to "knowhow", in the US and in the Common Market. But how helpful or well understood are those precepts?

VIEWPOINT OF THE PATENTEE, THE GOVERNMENT AND
THE COURTS

1. *From the viewpoint of the patentee*

He sees the situation simply as this: he is puzzled by the
reference to his having a monopoly, and he does not like the
term because it carries the connotation of something
wrong. He understands a monopoly to be dictatorial control over a market and a product which has already existed
and the monopolist having expanded his position in it to the
point of obtaining that dictatorial control. His invention, on
the other hand, is something which the world has never had
before. Indeed, it is the very definition of "invention" that
it is new to the world and the patent which he has received
gives him certain rights over that invention. He, the patentee, should therefore have the right to do whatever he
wants with his own patented invention. In particular he
should be able to decide who he wants to licence, for how
long, for how much and where, and what his licensee may
do in connection with the licence and what the licensee
should require from third parties to whom he might sell or
whom he might licence.

The patentee and the company employing him or the
company who owns the patent overestimate and perhaps
misunderstand the nature and the scope of power that has
been given to them by the grant of the patent.

2. *From the viewpoint of the government*

Each US Assistant Attorney General in charge of the antitrust division has advanced the fight to narrow and weaken
the scope of the patent because, regardless of their protes-
tations, they are embarrassed by the patent statute itself.
They see a patent as a repugnant monopoly totally contrary
to the spirit and intent of the entire body of antitrust law.
They see it as an unhealthy growth in the body of a healthy
freely competitive economy. One sometimes suspects that
they see the patent even as something which is anti-social

because it grants a legal privilege to certain individuals which is not given to the public at large.

3. *From the viewpoint of the courts*

Judicial cases involving patents come under the jurisdiction of the federal courts and there must be very few judges indeed who welcome the opportunity to hear cases involving patents. This is because there are very few judges on the federal benches who come from a patent background. The esoteric nature of the patent places the judiciary in a very difficult position. The judges do not understand patents but they instinctively suspect them as being something anticompetitive. A patent is not at all anticompetitive. In fact, it is very competitive because it defines a new product which, in order to find its way in the economic world, must itself compete with other products already in the market. This simple fact has, surprisingly, eluded a great majority of the federal judges. We think that the legal profession both in the private and public sector may have failed in their duty to educate the federal judges so that they might enforce the antitrust law more fairly and efficiently in matters involving the licensing and utilization of patents; indeed, of trademarks, knowhow and copyrights, as well. But of this group, there is little doubt that patents cause the most difficulty.

Let us first examine the business climate of patents. For the small, newly established company, the costly patent which it has obtained becomes a hope for much needed cash from licensing. Such a company is not interested in building an empire or carving up markets. It simply wants to licence the patent in order to obtain royalty income. For the medium-sized company, the patent becomes an adjunct to a developing direct sales programme. It will obtain a few foreign patents in selected countries where it hopes to licence them for "easy" royalty income. The success of the patent may lure the company to obtain additional related patents so that in time the company has composed a modest package to protect a small sphere of a product industry.

The company's balance sheet will appear that much more impressive and the value of the company will be enhanced thus benefiting takeover, joint venture, or merger aspirations. For the very large company, the patent is one of many forming a substantial budget item. The number of patents, rather than their quality becomes important because a large company, with few exceptions, does not rely on its patents either for protection against competitors or for licensing income. A company of that size probably has an excellent research and development division which, if necessary, is capable of analyzing competitors' products and patents. If market considerations are favourable, they may "design around" the competition.

Antitrust problems arise when management decides to use the company's patent portfolio in ways that unreasonably or unfairly restrain competition in other products and, in some cases, in the products covered by the patents themselves. The following cases and examples will illustrate illegal uses of patents and trademarks, and, we hope, will suggest lawful and profitable alternate uses.

Throughout what follows, it would be helpful to remember that an inventor need not obtain a patent. There is nothing to stop him from exploiting his invention. The patent is a franchise from the government giving legal sanction to the patentee to prevent others from making, using or selling the invention which is protected by his patent. The government has the right to object to misuse of the patent because it has committed itself by legislation to protect the patentee. If the patentee or copyright or trademark owner is going to enjoy all of the force of the government and the courts in his defence against infringement of his rights, then he must "play the game according to the rules". The rules, in these cases, are the antitrust laws. We will begin with copyright and trademarks because they afford a clear introduction of principles which ripen in the use of patents.

14

The unlawful use of copyright and trademarks

There are three landmark decisions which straddle this entire subject. They abundantly and clearly illustrate the two principles followed by the Commission and the Court of Justice in deciding legality of the use of copyright or trademarks. The cases are:

Grundig-Consten, Cases 56/64 and 58/64, C.M.R. 8064;
Deutsche Grammophon-Metro, Case 78/70, C.M.R. 8106;
Sirena-Eda, Case 40/70, C.M.R. 8101.

The principles illustrated by these cases are:

1. Once a copyright material has been placed in the flow of commerce by the copyright owner or by one authorized by him, the copyright protection has been exhausted. It cannot be reasserted to prevent its movement in trade within the Common Market.

2. The same trademark, though enjoying separate national registration in different countries of the Common Market, cannot be used to prevent parallel imports using the trademark from one Common Market country to another, so long as the trademarks stem from a common owner.

What is the basic problem of trademarks? This discussion is limited to what one can do with them, because obviously the real value of a trademark is to restrict competition with it. There is not much point in going to the expense of filing and obtaining registration of a trademark and applying it to goods if there is not some way that this trademark can be used to stop other people from using it on the same goods in one's market.

The Common Market is an economic theory. It is hoped eventually it will be political, but at the moment it is economic. The economic theory is that goods must flow freely across national borders. Anything which restricts that free flow is illegal. Articles 85 and 86 are the weapons to destroy such restrictions in the private sector. Yet, the individual national laws of trademarks must be respected. This is assured by art. 36 of the Rome Treaty. Thus there is a conflict between arts. 85 and 86 and art. 36. The Treaty of Rome on the one hand says that agreements and practices in restraint of interstate trade are illegal, and abuses of a dominant position are bad; but on the other hand, in dealing with industrial property rights, art. 36 permits the restraints inherent in such rights, in effect saying: "They are all right so long as they are not used in an arbitrary manner to discriminate, or they are not used as a diguised restriction".

In this presentation there is one particularly important feature of art. 85; in order for a violation of art. 85 to exist there has to be an agreement between two enterprises. The one particularly important fact about art. 86 is that it is not, in itself, an abuse of a dominant position to own and exercise a registered trademark.

The *Deutsche Grammophon (DGM)* decision involves copyright. DGM was a joint venture located in West Germany involving Philips of Eindhoven, Holland, as a joint venturer. It made records; it had recording artists under contract, and it had a subsidiary in France. It marketed records under the Polydor label. DGM required from their distributors a written undertaking that they would maintain a certain resale price on the records they purchased from DGM and would not permit imports from distributors in other countries or re-imports into Germany at a lesser price.

One of the German retailers obtaining records bearing the Polydor copyright was discovered by DGM not to have signed the standard undertaking about resale price maintenance so DGM cut them off from supplies of their records. DGM had been supplying the master pressings for record discs to its subsidiary in France. It owned 99.55% of the French company. The French subsidiary sold Polydor records to a wholesaler, who in turn sold to someone else, and eventually the later-rejected German distributor bought the records outside of Germany, brought them into Germany and sold them there at a price lower than the required resale price. DGM promptly sued the importer in the German court for infringement of the German copyright and obtained an injunction.

The defendant appealed as he could under the Rome Treaty on the ground that such use of a national copyright was a violation of art. 85. The case went to the Court of Justice, but the Court of Justice did not hold that it was a violation of art. 85. In order to put the matter under the jurisdiction of art. 85, there would have to have been an agreement between two enterprises. The Court held that as DGM owned over 99% of the French company, they constituted *one* entity; accordingly there was no agreement between two enterprises. Even though they were legally independent of each other they were not economically independent of each other. One completely controlled the other. That being the case, it was tantamount to having an agreement with oneself and, therefore, outside the scope of art. 85. The Court decided against DGM on other grounds. The Court used the German theory of the exhaustion of the protective right of copyright. When the French company sold the record discs legally, that sale exhausted the copyright, albeit the French copyright, and the German parent no longer could invoke the German copyright law to protect against reimportation. DGM argued that according to the German law of copyright, the copyright would attach against re-imports. That is where the Court said, in effect, "No, you cannot use a national copyright law to prevent the free flow of goods across borders once those goods have been validly placed in commerce". The copyright had been exhausted by the action of the subsidiary, which was a transaction authorized by the parent itself. Common Market law overrode German national law.

In the *Grundig–Consten* case, Grundig had an exclusive distributorship arrangement with Consten in France for Grundig products. Consten had agreed that it would not export to other countries and would not deal in competitive products. Grundig permitted Consten to register the "GINT" trademark in France. This was the Grundig trademark for its products in international trade. Grundig had this as a policy with other distributors throughout Europe. The European Court held this practice to be unlawful. This was the first decision of its kind by the Court involving trademarks. The Court said that although a trademark is a right protected by art. 36, it cannot be used as a disguised restriction of trade. Of course, this is exactly what Grundig had done. It had permitted Consten to register the "GINT" mark in its own name in France so that Consten would be able to invoke that registration against parallel imports from other countries. The Court struck this down as an improper use of a national trademark. There was something else that was wrong in the agreement, and that was the undertaking not to export, a direct violation of art. 85.

Grundig–Consten was the first decision establishing that a trademark could not be used in a manner to restrict the free flow of goods. The *Sirena–Eda* decision was a refinement of the principle pronounced in Grundig–Consten. Sirena was an Italian company to whom many years ago certain Italian trademarks, in particular the mark "Prep" for cosmetic cream, were assigned by an American company. Immediately after that assignment the American company stopped selling the trademarked product into Italy. It was a simple assignment of a trademark, without the business or goodwill of the business to go along with it.

In the meantime, the same American company who had assigned the trademark "Prep" in Italy to Sirena licensed a German company to use the "Prep" trademark that the

American company had registered in Germany. Cosmetic cream validly bearing the German "Prep" trademark was imported into Italy from Germany by Novimpex. Sirena sued Novimpex for trademark infringement in Italy. Novimpex invoked Treaty art. 85. In the Court of Justice Sirena put forward its arguments, the government of the Netherlands put forward its arguments, Novimpex put forward its arguments and the Commission itself put forward its arguments.

Sirena's case was very simple. It might be paraphrased, "We bought this Italian trademark in good faith. Novimpex is not licensed under the Italian trademark but nevertheless imported a cosmetic cream using the German equivalent of our Italian mark. Our Italian trademark also covers cosmetic cream and we have been selling cream in Italy under that trademark. This is straightforward trademark infringement, and should be stopped". The Commission itself agreed with Sirena. Novimpex argued that it had legally affixed the trademark in Germany, that it had received the formula for making the cosmetic cream that was covered by these trademarks; that the transfer of the Italian trademark was invalid because the formula had not been transferred with it; that this failure deprived the public in Italy from getting the genuine article "Prep"; and that this use of the trademark in Italy was a violation of art. 85 and also a violation of art. 86. It was a violation of art. 86 because Sirena was selling the "Prep" cosmetic cream in Italy for about 500 lire whilst Novimpex was selling the same thing for 250 lire, half the price. Novimpex's argument was that it was an abuse of a market dominating position to sell a trademarked article at such a high price.

The Court, the Commission and the government of the Netherlands were on the side of Sirena. They said it was a simple transfer. Sirena was exercising the traditional right of a trademark owner, i.e. protecting itself in the country in which the trademark is registered against infringement of it.

The Court was in a dilemma, because it could not see how art. 85 could apply. Where was the agreement between two enterprises? There was no agreement between Sirena and Novimpex using the German and Italian trademark to divide markets. The Court strained to find something wrong, and succeeded, because it said there was in fact an agreement. The Court made the distinction between obtaining a trademark by assignment of the trademark, and obtaining it as an absolute right from an original registration. As regards an absolute right, the Court meant obtaining the trademark as the originator of the trademark, i.e. the one filing the application, obtaining registration and using the registered trademark. The Court made the distinction between that and ownership of a registered trademark by assignment from the original owner and the subsequent use of it by the third party assignee. The Court said that there was in fact an agreement, e.g. the assignment itself. Article 85 applies where the owner of a trademark assigns the trademark to third parties and the effect is to permit third parties to restrict competition by preventing others from parallel importation of the trademarked article.

There was no question of intent by the American company or any of the parties to divide markets. There was no allegation or evidence that the American owner of the trademarks in Germany and in Italy intended to carve up the German and Italian markets by assigning the respective trademarks to different enterprises in each country. The Court held that the fact of assigning the trademark to one person in one country and to another person in another country would have the effect of permitting use of the national trademark law in each country to prevent import of the same competing product from one country into the other country. The Court said this effect resulted from the assignment itself, an agreement in restraint of trade under art. 85.

Dealing with the situation of Sirena under art. 86 was a different matter. No agreement is needed there. The argument was raised that the mere fact of having the trademark is a violation of art. 86 because the trademark automatically places its owner in a dominant position in the market.

This defence had been raised several times in earlier cases and was each time struck down. The interesting feature about this defence in Sirena was that the Court suggested that it is not a violation of art. 86 in itself to have a trademark, but that it could be. It could be a violation if the trademarked article dominates the entire market, not only in the goods covered by that trademark but also in similar goods. Then the Court will look at the pricing of the trademarked article. The Court did not say that Sirena had violated art. 86 but it did comment as to how art. 86 could be violated. It considered that the relevant market to be dominated would have to be not just the goods covered by the trademark but also similar goods, even though not covered by the trademark.

The three cases just discussed provide a basis for planning what can and cannot be done, particularly by multinational companies. The culmination of the principles is found in a Commission ruling. It involved the American Scott company, the people who make absorbent tissues. Scott wholly owned subsidiaries in several countries. There was a subsidiary in Germany and another in Holland. The trademarks in both countries were owned by Scott. Scott's policy was to licence the trademark in Germany to a German licensee exclusively, and the trademark in Holland to a Dutch licensee exclusively. The licensees agreed that they would not sell the trademarked articles into each other's market. Was this lawful? The Commission undoubtedly influenced by the relationship of companies, e.g. parent-subsidiary and common ownership, held the arrangement did not violate art. 85. Inferentially, if independent enterprises chance to register the identical trademark in different countries each might legally assert its trademark against the other.

In view of Sirena, a multinational company may licence all of its subsidiaries under the respective trademarks, and they may enforce their rights under them; but if the parent sells a subsidiary or assigns the trademark in one country to a third party it would seem to create a Sirena situation.

Suppose there is an identical trademark in each of two Common Market countries, but each is owned by a different person unrelated to the other. Would the Court permit one of the trademark owners to bring an infringement action against the other's import into his country?

In Case 6 U 1857/74: *Re Napoleon Liqueurs*, the Bavarian "Oberlandesgericht" held that as the Napoleon trademark in Germany was not of common origin with the owner of an identical trademark in France, there was no violation of either art. 85 or 86.

In view of the philosophy that has developed about trademarks in the Common Market, the indicated course of action is for the owner of a trademark in one country *not* to apply for a trademark in another country, but to permit a potential unrelated "licensee" to apply initially in its own name for the trademark in its own country. The danger in this method is that one approaches the Grundig–Consten situation. Grundig had done exactly what has been suggested. It gave Consten the right to obtain the "GINT" mark in its own name in France. This was illegal. The illegality theoretically could be avoided if the potential licensee applied for the trademark in its own name independently of any assignment of the right to so so.

AN EXAMPLE OF UNLAWFUL USE OF TRADEMARKS IN THE US

The primary area of trademark antitrust legality is the use of trademarks to allocate territories. There have been several major cases on this issue but probably the landmark case was *U.S.* v. *Sealy*, 388 U.S. 350, decided in 1967. But in 1972 the Supreme Court had to deal with the more modern use of trademarks as "private labels" for brand products sold through a retail grocery chain. It is this case which we think more accurately illustrates a more popular use of trademarks.

U.S. v. *Topco*, 405 U.S. 596

Topco was a cooperative association of about 25 small and

medium-sized independent regional supermarket chains operating in 33 states. The members' combined retail sales were exceeded by only three national grocery chains. A member's average share of the market in its area was often as strong as that of any competitor. Topco procured items having brand names owned by Topco and the members retailed these in the area allocated to them exclusively, under the rules of the association. Each member was licensed an exclusive territory by Topco within which only that member might sell the brand products. No member was allowed to sell Topco brand products outside of its licensed territory without the consent of the member into whose territory such expanded sales were desired. Topco members were prohibited from selling any products supplied by the association at wholesale, whether trademarked or not, without obtaining special permission granted with the consent of other interested licensees.

The government charged Topco with violating the Sherman Act because it divided markets and prohibited competition in Topco brand products among retail grocery chains. The government also challenged the wholesaling restrictions. Topco argued that it needed the territorial divisions (*a*) to maintain its private label programme and to enable it to compete with the larger chains; (*b*) that the association could not exist if the territorial division were not exclusive; and (*c*) that the restrictions on competition in Topco brand sales enabled members to meet larger chain competition.

The larger chains had developed their own private label programmes and the smaller chains had been competing unsuccessfully with them. Topco developed its own private labels and stated in court:

> "Private label merchandising is a way of economic life in the food retailing industry, and exclusivity is the essence of a private label programme; without exclusivity, a private label would not be private. Each national and large regional chain has its own exclusive private label products in addition to the nationally advertised brands which all chains sell. Each such chain relies upon the exclusivity of its own private label line to

differentiate its private label products from those of its competitors and to attract and retain the repeat business and loyalty of consumers. Smaller retail stores and chains are unable to compete effectively with the national and large regional chains without also offering their own exclusive private label products."

(*Private labels*: these products differ from other brand name products in that they are sold at a limited number of readily identifiable stores. By using private label products, a chain can achieve significant cost economies in purchasing, transportation, warehousing, promotion and advertising. Lower prices for the private label products are then possible, and national brand products can be offered at the same price offered in other stores, which is invariably higher than the private label product. If the profit margin is high on private label products the national brand products might be sold at reduced prices. Obviously there is great flexibility and profit in the use of private label products.)

The gist of Topco's defence was that the territorial divisions were necessary and that competition with the larger regional and national chains was actually enhanced by Topco's restrictions. The lower court recognized that Topco's members were restrained from *intra*-brand competition but held that "whatever anti-competitive effect these practices may have on competition in the sale of Topco private label brands is far outweighed by the increased ability of Topco members to compete both with the national chains and other supermarkets operating in their respective territories".

The Supreme Court disagreed with the lower court and struck down all of Topco's defences. It saw the arrangement as an agreement among competitors to divide markets, a *per se* violation of the Sherman Act which permits no appeal to the rule of reason. Thus it is clear that trademarks cannot be used in the US to divide markets, however noble or worthy the intent of the parties.

The restrictions that would be illegal in a patent licence would be equally illegal in a trademark licence, with the sole proviso that as a trademark, by its nature, requires control by the owner; the owner may impose certain tie-in restrictions for the sake of "quality control" of the product with which the trademark is associated. But even this must be treated cautiously. If quality control can be obtained by specifying the quality of the materials needed, the licensee should be allowed to choose his supplier.

15
The unlawful use of patents to divide markets

Patents present a problem analogous to that of trademarks. Patents in each of the Common Market countries protecting substantially the same subject-matter can be used to block imports and exports of that subject-matter. Indeed, a patentee may encounter difficulty in licensing his patent if he does not grant an exclusive licence to a licensee which would protect him in the natural market for his sales. Thus, if an exclusive licence is granted to A in France, another to B in Germany, and another to C in Belgium for the same product protected by patent, each licensee could prevent the import of the product into his country. Similarly he could not export from his country without infringing the foreign patent. The effect is a division of markets through the use of patents, which is precisely the anathema of the Rome Treaty.

This is the problem of "parallel patents". The Commission and Court of Justice solved it on the same principle relied upon in the *Deutsche Grammophon* case, i.e. "exhaustion of rights". When a patentee has once received his royalty payment for the sale of his patented product or the use of his patented process, either by his own action or by the action of his authorized licensee, he no longer has a patent right over that subject-matter. His patent right has been "exhausted". There are two aspects of this situation that need to be explained.

What if the product which was patented, say, in France and in Germany had not been patented in Belgium and a manufacturer, free of any licence in Belgium, exports the product into Germany or France, may the licensee in Germany and in France block the import of that product? This was one of the chief issues in Case 24/67: *Parke, Davis* v. *Probel, Reese*, [1968] C.M.L.R. 47, 29 February 1968. Parke, Davis is an American company which owned Dutch patents covering processes for the preparation of an antibiotic drug. Parke, Davis had granted a licence to a Dutch company under these patents. The defendants sold the antibiotic drug in the Netherlands but were not licensed or authorized by either Parke, Davis or its Dutch licensee to do so. Accordingly the defendants were sued in Holland for infringement of the Dutch patents. The defendants, in particular a defendant named Centrafarm, objected that this was contrary to Common Market principles because it had obtained the drug from an Italian company and to permit Parke, Davis to assert its Dutch patents against it, the effect would be to frustrate the free movement of the drug from Italy into Holland. The Italian Patent Law does not provide for the issuing of patents covering drugs or pharmaceutical products. Because of this both the Commission and the Court of Justice supported Parke, Davis's infringement action.

> "The questions submitted, which concerned the case where a product from a member state where no patent protection is given is exported to a member state where a patent has been granted, do not directly touch on the effects of parallel patents. In this instance, the patent protection is not used to share out and partition the markets, where patent protection already exists. It is, on the contrary, serving its main purpose, which is to guarantee that the patent holder can exploit its monopoly by enabling it to prevent entry of products for which it has not derived any profit from its monopoly, for the reason that the member state in question does not grant a patent for that product."

One wonders whether the Court would have come to the same result if the Italian patent law had provided for the protection of drugs or pharmaceuticals by patent and Parke, Davis had simply not applied for a patent. Or to put it another way, assume that Parke, Davis had applied for a patent in Germany (which *does* protect drugs and pharmaceuticals by patent) but had failed to obtain the patent on the grounds, according to the German patent examining authority, that there was not sufficient inventiveness to justify the grant of a patent. Assume, further, that a German manufacturer used the Parke, Davis process and sold the drug in Holland. Would the Court have come to the same result? If one were to keep strictly to the principle of the "exhaustion of rights" one would be disposed to allow Parke, Davis to bring its infringement action in Holland because Parke, Davis would not have received its reward which would have been due it at least under the Dutch law. The answer, of course, would be otherwise if Parke, Davis had attempted to take action against the German manufacturer in Germany because Parke, Davis had no patent protection there.

The proscription against such use of parallel patents should not be given a wider scope than it deserves. There is a distinction between a licensee in one country selling the patented product within the licensed territory and the purchaser then reselling into another country where there is another licensee; and the situation in which the licensee in one country itself attempts to sell the patented product outside of its territory into the territory of another licensee. This latter attempt would be an infringement of the patent in the other territory. The difference is that patent protection had not been validly exhausted when the first licensee sold direct into an unauthorized territory. When the licensee sold validly within its own territory, the patent protection had been exhausted and the patentee had received his reward. The landmark decision in the Common Market on the improper use of parallel patents is Case 10/712: *Centrafarm BV* v. *Sterling Drug* [1976] C.M.L.R. 1, 21 February 1975.

Sterling owned a trademark and a patent in Holland covering a certain drug. It sued Centrafarm, a Dutch company, for marketing in Holland (where it also had a patent) quantities of the drug which it imported from Great Britain. Centrafarm did this because the price of the drug in Britain was cheaper than in Holland. Centrafarm bought the drug validly and legally in Britain. The central issue was whether Sterling could assert its Dutch patent against Centrafarm. It could not, for the reason already discussed, i.e. exhaustion of the patent right. Sterling had exhausted its patent protection of the drug when it received its royalty for the valid sale of the drug in the UK to Centrafarm. Thereafter, Centrafarm could do whatever it wished with the drug. Concurrently, the court held the same way about Sterling attempting to use its Dutch trademark to prevent the import of the drug, i.e. trademarks could not be used to block imports.

ARE EXCLUSIVE LICENCES AS SUCH ILLEGAL UNDER ART. 85?

The answer is "yes and no". It depends on the effect of the exclusive licence. For example, the German firm Kabel-und-Metallwerke concluded an exclusive patent and knowhow licence with the French firm Luchaire concerning the use of the cold-extrusion process in the manufacture and sale of steel parts used especially in the automobile industry. Beginning with basic principles, the Commission recognized that the evil of exclusivity is that it forecloses the licensor himself from competing with the licensee and also prevents him from granting any other licences in the territory of the licence. Unless the facts show that it was essential that the licence be exclusive, the Commission would be unsympathetic about granting an art. 85(3) exemption to such a licence. The initial licence also contained certain restrictions which certainly infringed art. 85 and they had to be removed. As a matter of interest these restrictions concerned the licensee's obligation not to export within the Common Market; to assign to the licensee all improvements in the processes and also not to contest the validity of the licensed patents. Under the final licence Luchaire was granted an exclusive licence for the manufacture in France of the steel parts, using secret and patented manufacturing techniques. Luchaire was also granted the exclusive right to sell those products in Spain and Portugal as well as a non-exclusive right to sell those products in all of the Common Market countries. The issue of "exclusivity" is the one which interests us at the moment. The Commission took the view that an undertaking by a patentee to restrict the use of his invention to one single firm in a specified territory was not of the essence of the patent and could be a restriction of competition prohibited by art. 85. The licensee, Luchaire, had a substantial share of the market in these products within the Common Market. The exclusive nature of the licence was all the more dangerous from a competitive point of view. Notwithstanding its holding that the exclusive licence would violate art. 85(1), the Commission exempted the licence from the applicability of art. 85(1) because the grant of exclusive rights contributed to promoting economic progress. The reasons for the grant of the exemption are not particularly interesting. The value of this decision is that the Commission believed that an exclusive licence can in itself be a violation of Common Market rules of competition.

There was a case where the reasons for not granting an exemption were of some interest. The case did not involve an exclusive licence in the sense of the preceding one, that is, it was not an exclusive licence to one single firm in a specified territory. A Dutch company applied for a Dutch patent protecting a drainage system. It was of great economic importance particularly in Holland because the process was designed to lower the water table and the same process could be used for construction projects such as the laying of pipelines across national boundaries. Four companies opposed the grant of the patent to the Dutch company but the four companies withdrew their opposition after coming to an agreement with the Dutch company under which each of them was granted a licence under the patent that would be issued to the Dutch company. There was a taint of exclusivity in this agreement because the

Dutch company undertook not to grant any further licences without the previous consent of at least two of the four licensees. This undertaking tended to preserve exclusivity for the licensees.

The Commission felt there was no question but that these agreements violated art. 85(1). The sole issue was whether an exemption should be granted. The exemption was denied because the provision requiring the consent of the licensees before any further licence could be granted was not essential to improving the production or distribution of goods. The Commission said: "On the contrary by allowing the number of firms authorized to exploit the patented process to be restricted they hinder wider use of the process and prevent knowhow from being enriched by a broader range of experience". The patented process had already become well known and widely used in Holland, so "Confining its exploitation to a limited number of licensees has no beneficial economic effect such as might be expected of an exclusive licence having the prime purpose of facilitating the penetration of a new market".

16

The element of coercion
in licensing

In Part I of this book we saw that tying arrangements are *per se* illegal under the Sherman Act, and are illegal under s. 3 of the Clayton Act. In many boardrooms there still lingers the mistaken belief that the ownership of patents justifies tying-in to a licence the sale or lease of other products not covered by the licensed patent. This is not only incorrect; the assumption reveals a certain lack of understanding of the principle of tying clause illegality. A key requirement in illegal tying arrangements is that the guilty party have sufficient economic power over the tying product to compel the other party to obtain the tied product from him or from a source designated by him. A patent by its nature can be considered to be evidence of that power to compel the tying arrangement.

Apart from striking down virtually all forms of tie-ins in patent licensing, the courts have been reluctant to apply the US antitrust laws in such a manner as to threaten the existence of the patent system. Since 1969,[1] however, the momentum of antitrust development has carried the courts into such bold attacks on traditional views of patent licensing that there is some concern that the courts have done injury to the patent system itself. In the *Glen* case the US District Court for the Southern District of New York held

1 *Zenith Radio Corpn.* v. *Hazeltine Research, Inc.* 395 U.S. 100, 89 S. Ct. 1562 (19 May 1969) *Glen Manufacturing, Inc.* v. *Perfect Fit Industries, Inc.* 324 F.Supp. 1133, 5 Trade Reg. Reports, paragraph 71750 and paragraph 72791 (S.D.N.Y., 25 March 1969 and 1 May 1969).

that it was patent misuse[2] for a licensor to condition the grant of a licence on the payment of royalties on products not covered by the claims of a licensed patent. In the *Zenith* case the Supreme Court held that "conditioning the grant of a patent licence upon payment of royalties on products which do not use the teaching of the patent does amount to patent misuse". Both decisions distinguished from *Automatic Radio Manufacturing Company, Inc.* v. *Hazeltine Research, Inc.* 339 U.S. 827 (1950), the traditional precedent for preserving that royalty base. *Glen* and *Zenith* are, in turn, distinguishable from each other. The *Zenith* misuse was founded on licensor's "coercion" of licensee to accept a package licence.[3] In the *Glen* decision, only one patent was involved, no coercion was alleged, and the licensee had agreed to pay royalties on all products whether or not covered by the licensed patent. Both cases arrived at patent misuse, but for different reasons. The effect of either or both Zenith or Glen is such that a discussion of each is necessary, if not to test the reasoning of the courts, then at least to understand what certainty is left for exploitation of the patent system through licensing.

In the Zenith case, the District Court[4] ruled first that Hazeltine had "misused its domestic patents by attempting to coerce Zenith's acceptance of a five-year package licence, and by insisting on extracting royalties from unpatented products".

Various companies had pooled their radio and television patents in different countries (Canada, Great Britain and Australia). Zenith had been warned that they were infringing some of the patents in those pools and would need to take the standard package licence and also manufacture only in the countries where the pools were located. Zenith was interested in exporting into those countries, principally

---

2 Patent "misuse" occurs when the use of the patent does not amount to a Sherman or Clayton Act violation. It means that the patentee cannot enforce his patent.

3 Package licensing is the licensing of a group of patents even though perhaps only one or a few of them will actually be used.

4 239 F. Supp. 51 (1965).

Canada. There would seem to be little question that such a conspiracy to exclude imports would be a violation of the antitrust laws.[5] The standard five-year package licence agreement required royalties "on the licensee's total radio and television sales, irrespective of whether the licensed patents were actually used in the products manufactured". The District court had held that "a patentee has no right to demand or force the payment of royalties on unpatented products", but gave no reason why it was illegal. The Court of Appeals reversed that judgment and, basing its decision on the *Automatic Radio* decision, held that this did not constitute patent misuse. The Court of Appeals (C.A.) decision was not on the real issue. The C.A. obviously considered only the issue whether basing royalties on *all* products itself was wrong. It did not deal with the "coercion" aspect on which the District Court relied. The Supreme Court reversed the Court of Appeal and distinguished from the *Automatic Radio* case, holding that "conditioning the grant of a patent licence upon payment of royalties on products which did not use the teaching of the patent does amount to patent misuse". Here, again, there is confusion because the C.A. decided on the basis of coercion and did not pass on the mere pegging of royalties on all products, with or without coercion! The Supreme Court gave no reasons for its decision other than to say:

> "there are established limits which the patentee must not exceed in employing the leverage of his patent to control or limit the operations of the licensee. Among other restrictions upon him, he may not condition the right to use his patent on the licensee's agreement to purchase, use or sell, or not to purchase, use or sell, another article of commerce not within the scope of his patent monopoly."

The Supreme Court established the bare principle that coercion to pay royalties on unpatented products is wrong and the court remanded the case for trial as to whether such coercion had occurred. The Supreme Court, unlike *Glen*, found no *per se* violation in an agreement calling for royalties on unpatented products.

---

5 *Timken Roller Bearing Co.* v. *United States*, 341 U.S. 593 (1951).

It is difficult to isolate study of the coercion issue in the Zenith case from the context of the wider, surer antitrust violation by the pools conspiracy. As the court did not sufficiently explain its reasons for establishing coercion as the test for misuse (see Justice Harlan's separate opinion) and as there is no precedent for that test, there could be suspicion that the great antitrust net flung over the pools activities caught up the patent royalty aspect and as the reasons for violation by the pools conspiracies could not apply to the royalty negotiations the court felt constrained to find a reason to apply part of the evil to those negotiations.

The question as to what kind of coercion is bad needs to be answered. Hard bargaining by a patentee is certainly coercion, but cannot be called a misuse of patents. For example, what degree of insistence was used in *Automatic Radio* to obtain the royalty agreement? The Supreme Court in *Zenith*, therefore, did not really distinguish from *Automatic Radio* (again, see Justice Harlan's separate opinion). Even when the lower court hears evidence about coercion, it will have the problem to establish the point at which hard bargaining becomes illegal coercion.

The evidence which the District Court[6] heard consisted of this: when Zenith refused to renew its licence with Hazeltine, Hazeltine threatened infringement action and simultaneously persisted with offers of various kinds of licences. The feature of these alternatives that disturbed the District Court was that the royalty bases were grossly out of proportion to the royalty rate Hazeltine was asking for the entire package of patents. Hazeltine's objective was to make it economically unattractive for Zenith to take less than the whole package. These threats undoubtedly inconvenienced Zenith and when Hazeltine eventually lodged an infringement action, Zenith was further inconvenienced. The District Court said:

> "As of the date the trial began Defendant had been injured in its business and property as the proximate result of the acts and

6 239 F. Supp. 69-72 (1965).

demands of Hazeltine, referred to above, in the amount of $50,065. Defendant has been forced to make expenditures of money and to use the time of its officers, employees, and counsel to defend against this patent infringement suit and by virtue of Hazeltine's threats of suits on other patents, defendant has been forced to expend substantial amounts of money to investigate the scope and validity of the patents asserted. The injury to Zenith's business was occasioned by the necessity that defendant make a choice among alternatives each of which had an adverse economic effect on its business. It was forced either to cease manufacturing and selling its television receivers, pay tribute with consequent increase in its cost or incur the expenses incident to the defense of protracted patent litigation. Although defendant's choice determined the nature and amount of the resulting damages, *it was the necessity of having to choose that occasioned the injury*".[7]

The District Court held that "Plaintiff's demands on Defendant coupled with the bringing of this suit and the threat to bring other suits on other patents constitute an illegal effort to coerce defendant into signing the Hazeltine package licence". The Supreme Court then established the principle that coercion to accept a licence basing royalties on all products is patent misuse. The lower court on remand would have to be guided by the above mentioned observations as to what facts constitute coercion. If those guides are followed, an extraordinary restriction on the bargaining power of a licensor will have been imposed. It is extraordinary because it is the patentee who has something to offer and so lays down the terms that he wants before he will grant the licence, just as any merchant or seller who has a product to sell. It is up to the licensee either to accept, make a counter-offer or simply say that he is not interested. If the licensee rejects all offers, is it unlawful for the patentee to persist with alternative offers to induce the licensee to accept the licence on the patentee's terms? Hazeltine had made royalty demands and threatened infringement litigation if those demands were not accepted. It would be, indeed, a queer result to condemn that behaviour as

---

7 Italics added. Is this also coercion?

"coercion" because the threat of infringement litigation is precisely the weapon with which Congress has armed the patentee to induce the taking of a licence. A very large percentage of licences must surely find their birth in threats of infringement. It is not unlawful to threaten infringement litigation unless a licence is taken. Neither is it surprising. A licence is nothing more or less than a promise not to sue for infringement. It can hardly be unlawful for a patentee to make demands that are unacceptable to the potential licensee. No doubt the patentee is asserting his patent to compel the taking of a licence, but he is doing so on the basis of the patent itself and not on any extraneous unlawful economic restraint.

The implications of the Supreme Court decision go still deeper and wider on investigation. It suggests that if a patentee insists on a percentage of sales royalty on all products and the licensee refuses those terms and instead offers only to pay for actual use, not only has patent misuse been established but the patentee must also accept the licensee's terms. The court said:

> "We also think patent misuse inheres in a patentee's insistence on a percentage-of-sales royalty, regardless of use, and his rejection of licensee proposals to pay only for actual use. Unquestionably, a licensee must pay if he uses the patent. Equally, however, he may insist upon paying only for use, and not on the basis of total sales, including products in which he may use a competing patent or in which no patented ideas are used at all".

This certainly breaks new ground because the court has judicially created a right in the licensee that he never had before, i.e. to enforce the acceptance of royalty terms that he wants. Justice Harlan in his separate opinion has made that same observation. The unfairness of this is manifest. The patentee is the owner of the patent. If he cannot compel a licensee to take a licence, on what basis should the licensee be allowed to demand a licence? If the patentee offers a licence but cannot dictate his terms, on what basis should the licensee be allowed to dictate the terms of the licence?

A closer look at the facts in *Zenith* may be helpful. Zenith was a company in the business of making and selling radio and television sets. Coercion by the patentee, Hazeltine, would seem to lie in that if Zenith needed to use the patented devices, presumably Hazeltine had the power to compel acceptance of its terms in return for grant of the necessary licences. The difficulty with that argument is that Hazeltine could as well have refused to grant any licences at all. Or, to put it another way, could Zenith have compelled Hazeltine to grant the necessary licences? Even if one were to take a position that coercion would be wrong if it were unfair to the other party, i.e. Zenith, or illegal in the public interest, one would have to find more than just hard bargaining. In the *Zenith* case, presumably Zenith either had made radio or television sets without the patented devices and now wanted to incorporate the devices, or had been making them with the devices when the patents issued, in which case Zenith would find itself inadvertently to be an infringer. In the first instance Zenith may have wished to incorporate the new devices for some reason which would be profitable to Zenith. If the offer made by Hazeltine were to make the licence too expensive, Zenith always had the option not to accept. The second instance did not occur. Although Hazeltine threatened infringement and did bring an infringement action, the infringement action was brought on only one patent and the court held that there was no infringement. The District Court seemed concerned that Zenith was put to the expense of defending the suit, but this may not be any more than what any defendant has to face. It is not illegal in the US either to threaten or to bring an infringement action and it has never been held that that constituted illegal coercion. Illegal activity in connection with patent licensing or patent infringement suits must find its roots in something outside the course of events natural to the patent system, in something attributable to a separate illegal activity attendant on the bargaining sessions for the licence or the lodging of the infringement suit.

There are bound to be enigmas and contradictions at the interface of a system of legal monopoly such as the patent law and a system of anti-monopoly such as the body of antitrust laws. The peace in that co-existence is sometimes disturbed because the esoteric nature of a patent seems to have sensitized the non-patent-trained judiciary to find antitrust deviltry at times in the slightest assertion of the patent right. As a result the courts have evolved slogans such as "patent leverage", "extension of the patent monopoly"[8] and "patent power" that have no meaning. One sees them used again in the *Zenith* decision. These slogans imply an ability on the part of the patentee, merely on the strength of the exclusionary right in his patent to compel a licensee to accept his terms. That notion is more suited to theorists than to the slogging task of licensors. A patentee cannot compel a licensee to take a licence. If the patentee's demands are unreasonable the licensee will decide it is cheaper to invest its money to design around the patent, to contest the patent either in a separate suit declaring non-infringement and invalidity of the patent or, if necessary, in defending against an infringement suit. A licensee takes a licence purely as a matter of convenience. If these slogans mean that a patent can be used as part of a conspiracy among several parties to restrain trade, we are closer to the mark but the part played by patents in those schemes has many times been vastly overrated. The conspiracies were effective not because of patent power or patent leverage, but because of those parts of the agreements dealing with the much more immediately effective price-fixing, supply restrictions and distribution patterns. It is doubtful if conspirators even know what patents were involved, still less whether the patent claims could effectively restrain anybody. Nevertheless, one sees the same litany of cases recited to support the argument that the use or misuse of patents contributed to the damage. If the patent aspects were removed from those agreements, the anti-competitive restraints would be the same. This is not to say that patents are not effective to intimidate a competitor to keep him out of the market, but these matters should be kept in perspective and one day it is hoped that the courts

---

8 Baxter, Legal Restrictions on Exploitation of the Patent Monopoly: an economic analysis, 76 Yale L. J. 302 (1966).

will look more closely to see if the allegedly misused patents could in fact have foreclosed unlicensed users from the market. This is particularly important in Clayton Act tie-in violations where it is essential for the patent to be an effective economic power to compel the tie-in. To date, the courts have applied sanctions simply because of the existence *per se* of the patents, not whether the patent claims do, in fact, restrain the trade concerned. It is of some interest to note that in the *Zenith* case, not one US patent was shown to be effective to foreclose Zenith from the US market.

It is unfortunate that the court's attention should have been brought to the royalty provisions because Zenith's real complaint and real injury was not due to Zenith's demands for the domestic patent licence, but rather to Zenith's being prevented from importing into the pool areas because of the accumulated force of the pool. A further unfortunate result of the Zenith decision is this: if the licensee can demand a licence only on the basis of use of the patent, the licensee can legally suppress use of the patent. That becomes a matter of public concern which will be discussed in greater detail in connection with the *Glen* case. The *Glen* decision is perhaps of wider interest because whereas the Supreme Court in *Hazeltine* reduced the issue to coercion, *Glen* went further and attempted to create a *per se* violation with or without coercion in basing royalties on all products whether or not covered by the licensed patent. *Glen*, to support the scope of its proscription, did not go to the private rights of the contracting parties, but rather to public policy. (On remand, Judge Levet had to justify her decision on the basis of "conditioning" the licence on all-sales royalty.)

Judge Levet in the *Glen* case thus initially condemned all-sales royalties on a completely different footing from Zenith:

"By requiring royalties on all toilet tank covers manufactured or sold by defendant whether or not the toilet tank covers come within the scope of United States Patent No. 265874, plaintiff is guilty of a patent misuse. This royalty structure has the effect of raising the cost of non-patented, competing toilet tank covers, thereby restraining their output and tending to lessen competition in the toilet tank cover industry".

No evidence of such economic effect was presented to the court. Apparently Judge Levet saw it as an inevitable result of that kind of royalty base. Economic proof of the effect on the industry would have been extremely difficult and none has ever been convincingly assembled.[9] Any such proof would in any event be inconclusive because it is impossible to ascertain what effect licensee production or non-production of patented or non-patented goods would have on the industry at large. Moreover, economic evidence would not help to settle the more important issue latent in the court's decision. The existence of that issue is seen if one accepts the court's view that the "royalty structure has the effect of raising the cost of non-patented, competing covers, thereby restraining their output and tending to lessen competition . . .". If a licensee manufactures only the patented product, he cannot at the same time be producing the non-patented, competitive product and to that extent, it has been restrained. But is that an illegal restraint? The court can only have been referring to the output of the non-patented covers by defendant Perfect Fit and the only competition which could be lessened was that provided by Perfect Fit in the non-patented covers. This must obviously be so because non-licensees were completely free to produce non-patented covers. Accordingly, the real issue is whether it is wrong for a licensor to restrain the licensee's output of non-patented competitive products and thus lessen his contribution to that competition in the industry. That issue in turn rests ultimately on the effect of the patent system itself on the public welfare. It is not our purpose to challenge or to defend the patent system. One must accept it and then decide whether the kind of royalty base in the *Glen* case preserves or upsets the balance of competition in the public interest.

The patent grant is constitutionally based". . . to promote the progress of science and useful arts . . .". The Congress

---

9   Baxter, Legal Restrictions on Exploitation of the Patent Monopoly: an economic analysis, 76 Yale L.J. 267 (1966). Professor Baxter's Analysis was purely speculative.

decided the best way to do it was to grant exclusivity to the
inventor in return for his publicly disclosing his invention.
Simple disclosure to the public does not benefit the public.
The public is benefited by the use of the invention.[10]
Indeed, if the invention is not useful, or is intrinsically
incapable of working, the patent is invalid. Congress has
deemed that 17 years of exclusivity is sufficient to stimulate
inventors to invent and to file patent applications and
disclose their inventions to the public. Congress, therefore,
has decided that 17 years' exclusivity is a fair price for the
public to pay in return for free use of the invention after 17
years. However, during the 17-year period, the way the
public good is served is by use of the invention either by the
inventor himself of his heirs, or by his licensees or assigns.
It is rare, now that the inventor himself has the facilities to
manufacture to supply the market. His way is to grant
licences to others better able to produce and supply the
public. When a patentee grants a licence he is simply
contractually binding himself not to sue the licensee if the
licensee makes, uses or sells the subject matter covered by
the claims of the patent. The patent grant does not give the
patentee a positive right to make, use or sell the invention.
He always had that right. It gives him only a right to exclude
others. The patentee cannot compel the licensee to use the
patent, even though use of the patent is in the public
interest. Non-use can, in fact, be an antitrust violation.[11] If
the licensee agrees to pay a royalty based on sales of any
products, whether or not covered by the licensed patent
claims or, indeed, whether the products sold compete with
or are totally unrelated to the patent claims, it is not seen
that there is any more restraint on the commercial movement of those products than what would be if the licensee
had used the patent and paid royalties on the patented
products. If the licensee in *Glen* had produced and sold

---

10 *Ibid.* Baxter at page 174: "the principal determinant of the social value
of an invention is the extent to which it is useful and used".
11 See dissent in *Special Equipment Co.* v. *Coe*, 324 U.S. 370, 65 S. Ct. 741, 89
L. Ed. 1006 (1945); also Report of the Attorney General's National
Committee to study the Antitrust Laws 229–230 (1955).

toilet tank covers only covered by the patent, it follows that it would not be producing other kinds of covers. In that case, the situation could just as well be seen as a total suppression of non-patented covers, a somewhat worse effect than the production of the same non-patented covers subject to the royalty.

If the public will not pay the price of non-patented products, which price includes the use that is passed on to the licensor as royalty, the licensee will not produce those products. That is the restraint of output mentioned by Judge Levet. The same is true of the patented product, i.e. if the royalty is too high the ultimate sales price of the product will presumably be prohibitive. The royalty is a negotiated amount and licensees very carefully calculate the cost to them in order to determine whether their selling price will be acceptable to the market. The patented goods must also compete with non-patented goods. Thus, if the royalty is not commercially viable the potential licensee will not take the licence. He is not compelled to use the invention and can just as well carry on producing non-patented products. If a royalty is based only on use of the invention the licensee can choose not to use it and, therefore, pay no royalties. This is not an unknown manoeuvre. A licensee is often interested in suppression of the patent so as to prevent competition of the patented product with his presently produced products. He has, therefore, frustrated the patentee and public interest. In the case of an exclusive licensee the effect is dramatically suppressive because the patentee cannot grant additional licences and cannot himself make, use and sell his own invention.[12] Thus, the exclusive licensee by not working the invention can totally frustrate introduction of a new product into the market, an effect which is itself a form of restraint in that it obviously suppresses competition of the new product with the old products. The patentee tries to protect himself by requiring minimum annual royalties. A non-exclusive licence is somewhat better because the patentee can grant other licences.

---

12 In *Zenith*, the Supreme Court was aware of this, but begged the issue: "Of course, a licensee . . . is not used at all".

But is it really satisfactory to say that it is all right to grant one licence and if the licensee does not perform, search out another and grant another? Not only does this tend to mock the public interest in licenced manufacture of new products, it also must restrict the patentee's scope in the market because he cannot be guaranteed a rich supply of potential licensees to enhance his chances that one of them will produce the invention.

If the patentee and licensee agree on a royalty based on all sales, whether or not the products produced by the licensee are covered by the licensed patents, is there an effect so disadvantageous as to outweigh the public interest in the patent system? As mentioned above Judge Levet can only have meant that the output of non-patented goods by the licensee would be restrained and that the competition that would be lessened would be the competition provided by the licensee's supply of non-patented goods. So to the extent the public good is concerned, only the licensee's performance in non-patented goods is removed from the market. In return, however, the public receives the new, patented goods and new competition is introduced into the establishment market.

The dilemma can be summarized thus: if the licensor cannot base royalties on a percentage of sales of all products, production of the patented goods can be suppressed. On the other hand, if the licensor should require the licensee to produce only the patented goods, surely the courts would find an unreasonable restriction on the licensee's freedom to compete; indeed, such a restriction would be illegal. It is this danger which throws doubt on "best efforts" clauses because those clauses imply that producing other than the patented product is something less than a "best effort". Similarly, the *Glen* case clouds the legality of a licence on a fixed sum basis and even on a minimum annual royalty basis.[13] Each of those two payment schemes could be construed to involve the

---

13 Although Justice White in *Zenith* hedged that a minimum payment to cover expenses would be acceptable.

application of a portion of the consideration to non-patented goods being produced by the licensee, if the licensee does not produce patented goods—and the matter is again in the *Glen* court.

The statement of the problem suggests the solution. If the licensor could be permitted to require use of the licensed patent,[14] the Glen decision would make sense because then extraction of royalties on non-patented goods would be unjustified. If such permission is not judicially granted, the patent law should be amended to require use of the patent.[15]

The *Zenith* and *Glen* decisions must inhibit the development of licensing. If licensing is inhibited, patenting will be discouraged and inventions will be driven into the realm of secret knowhow, thus depriving the public of the disclosure and use for which it legislated.

No doubt coercion of a licensee to pay a royalty on all his production must be at least patent misuse, but the facts of coercion need to be proved. Often licence agreements continue until the expiration of the last-to-expire patent in the agreement. This can extend the term of a licence *ad infinitum*. If the licensee is required to pay royalties on all products indefinitely the antitrust problem, and coercion, seem obvious.

---

14 Some countries such as the Federal Republic of Germany permit a requirement that a licensee use the licenced patent. Busse, *Patentgesetz 3 Auflage*, page 225.

15 Almost all countries require in their Patent Law "working" of the patented invention.

17

The Schwinn principle and licensing

The Schwinn principle is that once a supplier parts with title to his product, e.g. when he sells it to a distributor, he can no longer put conditions on the distributor's right to resell the purchased product. The same principle applies to the licensor. He desires to control the further disposition of the licensed subject matter. To a certain extent he may do so. We have seen that so-called "field-of-use" restrictions can be lawful if they do not have the purpose of dividing markets. To a certain extremely narrow extent it may be possible for a licensor to control the price at which the licensee sells the licensed product. The licensor may also require the licensee to sell the product to a particular class of customers, subject always to the ready availability of competitive products to other customers. It is highly doubtful however that the licensee can be contractually prohibited from exporting the licensed product. If the licensee is to be inhibited at all in this respect, a licensor will have to rely on his foreign patents under which the licensee would not be licensed. The situation is not the same as in the Common Market where common ownership of several different national patents will not permit the patent-owner from frustrating the import of a licensed product from one country into another country of the Common Market.

One can say that the Schwinn principle is applicable to licence agreements and this can be illustrated by a decision of the US District Court for the Southern District of New York in 1950. The case is *U.S.* v. *Consolidated Car-Heating*

Co. Inc., civil case 34-312 decided on 20 June, 1950. Consolidated Car-Heating Company had developed a metal alloy which was useful for the preparation of dentures. It registered the name "Ticonium" as a trademark for the alloy. It also obtained five patents covering different compositions of the alloy, as well as patents on a furnace for melting alloys such as Ticonium and patents on a centrifugal casting machine for casting the alloy into moulds such as those used for casting dentures. It then proceeded to grant licences on these patents and there were some clauses in the licence which have particular antitrust significance.

> "1. The Company hereby grants . . . a personal, nonassignable . . . licence . . . to manufacture of the metal . . . in its own laboratory, cases, full or partial dentures, crowns, . . . and any other forms or parts used for dental restorations . . . and for no other purpose, it being clearly understood that this agreement grants a licence to use the aforesaid metal known as Ticonium only in manufacturing the aforesaid parts for the dental profession and to sell the same . . .
>
> 3. In order to facilitate the laboratory in taking advantage of the licence herein granted, and in order that the laboratory will be provided with the most efficient means known for making the articles mentioned in paragraph 1 hereof, the Company hereby agrees to loan the laboratory for use only on the premises . . . one of its Ticonium electric casting furnaces . . .
>
> 5. As a further consideration for the granting of this licence:
>   (*a*) The laboratory agrees to purchase from the Company the following equipment and supplies . . .
>   (*b*) To purchase exclusively from the Company, or from the Company's authorised dealers, all metal other than so-called precious metal used by the laboratory in the Ticonium electric casting furnace loaned by the company."

The US government succeeded in striking down para. 1 which prohibits the use of Ticonium for any purpose other than the manufacture of dentures etc. This was an illegal clause because it limited the use of the patented article after its sale. Note that the licensees were not licensed to manufacture the metal covered by the patent; they were licensed only to use the metal for certain purposes. The licensees purchased the metal alloy from Consolidated Car-Heating Company. Although the Schwinn case came much later than this one, obviously the Southern District court in New York was then thinking along the lines that would culminate in the Schwinn case in the Supreme Court. (Note the distinction from the example given below using the process and the catalyst for converting salt water to fresh water.)

The government also succeeded in having clause 5(*a*) declared illegal on the ground that it is obviously an unlawful tie-in. However clause 5(*b*) was declared to be lawful if the requirement refers only to Ticonium. The court reasoned:

> "That the requirement refers only to Ticonium, for the agreement was only a limited licence to the laboratory to manufacture dentures from the patented Ticonium and to use the patented furnace therefore. It was not a licence to use the furnace for any other purpose, much less to use it for melting other alloys, or metals, having a higher melting point than Ticonium which, if so used, would damage the furnace".

THE SIGNIFICANCE OF WHETHER AN AGREEMENT IS A SALE OR A LICENCE OF PATENTS

Patent-owners sometimes attempt to disguise a licence agreement so that it appears to be a sale of the patent. There is a tax advantage in doing this because if the arrangement is a sale, the income from the sale will be given capital gains treatment and will therefore be taxed at a lower rate. Ordinary royalty income is treated as ordinary income and is taxed at the ordinary corporate rate of tax, which is higher than the capital gains tax. This consideration is perhaps more important in the US than it is in Europe, but the significance of whether or not the transaction is a licence or sale has also to do with the antitrust aspect. As we have seen from all that has gone before, a licensor of a patent or a trademark is especially vulnerable to antitrust attack when he attempts to introduce certain restrictions in the licence. On the other hand, some restrictions which would be condemned if they were included in a licence would be lawful if they were part of a sales agreement for the patents or knowhow or trademarks. Under US law in order for a sale of a patent to take place there must be a transfer of all substantial rights in the patent. Anything less is a licence conveying no title or proprietary interest to the other party. A patent gives the patent owner the exclusive right to manufacture, use and sell the subject matter protected by the patent, for the lifetime of the patent. Accordingly the general rule governing whether a sale or a licence has taken place is that a transfer of less than all three rights for the term of the patent results in a licence rather than a sale. That is only a "general" rule and some qualification is necessary but we would refer the reader to a study of the regulations to s. 1235 of the US 1954 Internal Revenue Code. Section 1235 reads:

> "A transfer (other than by gift, inheritance, or devise) of property consisting of all substantial rights to a patent, or an undivided interest therein which includes a part of all such rights, by any holder shall be considered the sale or exchange of a capital asset held for more than six months, regardless of whether or not payments in consideration of such transfer are:
> (1) Payable periodically over a period generally coterminous with the transferee's use of the patent, or
> (2) Contingent on the productivity, use, or disposition of the property transferred".

US ANTITRUST LAW AND FOREIGN PATENT LICENSING

Shortly after the second world war there was little concern abroad about any restrictive effects of patent licensing agreements because the rest of the world was generally interested in obtaining as much technical assistance from the US as possible. However, times change and in 1973 the United Nations Conference on Trade and Development issued a report recommending that the following licence restrictions should be declared illegal by every country:

1. restrictions requiring the licensee not to contest the validity of the patent;
2. restrictions on the use of the subject matter of the patent and the related knowhow after the patent has expired;
3. restrictions on export of the patented product;
4. restrictions requiring the payment of royalties on patented products after expiration of the underlying patent.

We have already seen that in the Common Market all of the above recommendations have been implemented if not by legislation then by decisions by the Commission and by the European Court of Justice.

In the US, where US patents are concerned, the same is true. Any licensed arrangements, wherever concluded, which have an intended and direct effect on US foreign commerce is subject to the Sherman Act. The Clayton Act may also be applicable (e.g. if there is a tying arrangement or a clause requiring the licensee not to deal in competing products). In short, any agreement in which foreign licensees are prevented from selling in US commerce in competition with each other would be vulnerable to the application of US antitrust laws. A classic example of this is where an American licences for example a British patent and requires the licensee in England not to export to the US the product that he makes under the patent. Such a clause would very likely be a violation of US law because it is a direct restriction on US foreign commerce which is in no way reasonably justified (but see example 2 on page 299).

18

Examples of licensing clauses

The following four examples were supplied by the US Department of Justice to assist those contemplating foreign business with American companies.

EXAMPLE 1

An American company wishes to licence technology, either patented or unpatented. The company wishes to require the licensee as a condition of the licence to purchase from the American Company components for the product to be made using the licensed technology. It is further posited that (1) there are competing American manufacturers of these components and (2) foreign manufacturers generally have cheaper production costs.

If it can be clearly shown that foreign manufacturers have lower production costs, the tying agreement could be upheld on the basis that, without the agreement, no American company would be likely to export the components. Under these circumstances, American foreign commerce would not be restricted. Such tying, however, is illegal under the laws of some foreign jurisdictions. See, e.g., UK Patents Act, s. 57.

More generally, the second assumption will often be difficult to establish. If it is not true, that fact that there are competing American manufacturers means that the restriction, while of benefit to the one firm, would inhibit

Example 2 299

exports of other American companies. Consequently the restriction would hurt rather than benefit the US export trade. Even here, a tying agreement might be permitted when required to assure the proper functioning of the licensed technology.

(Cf., e.g., *Dehydrating Process Co.* v. *A. O. Smith Corpn.* (1961 Trade Cases No. 70,069, 292 F. 2d 653 (1st Cir. 1961), cert. denied, 368 U.S. 931 1961.)

EXAMPLE 2

Company A makes sophisticated electronic equipment in the US and wants to licence engineering knowhow in England. The licence agreement includes provisions for the export of machinery and components from the US. Company A would like to deny the licensee access to the US market because of the danger of building a competitor in its own home market, but fears that such restrictions would violate the antitrust laws.

Contrary to the example's implication, such restriction if properly drawn may in some circumstances be legal. To the extent that the knowhow could be patented under English law, the territorial restrictions could be created by transferring the English but not the US patent rights. Restrictions on knowhow ancillary to the patentable process would also be permitted to the extent that such restrictions on the patent are valid.

Although territorial restrictions on knowhow prohibiting re-export to the US pose more difficult antitrust questions, such restrictions may pass antitrust muster when reasonable under the circumstances and ancillary to the primary purpose of transferring knowhow. An important factor in this regard is how readily and how quickly a foreign firm could obtain the knowhow through other sources or its own efforts.

(Cf. *United States* v. *Dupont* 1953 Trade Cases No. 67,633, 118 F. Supp. 41, 219 (D.Del. 1953), aff'd. 1956 Trade Cases No. 68,369, 351 U.S. 377/1956.)

Territorial restrictions would not be permissible if unreasonable in light of the knowhow involved or part of a larger illegal plan to cartelize the market. See e.g. *United States* v. *National Lead Co.* (1944–1945 Trade Cases No. 57,394, 63 F. Supp. 513 (S.D. N.Y. 1945), aff'd. 1946–1947 Trade Cases No. 57,575, 332 U.S. 319 (1947); *United States* v. *Imperial Chemical Industries* (1950–1951 Trade Cases No. 62,923, 100 F. Supp. 504 (S.D. N.Y. 1951).

Thus in Case 2 the restrictions could be upheld if the knowhow being transferred is of substantial value, the territorial restrictions are limited to a reasonable period and the agreement is not part of a larger plan to divide markets between dominant firms.

Alternatively the licensor could protect itself through other means: (1) it could set the royalty rate high enough to off-set any cost advantage of the foreign firm, or (2) it could integrate forward (thereby providing a greater long-run improvement in the balance of payments) to insure control of the disposition of the products.

More generally, it is important to remember that licensing of knowhow in this situation may in fact have a negative impact on the balance of payments to the extent licensing is substituted for product exports or for foreign capital investment. The trade advantage of the US is highest in products involving new technology. Early foreign licensing tends to erode this source of export strength, and it may be very difficult on the basis of self-serving statements by the licensor to determine whether export alternatives to licensing are or are not feasible. Furthermore, restricting the English company from selling in the US could be injurious to US buyers, an injury which may offset any export benefit.

EXAMPLE 3

An American company would like to licence technology, either patented or unpatented. The American company would like to include in its licence agreement a provision that the licensee cannot sell the completed products in any

Example 4 301

country other than its country of domicile. The American company has determined that the licensee does not have the capability or experience to do an effective job of marketing the products in other countries, and the American company is negotiating with other similar companies to enter into similar licence arrangements in other countries.

The legality of restrictions involving sales back into the domestic US market is discussed in Case 2. Restrictions on sales in other foreign markets would not affect US foreign commerce and, therefore, not be subject to US antitrust jurisdiction. Consequently, no problems under the United States antitrust laws would exist. It should be noted, however, that exclusive national territories would probably violate European antitrust laws. See, e.g., Cases 56/64 and 58/64: *Grundig–Consten* decision, European Court of Justice (Common Mkt. Rptr. No. 8064).

If the domestic company's concern is that a foreign licensee may overextend itself and thereby dilute the quality of service, a "best efforts" clause and other contract performance criteria may solve the problem without the need for more stringent territorial limitations.

EXAMPLE 4

Licensing of American-owned patents affords another example of a type of situation where the US antitrust laws may hamper competition by American business with foreign competitors who are not similarly inhibited. If an Indian company, for example, is negotiating for the rights to use and develop a particular type of process for which an American and an English company hold competing patented processes, one important aspect of the negotiations may be the commitment of the patent holder to give the Indian company exclusive rights in, let us say, southeast Asia and to agree not to market the product in question in that area in competition with the Indian company.

The English or another foreign company can probably give this commitment without antitrust difficulties, but for the US company such a commitment poses US antitrust risks.

Contrary to the inference of the example, it is possible to give the foreign licensee an exclusive licence under the foreign patent rights which excludes the American patentee, and thus create the desired guarantee of exclusiveness. A licensee, however, must rely on the strength of the patent to exclude foreign licensees, and no contractual commitments not to compete should be made. Although legal it is worth noting that an exclusive licence by excluding subsequent US sales of the product in that market may have a detrimental effect on the US balance of payments.

EXAMPLE: FOREIGN LICENSOR OF A PROCESS IN THE US

British Processing Ltd. has obtained patents covering a process of manufacturing fresh water from sea water, as well as a catalyst for use in the process. It does not itself use the process or manufacture the catalyst but licenses the process to other corporations and the manufacture of the catalyst to various chemical manufacturing companies.

Ideally the corporation would licence the process users to employ the process only in certain licensed plants, and require them to use only the catalysts which it has developed and patented. Several American corporations show interest in using the process; and other American chemical companies show interest in manufacturing the catalyst.

For the process

British Processing grants a non-exclusive licence to American Processing Co. to use its US patents covering the process in a plant which American Processing is designing and constructing to use the patented process. Technical knowhow is included in the licence. The licence which will serve as a model for licensing other American process companies includes the following clauses:

" 4. If American company shall hereafter make, acquire or become entitled to any improvement in the Licensed Process whether patentable or not it shall forthwith communicate the improvement to British company together with all available information and documents respecting the way of working and using the same and shall assign to British company any such patent or American company's share of such patent.

5. American company shall keep confidential all information and know-how furnished by British company about or in respect of the Licensed Process other than

   (*a*) information which American company can prove was in its possession before such disclosure and which was not the subject of a confidentiality agreement;

   (*b*) information which becomes or is public otherwise than through the act or default of American company;

   (*c*) information obtained from a third party in lawful possession thereof and who was not in breach of any confidentiality obligation.

9. In further consideration for the benefit of this agreement, American company agrees to purchase catalysts for use in the process only from British company or a source designated by it.

14. This agreement shall continue for twenty years, but the obligation to maintain confidentiality shall continue in effect for twenty years after the date of termination.

15. American company agrees that it will not at any time during the term of this agreement export the product produced by the licensed process outside of the United States.

16. American company agrees from time to time to decide with British company the price it will charge to purchasers of the product produced by the licensed process."

British company insists on clause 4 because it does not want the American company to reap the benefits of the British knowhow and pass it on to someone who might be a competitor of the British company. It has been advised that such "grant backs" or "assignments back" will very likely be illegal. Can it be made lawful? The reason such clauses are out of favour in America is that they serve to frustrate inventive initiative in the licensee, i.e. the licensee would not be inclined to invent something if it had to assign it back to the licensor. If each party agreed to assign improvements back to the other exclusively there could be a serious problem of *per se* illegal division of markets.

The antitrust problem is the requirement to assign improvements back to British company. One way to lessen the problem is to have the American company grant to the British company a royalty-free non-exclusive licence with the right to sub-licence improvements developed by the American company. But British company has said that would not be satisfactory because it still would not prevent American company from doing what it wished with the improvements even though their development was made possible by what the British company gave to the American company under the licence. A step toward a solution might be to reword clause 4 as follows:

"4. If American company shall hereafter make, acquire or become entitled to any improvement in the Licensed Process it shall forthwith communicate the improvement to British company together with all available information and documents respecting the mode of working and using the same. British company shall have the right to file patent applications anywhere in its own name on such improvements, and such applications and US patents that may issue thereon shall fall within the licence but American company shall not be required to pay any royalty for their use and the licence to the American company under the improvements patents shall be for the life thereof. If British company elects not so to file patent applications then American company shall have the right to file in its own name on said improvements. In that event British company shall have a royalty-free non-exclusive licence with the right to sub-licence thereunder for any part or all of the life of any patents they may issue thereon, but should British company licence the same in the territory of this agreement it shall pay to American company   % of any royalties it may receive therefor."

The termination clause 14 is dangerous because under US law one cannot require payment of royalties when no patents exist (unless knowhow is also licensed, in which case the royalties would be deemed payable for the use of the knowhow). A US patent lasts 17 years, so unless British company obtains new patents during the agreement, the agreement could become invalid.[1] The requirement about confidentiality being kept for another 20 years thereafter may also seem to be illegal, but it is not, because it is subject to clause 5 which removes the obligation if the knowhow falls into the public domain. British company is also concerned about what effect there would be if the knowhow illegally falls into the public domain. Can it still keep American company to its bargain? This is a difficult point. British company's remedy is to sue American company, or whoever it was who disclosed unlawfully, for damages for such wrongdoing. One tactic which might help to solve both the termination problem and the unlawful disclosure of knowhow would be to use a clause like the following:

> "14. The term of this Agreement shall be for a period expiring on either (i) the date of the expiration of the last to expire of the patents or (ii) the date on which all of the knowhow validly falls into the public domain, whichever shall last occur."

It is doubtful that the word "validly" would change things; but it is rare for *all* knowhow to fall into the public domain.

Clause 9 is an unlawful tying clause. It should not be in the agreement at all. It is better taken care of in a separate agreement with the catalyst manufacturer (as we shall soon see). But for the purpose of discussion, if such a clause is insisted upon, it *may* be more acceptable if all signs of coercion are removed. The element of "coercion" on the licensee, or conditioning the licence on the licensee's agreeing to purchase other products, is essential for an antitrust violation in the US. It would help to blunt the antitrust danger somewhat if the words "In further consideration for the benefit of this agreement" were removed. They add nothing to the agreement and suggest that the clause is a condition for the grant of the licence.

Further alleviation might be obtained by the licensee's purchasing the catalysts for a short period of time, one or

---

1 But see page 292 for caution about payments indefinitely.

two years, simply to be sure that the process is started up correctly. Thereafter the licensee should be free to purchase the catalyst (meeting certain specifications) from anyone.

Clause 15 is very likely to violate US antitrust law. The argument has been made that it does no harm because as the licence is only for the US the licensee could not export the product into a foreign country where the licensor has a patent without infringing that foreign patent. The argument will not succeed. First of all, British company might not have a patent in the country where American company might want to export. Secondly, the Justice Department has said that such clauses would inhibit the licensee's right to challenge the validity of the patent. (It is now wellknown that in America, and probably also in Europe, a licensor cannot require a licensee not to challenge the validity of the licensed patent.) By permitting the inclusion of a clause restricting exports, the licensee might still challenge the patent's validity, but nevertheless be prevented, contractually, from exporting. Such a clause is unlawful in the Common Market and would be very difficult to exempt under art. 85(3).

Clause 16 at one time was clearly permitted by the courts in America under the so-called "General Electric doctrine". Briefly, this meant that a patentee could fix the price of the licensed patented article. This doctrine has been narrowed almost into non-existence. In Europe such price-fixing can be all right, and would be viewed in the same way as any other restriction, i.e. a perceptible effect on inter-state trade, and might be absolved by the art. 85(3) exemption. But in our illustration the problem is even more subtle. The GE doctrine applied only to patented articles. Under US patent law the product produced by a patented method (here, it would be the fresh water) is not automatically protected by a patent covering only the process of making the fresh water. Accordingly, even if the GE doctrine remained totally valid, it would not apply because fixing the price of the fresh water would be price-fixing outside the scope of the patent. In most European countries the

product of a process is automatically protected by a patent
covering only the process.

For the catalyst

British company now must arrange non-exclusive licences
for the manufacture of the catalyst. It is interested in having
the catalyst manufactured and sold only to those who have
been licensed to use the patented process for converting
salt water to fresh water. The following clauses appear in
the proposed licenses:

"1. British company hereby grants to Licensee a non-exclusive
licence under its US patents covering the XYZ catalyst
(herein-after called the "Catalyst") and the confidential
knowhow pertinent thereto to manufacture the Catalyst
for the purpose of supplying the same to the Process
Licensees.

2. Licensee shall not without the written consent of the British
company supply the Catalysts to anyone other than the
Process Licensees where such Catalysts are manufactured
under any of the patents or knowhow.

7. Licensee shall not during the term hereof manufacture or
sell any Catalyst to a Process Licensee for use in the
Licensed Process other than a Catalyst manufactured
hereunder or supplied by any licensee of the British company.

(2) Licensee covenants that it will not use any of the
knowhow received directly or indirectly from the British
company to make catalysts other than as provided in this
Agreement".

(3) Licensee shall advise British company if it shall make
any catalysts independently of the patents and knowhow
licensed herein and which licensee knows or believes can
be used to make fresh water out of salt water and in such
event the British company may terminate this Agreement
by written notice but without prejudice to any antecedent
right or obligation".

As to clauses 1 and 2—the licence is non-exclusive and the
purpose is to be sure that there is a supply of the Catalyst for
the licensed users of the process. It is lawful to limit the use

of a patented product, so long as the limitation is not a device to establish a monopoly or divide markets. That is not the case here. If the licence had been exclusive, antitrust problems would have arisen because the result would have been to deny others the chance to make the Catalyst to supply the licensed process users.

If the Catalyst is specific to the patented process, there would be still less objection to limiting the licensee's customers. If the Catalyst can be used in other processes, the antitrust danger may be more imminent, unless there are other catalysts readily available to users other than the licensed process users.

Clause 7 could be illegal for the same reason that exclusive dealing clauses are illegal. These were discussed earlier. One cannot forbid a dealer or a licensee from dealing in competitive products. The reader is reminded of the "area of primary responsibility" discussion earlier in this book, and of the possibility of legality of the restriction if the exact nature of the catalyst is unique and particular.

Clause 7(2) however, is lawful. It does not prohibit licensee from making other catalysts, just that the licensee cannot use British company's knowhow to do so.

Clause 7(3) may cause a problem. It resembles the kind of clause permitting a supplier to refuse to continue to deal with a distributor who deals in competitive products. It is based on the theory that any individual (not enjoying a monopolistic position in a relevant market) can choose with whom he wishes to deal. This unilateral right becomes illegal if it is done by agreement with another. That is not the case here, nor is British company in a monopolistic position in respect of catalysts to convert salt water into fresh water. Nevertheless, Clause 7 would be better written as follows:

"7. (1) Licensee undertakes to assist Process Licensees in the best use of the Process by supplying them only with the Catalyst or catalysts meeting the standards, tests and analyses set out in Appendix A to this Agreement.

(2) [same as before]

(3) Notwithstanding anything contained in this Agreement, Licensee shall not be restricted from manufacturing

or dealing in catalysts useful for converting salt water into fresh water independently of the patents or knowhow licensed herein. If Licensee does so manufacture or deal, it shall notify the British company, and in such event, the British company may terminate this Agreement by written notice, irrespective of notification from Licensee of its manufacture and dealing. Such termination shall not operate as a waiver of any right of action which the British company may otherwise have under this Agreement".

19

US jurisdiction over a foreign person

If the potential defendant is physically present within the US there is no problem in obtaining jurisdiction over him. Section 4 of the Clayton Act says that "Any person who shall be injured in his business or property by reason of anything forbidden in the antitrust laws may sue therefore in any district court of the United States in the district in which the defendant resides or is found or has an agent . . .". Section 4A of the Clayton Act gives the same right to the US government. The key requirement is that the defendant reside or be found or have an agent anywhere in the US. We think that one example will illustrate all of the essential parts of which anyone foreign to the US should be aware.

In the 1950s the manufacture and sale of quinine and quinidine (products useful as drugs for the treatment of malaria and certain heart diseases) was on the decline because the price of quinidine was dropping. As a consequence of the lowering price of quinidine the growers of the cinchona tree from which the starting material for the eventual production of quinine comes were gradually turning over the land on which they had been growing the cinchona tree in order to grow other more profitable products. The manufacturers of quinine were alarmed. They comprised Dutch companies, a German company and an English company. They met to decide on a course of action to keep up the price of quinine. The US government had announced an auction of a stockpile of raw material for the production of quinidine and quinine. The manufacturers agreed to have one bidder for the stockpile so that it would not be purchased at too low a price which must be the result in the event of truly competitive bidding. They also agreed that once the stock pile had been purchased each of the members would be allocated a proportion of it and they also agreed on the fixing of prices and rebates for exports as well as allocation of export quotas, each of the manufacturers reserving for himself certain markets outside of the Common Market. The US government investigated the activities of this international quinine cartel because of the nature of the purchases of the US stock pile. There was an alleged violation of the Sherman Act and the Common Market authorities were convinced that there had been a violation of art. 85 as well as of art. 86. In the US a grand jury was convened and all of the defendants were indicted. The problem was how to obtain jurisdiction over them in the US. Certain individuals as well as the companies were posted complaints issued from the District Court for the Southern District of New York. We will concentrate on one of the defendants for the purposes of this illustration.

Lake and Cruikshank, the English member of the alleged cartel, and its president duly received their summonses and complaints. But the US government had no jurisdiction over either of them. There was no subsidiary in the US nor was there an agency for the sales by the company into the US. Lake and Cruikshank sold through an independent distributor. There is a provision in most states of the US called a "long arm" statute. This statute permits jurisdiction over any foreigner if that foreigner has done some measure of trading or business in that state. The general test is whether the foreigner had had sufficient contact within the state in the form of business trading. If that contact had occurred, the state would be considered to have given due process to the defendant by serving him with the summons and complaint in a prescribed manner. In the case of Lake and Cruikshank, they did not come within the New York State "long arm" statute. If they had had an agent, the presence of the agent could have been enough to give jurisdiction over Lake and Cruikshank. Of course, if the president of the company should be found personally within the US, jurisdiction could be obtained over him, and probably over his company. If the company had had a subsidiary in the US, service of process on the subsidiary would not have obtained jurisdiction over the English company, unless the English company so controlled the subsidiary that the subsidiary was in effect its agent in the US. The lesson is clear: it is safer to do business in the US through a distributor.

US Patent Law provides jurisdiction over a foreigner who is the owner-of-record of a US patent, but only in matters concerned with the patent.

20

Technical assistance (knowhow)

This topic has been left until last, though it is at least as important as patents and trademarks from a commercial point of view. From an antitrust point of view there is less reason to permit restrictions in knowhow agreements than in patent and trademark licences. Knowhow is not protected by any national grant (such as a patent or registration of a trademark). It knows no boundaries at all. The essence of knowhow is its secrecy. It is the special knowledge about doing something that one may possess. In America and the Common Market it is recognized as worthy of protection and is something of value which may be sold or licensed by its owner. If it is not secret or confidential, it is not protectible. If it is secret or confidential, how can it be protected? By restricting the licensee to keeping the information secret and confidential. In the US and in Europe, if the knowhow becomes public knowledge, i.e. loses its secret or confidential nature, validly or invalidly, the licensor can no longer compel the payment of royalties. An argument might be made that the transfer of the knowhow, although it may later become public, did nevertheless give the receiver of it valuable "lead time" over his competitors so he should be required to continue payments. This theory has not been tested in either jurisdiction. The best course would be to *sell* the knowhow for a lump sum because the sale would not be affected by a later public disclosure.

The problem with secret knowhow is not so much legal (antitrust) as it is commercial practicality. For example, one giving knowhow would like to have some "feedback" of improvements made by the licensee. Should these improvements be patented? If they are, the patent specification may make public that which had been secret. Knowhow may be very short-lived, yet some secrecy has lasted a long while, e.g. the Coca Cola formula and the Angostura Bitters formula. Business decisions about knowhow should be based on practical business considerations and not antitrust worries. A good rule of thumb is that one may compel a knowhow licensee to maintain secrecy and may restrict him to using the knowhow in a given geographical area, but the possessor of knowhow has no greater rights (indeed, less) than a patentee or trademark owner.

When anyone licenses another to use his patents or knowhow one of his concerns is to obtain from the licensee rights in any improvements that the licensee may devise in the subject matter related to the licence. This has been called a "grant-back" in the US because the licensor requires an express undertaking by the licensee to assign or license back to the licensor rights in any improvement made by the licensee in the licensed product or process.[1] In the case of a licensed patent the licensor will want to have any patent obtained by the licensee on improvements, or an assignment back to him of rights to obtain a patent in the name of the licensor on such improvements.

The Antitrust Division has consistently attacked such arrangements, but the courts have upheld them so long as they did not form part of a wider anticompetitive scheme. The US Patent Code expressly permits assignment of patents but grant-backs exercised between competitors or involving a party dominant in the technology may go beyond the permitted simple assignment. For example, grant-backs between competitors can have the effect of dividing markets or perpetuating dominance in an industry. If a grant-back is coupled with price-fixing it is *per se* illegal.

---

1 See pages 303 and 304.

Former Assistant Attorney General Donald F. Turner, of the Antitrust Division, expressed his intention to overrule judicial precedent and have the courts find grant-back provisions illegal *per se.* In particular he declared his war on grant-back of future improvement patents simply because such a requirement went beyond what was necessary to protect the licensor's proper interest in the licensed subject-matter. He did, however, also say that he would not attack grant-backs of non-exclusive licences.

Whatever the merits of his argument the fact is that US courts have not applied *per se* illegality to grant-back patent clauses and have declared them illegal only, as mentioned above, when they have been involved or combined with other clauses or purposes which altogether formed an illegal antitrust restraint.

If a company is anxious to obtain improvements from its patent licensee, it is still more keen to obtain improvements from a licensee who is obtaining its knowhow. In many respects, knowhow is more valuable than a patent. Certainly it is more practical because the possessor of knowhow actually teaches his licensee how to do something. It affords quick entry into an industry. But the licensor of know-how has a real concern about the effect of licensing his knowhow. It is not like a patent. A patent is a public disclosure. Knowhow is secret and can be obtained only by special agreement with the owner having it. Accordingly when a company licenses another to use its knowhow it is very much concerned that the licensee does not disclose it to others. Once that knowhow becomes public knowledge, the original owner of it cannot continue to extract royalties from its licensee and, more important, finds himself with new competition using his own knowhow.

In the case of the licensing of knowhow, therefore, the use of a grant-back clause becomes a matter of considerable practical importance. A licensor would not be happy to have his licensee develop its own improvements based on the transmitted knowhow and then have the licensee dispense the improvements to others.

EXAMPLE OF THE PROBLEM

Company A possesses knowhow for a certain chemical process. It has licensed others in the US. It does not enjoy a dominant position in the technology and there are other competitive processes and other competitors. Company B wants A's knowhow. Company B has never been in this particular industry and is not a competitor of A. Company A has insisted on the following clause which B argues is a violation of US antitrust law:

> If Licensee shall hereafter acquire or become entitled to any improvement in the Licensed Process it shall forthwith communicate the improvement to Licensor together with all available information and documents respecting the mode of working and using the same. Licensor shall have the right to file patent applications anywhere in its own name on such improvements and such applications and patents that may issue thereon shall fall within this licence but Licensee shall not be required to pay an additional royalty for their use. If Licensor elects not to file such patent applications then Licensee shall have the right to file patent applications in its own name on said improvements. In that event Licensor shall have a non-exclusive licence with the right to sub-license thereunder for any part or all of the life of any patents that may issue thereon. For the purpose of this clause the expression "improvement" shall include any discovery or innovation which if used in the Licensed Process would make it cheaper to operate or more effective or in any way more beneficial.

The issue is whether this clause violates US antitrust laws or runs a substantial risk of violating them. If the above clause is illegal under US antitrust law, it must be illegal *per se* or illegal because it imposes an unreasonable restraint on competition. Assume that the agreement comes within the Sherman Act in that a sufficient amount of inter-state and/or foreign commerce would be affected.

Per se illegality means simply that the clause itself, i.e. the requirement to grant-back improvements by a licensee to a licensor is illegal in itself. There has been no decision establishing such *per se* illegality.

It is of some interest that Mr Richard McLaren in 1969, then head of the Antitrust Division of the US Department of Justice, announced his intention to attack grant-back clauses; but he did not allege *per se* illegality as Mr Turner did in 1965. It is perhaps more interesting to note that since his speech there has been no decision declaring grant-back clauses to be illegal, independently of their relationship in agreements which were otherwise illegal because they contained other clauses or unlawful purposes.

In 1973 the United Nations Conference on Trade and Development was concerned with the anticompetitive effects of certain clauses in licence agreements. The Conference recommended that four clauses be declared *per se* illegal by all countries.[2] "Grant-back" clauses were not mentioned. If the clause above mentioned is not illegal, *per se*, it must be subjected to the "rule of reason". If the clause is evidence of an attempt to monopolize the market in the particular chemical process, or if it unreasonably and substantially restrains competition, it could be illegal.

There are no circumstances suggesting monopolization and the clause is not evidence of any monopolization attempt. No monopolization is possible. Licensee is not in the business of this chemical process and licensor has no monopoly or dominant position in this field in the US. The market has several competitors. The agreement contains no clauses which alone or together with the above mentioned clause would indicate an attempt to monopolize. There is no exclusive arrangement between the parties, no division of markets or any indication of monopolization.

Is there any unreasonable restraint of competition? It would be difficult, for a start, to identify the competition at all. Licensee was not a competitor and is entering this technological field under the auspices of the licensor in this agreement. As there is no restriction affecting either party's relationship with third parties, there would be no restraint on competition. If one takes the broadest view, one might argue that licensee is itself unreasonably restrained in its use of its own improvements. Even if it were not a competitor, it might have become a competitor so this restriction unreasonably restrains competition because it restrains licensee.

2 See page 297.

Assume that licensee is, in fact, restrained in its use of its own improvements. The question then is whether the clause set out above is a reasonable restraint ancillary to a main lawful purpose. The purpose of the agreement is lawful. One is then left only with the issue of the reasonableness of the above mentioned clause. It appears reasonable for licensee to agree to assign improvements back to licensor. Whilst there are no decisions declaring grant-backs illegal (absent their being caught in a wider net of illegal activity), there is at least one landmark decision supporting the view that they may be legal. It is *United States* v. *National Lead Co.*, 332 U.S. 319. Another is *Transparent-Wrap Machine Corpn.* v. *Stokes and Smith Co.*, 329 U.S. 637.

If licensee develops its own improvements based upon information it receives from licensor, licensee could reasonably be required not to disclose those improvements if, in doing so, it would disclose that which is confidential and secret. The improvements would obviously be coloured with the knowhow provided by licensor, so licensor has a proprietory interest in them. If the licensor can restrain licensee's disclosure of improvements it might reasonably require grant-back of rights in those improvements. There is no unreasonable adverse effect on licensee because it is not restrained from using its improvements.

We suspect that at least one reason why there has been no declaration that grant-back clauses are illegal on their own is that if a licensor of knowhow could not protect himself as to improvements arising out of the soil of his own knowhow, he would be discouraged from imparting knowhow—which must be against the public interest.

Common Market authorities have declared their intent to have grant-backs condemned. Their principal reason is that a licensee would be discouraged to innovate if he would be required to assign his improvements back to the licensor. There have already been decisions on this point but no decision has declared out-of-hand that such clauses are illegal. Their illegality was wrapped up in other considerations, e.g. the dominant position of licensor and the fact that the licence was exclusive and tended to preserve the dominance and frustrate wider use of the subject-matter.

Appendix

Summary of Commission decisions on exemptions under article 85(3)

I. RESTRICTIVE PRACTICES

A. Price-fixing

The Commission has struck down any attempted price-fixing or concerted practices to fix prices and denied exemption or imposed fines in all sixteen cases, seven of which were appealed to the Court of Justice but turned down by the Court acting in accordance with the Commission.

In Case 41/69: *A.C.F. Chemiefarma* v. *E.C. Commission*, 15 July 1970, 16 REC. 661, Case 44/69: *Buchler and Co.* v. *E.C. Commission*, 15 July 1970, 16 REC. 733, Case 45/69: *Boehringer Mannhein GmbH* v. *E.C. Commission*, [1973] C.M.L.R. 864 (Quinine Cartel) the parties had concluded an export and sales agreement concerning trade with third countries and providing for the fixing of prices and rebates for exports of quinine and quinidine and for the allocation of export quotas.[1] Two "gentlemen's agreements" between the same parties extended these provisions to all sales within the Common Market. Moreover it contained the principle of

---

1 See pages 310–312.

protection of home-markets for each producer. This led to a price increase of 50% in 1964. The Court agreed with the Commission that the parties of the export cartel had complied with the gentlemen's agreements and participated in a cartel that is prohibited by art. 85. Since there was insufficient proof that the quota system was continued the Court reduced the fines.

The decision contains interesting statements concerning the Statute of Limitation which was in dispute. Though the Court acknowledged the purpose of the Statute of Limitation, namely to ensure legal security, it held that the periods of limitation must be set in advance. Since this was not dealt with in reg. 17 it could not be considered until the Community legislator decided. This meant that it was up to the Commission whether and when it would grant this legal protection because an amendment of reg. 17 depends on whether the Commission exercises its right to propose regulations.

One member of the Quinine Cartel, Boehringer, made a request to the Commission that the fine imposed by the US District Court, Southern District of New York, on Boehringer for its participation in the quinine cartel should be deducted from the fine in the above-mentioned decision. The Commission refused to offset and the Court dismissing the appeal agreed in Case 7/72: *Boehringer Mannheim GmbH v. E.C. Commission*, 14 December 1972, with the reasoning that not the agreement as such is fined but the act of restriction which is prompted by the agreement and that the two fines imposed under different legal systems were justified as two different acts were involved, one in the US and one in the Common Market.

In Case 48/69; *Imperial Chemical Industries Ltd.* v. *E.C. Commission*, [1972] C.M.L.R. 557, 14 July 1972 the Commission and the Court had to deal with unclear alleged concerted practices by dyestuff manufacturers in the UK and throughout Europe. There was no obvious association or expressed recommendation of prices such as in the two cases just mentioned. The pricing by the manufacturers on three separate occasions seemed to follow a uniform pattern. The major issue was whether there had been a concerted practice in pricing by the manufacturers. Both the Commission and the Court dismissed the US precedents on evidence of a conspiracy and "conscious parallelism". In the US, there must be evidence of an intent with concerted action and a common design among competitors. The Commission referred vaguely to a "shared intent" regardless of whether it resulted in action by other parties. The Commission stated flatly that the mere exchanging of pricing information is sufficient to amount to price-fixing because it consciously eliminates

> "the risk of not knowing their future market behaviour . . . and in doing so co-ordinate their conduct . . . . The dyestuffs manufacturers followed a uniform course of conduct in their pricing. On that basis alone it sufficiently proved the existence of concerted practices . . .".

The Commission apparently believed that any prior consultation, regardless of the absence of a common design or intent by all the parties is sufficient to be a concerted practice fixing prices if only because it "eliminates the risk of not knowing their future market behaviour".

The Court was equally unclear but not so sweeping. The Court was unwilling to accept the Commission's extreme view and although it agreed with the Commission, it did so on grounds closely resembling those for the US "conspiracy". The Court, unlike the Commission, inferred from the "consciously parallel" behaviour in pricing that there *was* an intent and a common design to fix prices. This is quite different from the Commission's opinion. Yet, the Court also followed the Commission's thrust that by announcing prices, the manufacturers eliminated the risk of not knowing about future conduct.

The Court was clearly confused by the Commission's absolute condemnation based almost solely on the ground that the manufacturers announced their prices and were thereby able to adopt a uniform pricing policy. The Court accepted this and yet muddied the principle by suggesting there had to be a concerted act by the manufacturers. For example, the Court said, ". . . that they did not act otherwise *than in* concert is corroborated . . ."; and later ". . . it is hard to imagine that such parallel conduct . . . could come about without some *prior arrangement* . . ."; and still later ". . . the only explanation . . . is that the enterprises *had the same intention,* i.e. to improve the price level . . ." (our italics). The Court also required that an actual affect on competition should result.

The Advocate-General very nearly adopted the US view and advised the Court that parallel conduct was insufficient in itself to establish a concerted practice; that there had to be an intent of the parties to act together and there had to be a causal connection between the common intent of the parties and their conduct. Moreover, and very significantly, the Advocate-General said that there need not be an actual effect on competition and that the offence would occur if the parties only attempted to establish uniform pricing.

We think that this particular area of "concerted practices" of Common Market law is unfortunately confused and unsettled. In the ICI case the Commission, the Court and the Advocate-General had varying opinions but we suspect that the law may develop along the lines indicated by the Advocate-General.

In Cases 8–11/66: *S.A. Cimenteries C.B.R.* v. *E.C. Commission,* [1967] C.M.L.R. 77, 15 March 1967, the Court disagreed with the Commission on a procedural point of some importance to the liability of parties. A cartel of German, Belgian and Dutch cement suppliers notified the Commission of their agreement fixing prices and dividing markets. The Commission told the cartel their agreement violated art. 85 and could not be exempted under art. 85(3). The Commission did not specify its reasons; moreover, it told the parties that they were no longer immunized against imposition of fines by the Commission. The Commission took the position that certain parts of the agreement were invalid even without their having to make a formal decision to that effect. The Court disagreed in two important respects: It criticized the Commission's failure to detail its objections and submit reasons why art. 85 was infringed and why an exemption under art. 85(3) was not available.

It also contradicted the Commission and held that an agreement which has been notified is valid until declared illegal by the Commission.

In Case 8/72: *Vereeniging van Cementhandelaren* v. *E.C. Commission*, [1973] C.M.L.R. 7, 17 October 1972, a totally Dutch association of cement dealers recommended prices at which its members should sell certain quantities of cement and provide for uniform discounts and sales conditions. The Court and the Commission agreed the practice was illegal because by recommending prices the association members were made capable of adjusting prices uniformly. Similarly the Commission denied exemption for the *Nederlandse Cement Handelmaatschappij NV*, 23 December 1971, O.J. L22/16 [1972] C.M.L.R. D94, a Dutch sales agency for 38 German cement manufacturers. The agency offered the cement produced by its members at uniform prices and conditions. Members were obliged to deal exclusively with the agency which allocated quotas to them and provided for the pooling of certain discounts and freight costs. The Commission held that the agreement eliminated competition totally. In the third decision concerning the Benelux Cementmarket *Re Cimbel*, 22 December 1972, O.J. L303 24, [1973] C.M.L.R. D.167, the Commission held the same view for the Belgian cement industry association which allocated quotas and applied uniform prices and conditions except for privileged buyers approved by the association. Exemption was denied because competition would be eliminated.

In four decisions the Commission could only apply art. 85(1) since the agreements had not been notified. In *GISA*, 22 December 1972, O.J. 1972 L303/45, [1973] C.M.L.R. D125, 31 December 1972, p. 45, a Dutch association of wholesale dealers in sanitary ware had fixed prices and sales conditions on Dutch products as well as on Common Market imports and were allowed to grant only approved discounts. Dealers had to purchase a minimum quota from Dutch manufacturers. The whole agreement was regarded as restricting competition and a violation of art. 85(1).

In *Deutsche Philips GmbH*, 5 October 1973, O.J. L293/40, [1973] C.M.L.R. D241, the German subsidiary of a Dutch concern neglected to amend its agreements with its purchasers following an order by the Dutch parent company to eliminate export bans. The Commission considered Philips' network system of bans on horizontal supplies of wholesalers and retailers, the bans on direct supplies by wholesalers to consumers, and the bans on reverse deliveries, where retailers were not allowed to sell to wholesalers, and the export ban together with the re-import price-fixing an infringement of art. 85(1). The network was bound to a fixed resale price. The Commission, for the first time, expressed its view on this legally permitted system of resale price-fixing in Germany and pointed out that it fell within the scope of art. 85(1) if it created artificial barriers between member states.

In the *Preserved Mushroom* case, 8 January 1975, O.J. L29/26, five French producers of canned mushrooms and the association of all Taiwan exporters divided the German market between them through an export quota system and fixed prices in order to avoid competition. Taiwan and France are the two largest canned mushroom producers in the world. The Commission announced that even in case of notification, an exemption could not have been given and imposed fines because of the gravity of the infringement and the intention of the parties to divide the market, although the agreement had not yet had significant adverse effects.

In another case the Commission stated that an exemption could not have been given even if the agreement had been notified since the provisions of art. 85(3) were not met: *Re Franco–Japanese Ball Bearings Agreement* 29 November 1974, O.J. L343/19, [1975] 1 C.M.L.R. D8. The major ball-bearing manufacturers in France and in Japan had agreed to raise the cheaper Japanese price to the French level. The Commission had to consider what constituted an "agreement" and said that it was sufficient that one of the parties voluntarily undertakes to limit its freedom of action with regard to the other. But it does not require all the elements of a contract as long as there is a common understanding between the parties that the price will be increased. As to the relevant market, only the standard type of ball bearings was taken into consideration to the exclusion of special type bearings for which there was no substitute. The Commission abstained from imposing fines because the agreement was concluded before the publication of the Commission Notice that art. 85 is also applicable to measures designed to restrict imports from Japan.

In *Re Pittsburgh Corning Europe–Formica Belgium Hertel*, 23 November 1972, O.J. L272/35, [1973] C.M.L.R. D2. Formica and Hertel agreed to use PCE's discriminatory price list to prevent cheap parallel imports from Belgium and the Netherlands to Germany. A 20% price reduction was given if it could be shown that goods were used in Belgium or the Netherlands. Although the infringement of art. 85(1) resulted from a concerted practice between Formica, Hertel and PCE, only the latter was fined because it was primarily responsible for the concerted practice and the only beneficiary of it.

In 1974 and 1975 two "fair trading" agreements were denied exemption. Both cases were, according to the parties, designed to prevent unfair competition but in fact restricted price competition. In *Re Agreements between Manufacturers of Glass Containers*, 15 May 1974, O.J. L160/1 [1974] 2 C.M.L.R. D50, the major manufacturers of glass containers of five member states agreed that it was unfair to offer goods below a competitor's price or at a discount and under special conditions. The *IFTRA rules of producers of Virgin Aluminium*, 15 July 1975, O.J. L228, 29 August 1975, p. 3, concluded by aluminium producers of four member states also restricted price competition and excluded competitive rebates.

In Case 73/74: *Groupements des Fabricants de Papiers Peints Belgique* v. *E.C. Commission*, 26 November 1975, the Court disagreed with the Commission on procedural matters. A cartel of Belgian wallpaper manufacturers notified the Commission of their agreement fixing prices, conditions of sales and discounts. The Commission considered the agreement a violation of art. 85(1) and denied exemption. Any aggregated rebate system, even if purchases from non-members are taken intó account, is regarded as a restriction of competition. Fines were imposed on the members of the cartel for organizing a boycott against a dealer who refused to comply with the cartel's conditions. The Court criticized the Commission's failure to detail its objections and to give an account of its reasons why art. 85(1) was infringed, instead of simply referring to the decision of the Court of Justice in the Dutch Cement Cartel. Though the Court agreed that an agreement extending over only one member state might by its nature have the effect of re-enforcing compartmentalization and hold up interpenetration of national markets it stated: "Since the decision went appreciably further than the Commission's earlier decisions it ought to have supplied more detailed statements of the grounds on which it was based".

Court and Commission agreed in Case 71/74: *Frubo* v. *E.C. Commission*, [1975] 1 C.M.L.R. 647 that an association of Dutch fruit and vegetable merchants requiring their members to buy fruit and vegetables at auctions had a price-fixing effect. The obligation was not regarded as indispensable to attain advantages from the agreement. The Court confirmed the Commission's refusal to grant an exemption.

Another agreement concluded between parties of only one member state, *Stove and Heaters*, 3 June 1975, O.J. L159, 21 June 1975, p. 22, was denied exemption because it blocked parallel imports and access to the distribution network. Dutch manufacturers and traders of all levels (wholesalers, retailers, importers, agents) in coal and oil heating appliances who accounted for more than 90% of the trade concluded agreements that sales and purchases should only take place between approved members and that vertical sales should be excluded. This was regarded as preventing the interpenetration of markets.

In the Sugar Industry decision Cases 40–48/73, 50/73, 54–56/73, 111/73, 113/73, 114/73: *Coöperative Vereeniging "Suiker Unie" U.A. et alia* v. *E.C. Commission*, 16 December 1975, the Court disagreed with the Commission on several points and reduced the fines by 60%–90%. The Commission had imposed the fines on the principal producers and sellers of sugar in the Common Market because they had—according to the Commission—engaged in concerted practices to protect their respective markets and reduce competition by consigning sugar directly to the producers of countries in short supply. They also refused to consign to buyers other than producers or only with the authorization of the national producers or with increased prices. The decision mainly deals with art. 86 but contains fundamental interpretations on concerted practices where Court and Commission disagreed. To prove concerted practices the Commission had simply mentioned isolated actions such as, consignment of sugar directly to producers in other countries. This view was struck down as insufficient by the Court who emphasized that all the facts have to be considered together with the special features of the market in question. However, Court and Commission agreed that concerted practices do not require a plan but only a direct or indirect suggestion which enables the parties to eliminate uncertainty about the competitor's future actions.

B. *Market division*

The Commission's policy has been to strike down any attempt that could prevent the "interpenetration of markets" and all notified agreements that divided or intended to divide markets were denied exemption. In instances of three agreements which had not been notified the parties were fined.

In *Re Agreement of Julien/Van Katwijk*, 28 October 1970, O.J. L242/18, [1970] C.M.L.R. D43, the two leading Belgian and Dutch manufacturers and exporters of cardboard tubes for the textile industry concluded an agreement to restrict exports to the Netherlands and to cease selling in Belgium altogether. Since the Agreement did not fulfil any of the conditions required under art. 85(3), an exemption was not granted.

Two requests for exemption concerned the Benelux and particularly the Dutch cement market, which depends on imports from Belgium and Germany for about 33%

of its consumption. In *Re Nederlandse Cement–Handelmaatschappij NV*, 23 December 1971. O.J. L22/16; [1973] C.M.L.R. D257, a Dutch sales agency for 38 German cement manufacturers regulated the trade between Germany and the Benelux countries, especially Holland. The contract allocated quotas to the members and required them to deal exclusively with the agency which offered the cement at uniform prices and conditions. The Commission rejected the parties' argument that the restrictions were essential for competition among German, Dutch and Belgian manufacturers since distribution costs were reduced and marketing was improved. Any possible improvement that might result from the contract was considered disproportionate to the restriction.

The Commission held a similar view in *Re Cementregeling Voor Nederland*, 18 December 1972, O.J. L303/7; [1973] C.M.L.R. D149. This agreement divided the Dutch market among Dutch (69%), Belgian (17%) and German (14%) cement producers and allowed only a minor quantity (250,000–500,000 tons) to be sold under open competitive conditions. Each year the parties made a forecast for the Dutch demand and allocated quotas according to the division. They regarded the quota system as essential to supply the Dutch market adequately. This view was not shared by the Commission. It felt that the import needs of the Dutch market could be met by the excess capacities of the German and Belgian producers and that Dutch parties could enter into medium as well as long-term delivery agreements with foreign manufacturers.

In *Re WEA Filipacchi Music S.A.*, 22 December 1972, O.J. L303/52; [1973] C.M.L.R. D43, a decision on art. 85(1) was issued. The French firm manufactured and distributed pop records in France at a substantially lower price than WEA GmbH in Germany. To prevent exports from France to Germany French distributors had to return a signed and stamped circular to WEA Filipacchi S.A. that no exports would be made by third parties. The Commission imposed an especially high fine because it was well established as early as the Grundig–Consten decision that such export bans constituted a violation of art. 85(1).

Two very important decisions dealt with the use of trademarks for market-partitioning. The Commission had already stated in the Grundig–Consten decision that partitioning of the Common Market on the basis of trademark rights is contrary to the objectives of the EEC Treaty and this principle was confirmed by the Court in the *Sirena* and *Van Zuylen Frères* v. *Hag* cases. In 1974, however, the Commission had to decide whether an exemption could be granted for such trademark agreements.

In *Re Advocaat Zwarte Kip*, 24 July 1974, O.J. L237/12; [1974] 2 C.M.L.R. D79, the Dutch firm Van Olffen had transferred the trademark "Advocaat Zwarte Kip" to the Belgian firm Thissen for use in Belgium and Luxembourg. Thissen assigned the trademark later to another Belgian firm which in turn assigned it to Cinoco S.A. (Belgium). The latter tried to prevent imports from Holland. The advocaat liqueur put into circulation by Van Olffen in Holland under the same trademark as Cinoco's differed in composition, alcohol content and presentation. The Commission considered it to be incompatible with the provisions of the free movements of goods (arts. 30, 36) to prevent imports of products legally trademarked in another member state on the sole ground that an identical trademark of the same origin had been registered in the first member state. An assignment cannot prevent the application of art. 85(1) if the original agreement contained a partitioning of markets and if there exist links of a legal, technical or economic nature between the two later owners. Despite the fact that the agreement was not notified, the Commission declared that the requirements of art. 85(3) were not satisfied and that the agreement hindered the distribution of advocaat.

The second decision concerned an agreement which demarcated territories for non-identical but similar trademarks. In *Sirdar–Phildar*, 5 March 1975, O.J. L125, 16 May 1975, p. 16, an English and a French manufacturer of knitting yarn concluded an agreement in 1964 not to sell yarn under their respective trademarks Sirdar and Phildar in the other's territory because of danger of confusion. The Commission regarded the agreement as a violation of art.

85(1) and stated explicitly that market-sharing was not justified even if there might be danger of confusing the trademarks. In the Commission's view the agreement did not satisfy the requirements of art. 85(3) but in fact hindered the distribution of goods and harmed consumers because they would obtain only one type of knitting yarn.

C. *Agreements concerning exclusive purchases and exclusive sales*

In *Re ACEC–Berliet*, 17 July 1968, O.J. L201/7; [1968] C.M.L.R. D35; CMR 9251, the Belgian firm ACEC which had invented an automatic transmission agreed with the French motor coach producer Berliet on technical co-operation and joint research. Berliet in return would purchase electric transmission systems only from ACEC. The Commission regarded the restriction on third parties from selling to Berliet as an infringement of art. 85(1) but granted exemption because of the positive effects of the cooperation agreement.

Exemption was denied in *Re Central Heating*, 20 October 1972, O.J. L264, 23 November 1972, p. 22, because the agreement prevented interpenetration of markets. Two Belgian associations, the manufacturers of heating equipment (CSM) and the installers of heating and ventilation equipment (UBIC) agreed that the latter would buy only approved equipment and exclusively from CSM. Members of CSM were prohibited from selling to wholesalers or contractors. Article 85(1) was infringed, because both parties were limited in their choice for sale and purchase. Common Market producers were virtually excluded from supplying the Belgian market since a large amount of their equipment was not approved. UBIC controlled about 70% of sales and installation.

In *Re Agreement of Prym–Beka*, 8 October 1973, O.J. L296/24; [1973] C.M.L.R. D250, the Commission approved the agreement between a German (Prym) and a Belgian (Beka) manufacturer of sewing machine needles. Prym would cease to produce sewing machine needles and buy them exclusively from Beka. The agreement had effects similar to those of a specialization agreement because, as a consequence, Beka could introduce a production line.

In a recent case the Commission and the Court disagreed on what constituted the relevant market. In Case 19–20/74: *Kali und Salz A : G* (K & S) and *Kali–Chemie* (KC) v. *E.C. Commission*, (1975), Times 22 May 1975, K & S and KC were the only German companies manufacturing potash. KC agreed to sell its surplus straight potash (as compared with compound potash) to K & S for resale everywhere. The Commission objected that this effectively removed all competition in Germany in straight potash and therefore the exclusive sales agreement must affect trade between member states. KC explained it did not have the facilities to market straight potash and that, in any event, competition was not affected because there were many other suppliers of compound potash, that compound potash and straight potash were interchangeable; and that both potashes constituted the relevant market. If that were so, then the effect on trade, if any, would only be in straight potash and this would be minimal compared to the wider potash market.

The Court disagreed with the Commission and said the relevant market was the entire interchangeable compound and straight potash market. As the Commission had not investigated the correct (or relevant) market it could not find a violation of art. 85. The Commission had also said that KC would have set up its own marketing of straight potash and thereby competed with K & S. The Court disagreed with the Commission also on this point because the Court believed KC's argument that it could not have afforded the costs of setting up such a market programme, particularly in view of the declining market for straight potash (see also pages 72, 73 above).

D. Discount systems

The Commission has taken a very strict view of discount systems granting fixed or aggregate rebates. They are considered violations of art. 85(1). In all five decisions on the issue the Commission denied exemption since no agreement brought any advantages for the consumer.

Re Association of German Tile Manufacturers, 29 December 1970, O.J. L10/15; [1971] C.M.L.R. D6. A German association, which could not be joined by foreign manufacturers, granted discounts to their customers at the end of the year for purchases from all German manufacturers (members and non-members).

In *Re Gas Waterheaters and Bath Heaters*, 3 July 1973, O.J. L217/34; [1973] C.M.L.R. D231, Belgian manufacturers and importers of gas and water heaters agreed on purchasers to whom manufacturers might sell, thus excluding large shops, cooperatives and chain stores. The purchasers were given an aggregate rebate depending on their total amount of purchases from members or non-members.

In both cases the Commission saw a violation because the discount was not related to the individual relationship between a particular manufacturer and a particular purchaser but was given on the basis of sales by and purchases from any manufacturer.

In *Groupement des Fabricants des Papiers Peints Bélgique* the Commission took the position that any aggregate rebate system even if purchases from non-members are taken into account, constitutes a restriction of competition. The Court did not express an opinion on that conclusion but agreed with the Commission that restrictive agreements over the whole territory of one member state by its very nature reinforce compartmentalization and thereby inhibit market interpretation. However, the decision was annulled for procedural reasons because the Commission had assumed a violation of art. 85(1) without reviewing all of the facts (see pages 325, 326).

In the *Agreement between Manufacturers of Glass Containers* the exclusion of discounts for certain enumerated types of purchases and the fixed rebate system in *IFTRA rules for producers of Virgin aluminium* were considered an infringement of art. 85(1) because they suppressed competitive discounts.

II. LICENSING AGREEMENTS AND INDUSTRIAL PROPERTY
RIGHTS

In two decisions the Commission held the view that
exclusive licensing agreements violated art. 85(1) because
the licensor was prevented from granting licences to
interested third parties. However, an exemption might be
granted if the exclusive licensee is thereby encouraged to
penetrate a market not yet entered by the licensor.

In *Re Davidson–Rubber Co.'s, Agreement* 9 June 1972, O.J.
L143/31; [1972] C.M.L.R. D52, an American firm concluded
exclusive patent licensing agreements with respectively a
German, French and Italian manufacturer for the manufacture of armrests for automobiles. After the parties
removed the no-challenge clause (that neither licensee nor
sublicensee will contest the validity of patents for the duration of the contract), and export bans, exemption was
granted.

In *Kabelmetal–Luchaire*, 18 July 1975, O.J. L222/34, 22
August 1975, Kabelmetal (Germany) granted to the French
firm Luchaire an exclusive patent and knowhow licence in
France for a cold extrusion process. Again the parties
removed an export ban, the no-challenge clause and the
obligation to transfer the ownership in improvements
whether patentable or not to Kabelmetal. The exemption
was under the condition that Kabelmetal would communicate to the Commission any judgment under the arbitration
clause.

In *A:O.I.P.–Beyrard*, 2 December 1975, O.J. L6/8, 13
January 1976, a self-employed inventor Beyrard concluded
an exclusive licensing agreement with A.O.I.P. (France)
which was not exempted because the majority of the restrictive clauses did not meet the requirements of art. 85(3).
However, an exemption would be granted for a clause
banning exports for a first sale and for a short period.
Exclusive clauses came within the scope of art. 85(1) but were
exempt because the licensee would not otherwise have been
prepared to make the necessary investment.

The two important questions whether the *duration of a
licensing agreement* could be extended by the term of each

new improvement patent and whether the licensee might still be obliged to pay *royalties* after the basic patent expired, are not settled. The Commission decided these clauses could not be exempted in view of their combination with other restrictions. The *no-challenge* clause and the *no-competition* clause were not exempted. The Commission enumerated four clauses which normally would not come within the scope of art. 85(1), though a restrictive effect on competition might be possible in specific cases: The *most-favoured licensee clause* which obliges the licensor not to grant a further licence on terms more favourable than those of the licensee; a *grant-back clause*, which obliges the licensee to grant the licensor a non-exclusive licence for improvements; the obligation to keep *knowhow secret* (Kabelmetal); and an arbitration clause (see pages 254–258).

In *Bayer/Gist–Brocades*, the Commission granted an exemption for the mutual obligation of the parties to grant each other not only licences for improvements to existing processes but also for new, independently developed processes.

In *Bronbemaling* v. *Heidemaatschappij* 25 July 1975, O.J. 249, 25 September 1975, p. 27. Heidemaatschappij, a Dutch drainage undertaking, granted licences to four other Dutch drainage undertakings. It agreed to grant further licences only with the consent of at least two licensees. The Commission said that such clauses requiring the consent of existing licensees infringe art. 85(1). It denied exemption because the agreement frustrated wide use of the process (see pages 277 and 278).

III. SELECTIVE DISTRIBUTION AGREEMENTS

The Commission granted exemptions for three selective distribution agreements.

In the *OMEGA* decision, 28 October 1970, O.J. L242, 5 November 1970; [1970] C.M.L.R. D49, the Commission considered an exemption necessary to achieve better sales promotion and better provision of services because OMEGA produces only a relatively small number of watches.

With the exemption of the dealer contracts of *Re Bayerische Motorenwerke AG (BMW)*, 13 December 1974, O.J. L29/1, 14 December 1974, p. 2, the Commission authorized a distribution system where only selected specialized dealers, i.e. franchised retailers were allowed to sell the products of the manufacturer.

The principles of the *BMW* decision were not only confirmed but the Commission's view on several restrictive clauses were thoroughly substantiated in the *SABA*-decision, 15 December 1975, O.J. L28, 3 February 1976, page 19 (see pages 154–156).

The Commission exempted six out of eight notified exclusive distribution agreements. In *DRU–Blondel*, 8 July 1965, O.J. 131, 17 July 1965, p. 2194, a Dutch firm had granted sole selling rights for its products in France to the French firm Blondel.

In the decisions *Hummel–Isbecque*, 17 September 1965, O.J. 156, 23 September 1965 and *Maison Talatte*, 17 December 1965, O.J. 3, 6 January 1966 the manufacturers had granted exclusive rights to one person and had agreed not to sell to others in these territories; but the manufacturers had not undertaken to prevent parallel imports and the distributors were not prohibited from exporting.

An agreement between a German and a French producer of servo control equipment to supply to each other exclusively and to abstain from developing or selling competing equipment was granted exemption. *SOPELEM–Langen*, 20 December 1971, O.J. L13/47, 17 January 1972; [1972] C.M.L.R. D77.

In *Goodyear Italiana–Euram*, 19 December 1974, O.J. L38, 12 February 1975, p. 10, an agreement between two enterprises of the same member state was exempted. Since the agreement did not contain any restrictive clause other than those exempted by reg. 67/67, it could benefit from art. 85(3).

The same reasoning applied in *Duro–Dyne/Europair*, 19 December 1974, O.J. L29, 3 February 1975, p. 11. The American firm Duro–Dyne appointed the Belgian firm Europair its exclusive distributor in the EEC.

Another national agreement which insulated home markets was denied exemption: *Bomée–Stichting*, 21 November 1975, O.J. L329, 23 December 1975, p. 30. A Dutch association of manufacturers and exclusive representatives of perfumes, cosmetics and toiletry products sold their products only through wholesalers and retailers who accepted the sales conditions fixed by the association. Their aggregate share of the market was considerable: approximately 90% for perfumes, 70% for cosmetics and 40% for toiletries, half of which were imported from other member states. The association's network made goods available only within the circle of member manufacturers, importers and recognized dealers. Recognized dealers could obtain articles marketed by the association from firms outside the Netherlands. Nevertheless the Commission considered that the collective systems of reciprocal exclusive sale and purchasing commitments assured the market position of the members and prevented the free access of other resellers to the Dutch market.

IV. COOPERATION AGREEMENTS

The Commission granted exemptions to fifteen out of sixteen cooperation agreements. Three decisions concerned the *Transocean Marine Paint Association*. A group of medium sized paint manufacturers received Commission approval under art. 85(3) to form an association to sell marine paint under the same trademark and allocate markets on the grounds that it was necessary in order to compete with the giant paint manufacturers 27 June 1967, O.J. 163/10, 20 July 1967; [1967] C.M.L.R. D9. When the exemption had to be renewed after five years the Commission imposed stricter obligations on the manufacturers (21 December 1973, O.J. L19, 23 January 1974, p. 18) and required them to inform the Commission about their relations with any other paint manufacturer, even those outside the Community, information such as the identity of common directors or managers between an association member and any other manufacturer or any financial participation in such company. The Association appealed to the Court of Justice and the Commission had to redraft its decision (23 October 1975, O.J. L286, 5 November 1975, p. 24). The Association is now required to inform the Commission about relations between members or between a member and any other paint manufacturers operating within the Community, information such as a financial participation amounting to 25% or more of the share capital by way of common directors or managers.

The Court (Case 17/74: *Transocean Marine Paint* v. *E.C. Commission*, 23 October 1974; [1974] 2 C.M.L.R. 459) had struck down the Commission on the procedural issue and said that the Association must be given opportunity to argue the merits of the requirement for information. The Court, however, did not comment on whether the Commission had the authority to obtain information about foreign companies. The Advocate General also expressly refused to comment on where the line should be drawn to limit the scope of information that the Commission could require but he could not restrain himself from saying on this point:

> "As a matter of law, the power of the Commission is subject to two limitations only: the information should be relevant to competition in marine paints within the Common Market and should not be oppressive . . .".

In *ACEC–Berliet* the exemption was granted because the cooperation would enable mass production to make the new product more readily available for consumers.

The Commission exempted six specialization agreements for periods between five and ten years. In *Clima–Chappée/Buderus*, 22 July 1969, O.J. L195/1; [1970] C.M.L.R. D7, a French and German firm agreed to restrict their production of airconditioning equipment and to produce only specific types for which the other party would be the exclusive distributor in its own home market. The parties thus avoided duplication of studies, research and investment, and were granted exemption. In *Re JAZ –Peter Agreement*, 22 July 1969, O.J. L195/5; [1970] C.M.L.R. 129, the

French firm JAZ and the German firm Peter–Uhren concluded an agreement under which JAZ would manufacture electric clock movements and Peter–Uhren large mechanical alarm clocks. The agreement included exclusive reciprocal supply and purchasing rights for France and Germany. The reasons for exemption were that production costs were reduced by an increase in production and that the exports to the partner's territory carried the partner's trademark and enabled the importing partner to profit from the other partner's reputation.

In *Re Fabrique Nationale d'Armes de Guerre* (Belgium) and *La Cartoucherie Française* (France), 28 May 1971, O.J. L134/6, 20 June 1971, p. 6, two firms agreed to restrict their production on special types of ammunition which was exclusively delivered to the partner's territory and to exchange technical information relating to new products. The Commission wanted to survey the development and exempted the agreement under condition that the parties submitted a report every other year on the specialization measures taken and on the effects of cooperation, such as expansion of production lines, new investments and the estimated market share in the member states.

In *Re MAN/SAVIEM Agreement* 17 January 1972, O.J. L31/29; [1974] 2 C.M.L.R. D123, German and French firms wanted to produce a common line of industrial vehicles over 12 tons. They split their production according to tonnage, MAN producing vehicles over 12 tons and SAVIEM up to 12 tons. Both parties would collaborate in research, development, finishing and assembly, and customer service. Mutual consent of the parties was required for sale to third parties. Neither was allowed to sell its entire line in the other partner's territory or to sell the partner's tonnage other than in its home country.

The Commission again imposed conditions and wanted to be informed every three years on the effect of the specialization measures (e.g. extraordinary investments, increase in regular production). The parties had to assess their market shares in the member states as well as notify the Commission of any further agreements concluded between them or with third party automobile makers.

In *Lightweight Papers* 26 July 1972, O.J. L182, 10 August 1972, p. 24, the Commission exempted an agreement between the principal French manufacturers of lightweight paper to concentrate production on certain types of papers.

Some months before the Kali & Salz and Kali–Chemie decision the Commission prohibited a cooperation agreement in the potash fertilizer sector between *Société Commerciale des Potasse et de l'Azote (SCPA)* and *Kali & Salz*, 11 May 1973, O.J. L217/3, 6 August 1973. The two firms were the largest producers of potash in the Community. Each provided about 95% of its respective national requirements and more than 50% of the requirements of other EEC Markets. SCPA and K & S wished to fix prices, quantities and quality of potash salts for exportation and to coordinate delivery and distribution. The coordination was achieved by the appointment of joint distributors in Italy and the Netherlands and resulted in standardized prices and sales conditions. The Commission opposed the scheme because it eliminated competition between the two undertakings in the market in question.

The Commission approved the establishment of a joint research company for washing powders: (*Re Henkel/Colgate*, 23 December 1971, O.J. L14/14, 18 January 1972; [1972] C.M.L.R. D94. Henkel (Germany) and Colgate–Palmolive (New York) decided to coordinate the development of laundry soaps and detergent through a jointly owned Swiss research company. The two firms were the third and fourth largest producers in this sector in the world. The Commission granted an exemption because the joint venture did not include any restriction on production and distribution. However, a number of conditions were imposed: the parties had to submit to the Commission an annual report of the volume and value of annual sales for products resulting from the joint venture. The Commission had to be informed immediately of any patent and knowhow licensing agreement entered into by the Swiss joint venture company. The partners had to inform the Commission of any overlapping of capital and personnel between them.

The *Rank/SOPELEM* decision, 20 December 1974, O.J. L29/20, 3 February 1975, concerned an agreement in the field of precision optics and precision tools. Rank (England) accounted for 75% of total British production and SOPELEM (France) for 25% of total French production. Their cooperation covered joint research and development, manufacture and distribution. Each party, however, was free to carry on research on its own or with third parties. After the parties had removed certain restrictions, mainly involving industrial property rights and an export ban on lenses to sales territories reserved exclusively for the other partner, the Commission granted an exemption.

The Commission reviewed three agreements concerning the service market for fairs and expositions: *European Machine Tool Expositions (EEMO)—European Committee for Cooperation in the Machine Tool Industry (CECIMO)*, 13 March 1969, O.J. L69, 20 March 1969, p. 13; *CEMATEX*, 24 September 1971, O.J. L227, 8 October 1971, p. 26 and *UNIDI*, 17 July 1975, O.J. L228, 29 August 1975, p. 14.

CECIMO was an association of 12 European associations of machine tool manufacturers. It presented an exposition every other year in a member country. CEMATEX was an association of the national trade associations of manufacturers of equipment for the textile industry and organized an international exposition every four years. The majority of manufacturers of dental equipment were members of UNIDI which organized, every 18 months, an EXPO-dental trade fair. The exposition rules of the three associations contained a clause that exhibitors were not permitted to exhibit products at other exhibitions for a certain period of time beforehand (CECIMO: the same year of the EEMO exposition; CEMATEX: the same year of the exhibition and the previous one; UNIDI: the nine preceding months). All three agreements were exempted on the basis that the consumer became acquainted with the entire range of production in the industry and with more detailed information and better guidance by the manufacturers.

The Commission exempted two agreements in the nuclear fuel reprocessing sector: *United Reprocessers GmbH/KEWA*, 23 December 1975, O.J. L51, 26 February

1976, pp. 7 and 15. The first decision authorized an agreement between two Common Market undertakings already operating large-scale plants for the reprocessing of nuclear oxide fuel: British Nuclear Fuels Ltd. (BNF) and the French Commisariat de l'Energie Atomique (CEA)—and an undertaking that had decided to build such a plant Kernbrennstoff-Wiederaufarbeitungsgesellschaft GmbH (KEWA). As soon as BNF (800 metric tons) and CEA (800 metric tons) operated at full capacity KEWA would operate its own plant with 1500 metric tons. The agreement provided for the coordination of investment of the three undertakings and for the creation of a joint subsidiary, United Reprocessers Gesellschaft mbH (URG), which would organize the marketing of the processing services of the three partners, distribute the workload among their plants and pool research work. The partners fixed prices for the processing services and agreed to exchange knowhow and to grant each other licences.

The second decision authorized an agreement concluded between four German firms—Bayer, Hoechst, Kelsenberg AG and Nukem—to establish KEWA as a joint subsidiary through which they would operate exclusively and jointly own the shares of URG.

The Commission noted the importance of the new industry and held that in the absence of the agreement consumers would have suffered harm through the creation of unprofitable ventures financed by public funds. However, the Commission demanded that competition be reintroduced among the four companies after certain conditions were met. One condition was that the investment was not to be extended beyond the three plants or to other parties. URG was required to forward to the Commission any contracts concluded, information about prices and conditions, the annual balance sheets and the profit and loss account. Moreover, it had to inform the Commission every two years about the exchange of knowhow and the granting of licences.

In *Bayer/Gist–Brocades*, 15 December 1975, O.J. L30, 5 February 1976, p. 13, the Commission exempted an agreement between two large European drug manufacturers in the penicillin market. Bayer (Germany) and Gist–Brocades (Netherlands) concluded an agreement under which raw penicillin manufacture was undertaken mainly by Gist–Brocades and intermediate products by Bayer. In this industry different relevant markets in the various manufacturing stages had to be distinguished: raw penicillin, 6-APA, an intermediate product, semi-synthetic penicillin in bulk form and end products. This specialization agreement was matched by a reciprocal long-term supply contract, joint investment arrangements and another agreement to issue licences to each other not only for improvements in existing processes for the manufacture of 6-APA but also for independently developed processes. Gist–Brocades granted Bayer a non-exclusive, non-transferable licence and the necessary knowhow for its chemical process for the manufacture of 6-APA. Before entering these agreements both firms were active independently in the various stages of production.

This decision was of particular interest because the Commission developed its policy regarding jointly owned subsidiaries by two competing Common Market enterprises. Originally the parties had intended to transfer the plants for the production of raw penicillin and of 6-APA to two joint subsidiaries in which both parties were to own equal shares and appoint an equal number of directors. The Commission held the view that this had the effect of bringing production and investment under joint control. Because of equal representation neither firm would have been able to veto any management decision. The result that the output would have been determined by joint agreement was regarded as impossible to exempt, since the anticipated specialization and relationalization could have been achieved by other measures. Both firms therefore agreed to terminate this agreement and carry on with the above mentioned agreements. The Commission exempted the specialization agreement because it concluded that production could be more economic as a result, but attached extensive reporting obligations.

Index

ABUSE OF DOMINANT
 POSITION
practices constituting, in EEC, 190
refusal to deal with customer, 160
tie-ins, 187–188
trademark, use of, 263

ACQUISITIONS   see also
 MERGERS AND ACQUISITIONS
definition, 237

ADVERTISING
distributor's investment in, 135^{n}, 151
expenditure level indicating
 monopoly, 195–196
research scientists employed in, 245

AGENCY
buying—
 legal use by competitors, 163
 stabilizing measure, as, 96–98
in conspiracy with company, 61
selling, elements of illegality in, 96,
 108, 242
termination of, legality, 152
US jurisdiction over, 310–311
vertical territorial limitation, 134

AGREEMENT   see also subjects of
 agreements e.g.: CO-OPERATION;
 DISTRIBUTION; LICENSING
absence of, legality of practice in,
 70, 124, 163
in EEC—
 concerted practice distinguished,
  71
 construction in price-fixing case,
  324
 co-ordination of activity, 73
 "fair trading" exemption denial,
  325

AGREEMENT—cont.
in EEC—cont.
 jurisdiction of Commission, 158
 notification of, effect, 26–27   see
  also NOTIFICATION OF
  AGREEMENTS
 US "contract", equated with, 68
 validity or invalidity, dating of, 3,
  27
in US, "contract" equated with EEC
 "agreement", 68

ANTITRUST LAWS   see also EEC
 LAWS; US ANTITRUST LAWS
aim of, 1, 7–9, 191
business practices vulnerable to,
 207, 238, 314   see also BUSINESS
 PRACTICES
Canadian, on mergers, 235
courts, interpretation by, 9, 17   see
 also COURTS
English Common Law as origin, 18
government activities in EEC,
 jurisdiction, 14–15
jurisdictions, extent of, 24
patent licensing, international, 273–
 278, 286   see also INDUSTRIAL
 PROPERTY RIGHTS;
 PATENTS: LICENCES AND
 LICENSING
understanding of, essential to
 business, 12
US laws compared with EEC   see
 under EEC LAW

AREAS OF PRIMARY
 RESPONSIBILITY
legal status of clauses, 142, 145, 149

ASSOCIATIONS, TRADE   see
 TRADE ASSOCIATIONS

ASSOCIATIONS OF COMPANIES
intracorporate structures, as, 63

ATTORNEY GENERAL'S
COMMITTEE, US
function of, 32, 34
policy of—
exclusive dealing legality, 219
price-fixing with subsidiary, 56
summary of, 52
test for conspiracy, questions in, 67

BANKS AND BANKING
antitrust laws, susceptibility to, 207
joint ventures, 242

BENEFICIAL EFFECT *see* PUBLIC
BENEFIT

BLACK, JUSTICE
on foreign subsidiaries, 46–47

BOYCOTTS *see* GROUP BOYCOTT

BRANDEIS, JUSTICE
quoted on—
information exchange, 122–123
test of legality of agreement, 87

BRENNAN, JUSTICE
on vertical territorial restriction,
133–134

BUSINESS JUDGMENT RULE
in US state laws, 21

BUSINESS PRACTICES
antitrust laws, conflict with, 207 et
seq., 238, 314
coercion and hard bargaining,
282 *see also* COERCION
exclusive distributorships, 136–
137 *see also* DISTRIBUTION
failing or new company, allowance
for, 147, 214
franchise, manufacturer's right to,
140 *see also* FRANCHISE
AGREEMENT
joint ventures, 238 *see also* JOINT
VENTURES
legality, factors in determining, 1,
105, 111
litigation threat as coercion, 284,
285 *see also* COERCION;
LICENCES AND LICENSING

BUSINESS PRACTICES—*cont.*
market division (135–136) *see also*
under MARKET
mergers, 209–236 *see also*
MERGERS AND
ACQUISITIONS
patent licensing, 260 *see also*
LICENCES AND LICENSING;
PATENTS
reasonable, 85
research and development, 245 *see*
also RESEARCH AND
DEVELOPMENT
secret knowhow, feed back of,
314 *see also* GRANT-BACK;
KNOWHOW
tying arrangements, 179–184 *see*
also TYING ARRANGEMENTS

CARTEL
aggregated rebate system as
restriction, 326
price-fixing agreement case, 322

COERCION
as factor in antitrust illegality, 175,
178
element of illegality, in, 282
in licensing, 279 *see also under*
LICENCES AND LICENSING
litigation threat as, 284, 285
reciprocity as, 230
sale conditional on other purchases,
as, 181

COMBINATION OR
CONSPIRACY *see also*
CONSPIRACY
meaning, in Sherman Act, 30

COMMISSION OF THE COURT
OF JUSTICE *see* EEC
COMMISSION

COMMON MARKET *see* EEC

COMMON OWNERSHIP
affiliated companies under, 40
conspiracy between companies in,
32
single trader defence, element of,
64 *see also* SINGLE TRADER
DOCTRINE

COMPANIES
  associations of, 63
  behaviour conducive to avoiding
    conspiracy charge, 68, 221
  board, function of, 19–20   *see also*
    COMPANY DIRECTORS AND
    OFFICERS
  failing—
    acquisition of, 214
    allowances for practices, 147
  fines on, as penalties for violations,
    22
  foreign—
    acquisitions by US firms, 229
    mergers with, 222, 228–229
    US jurisdiction, 21, 310–312
  holding company as conspiracy,
    235–236
  large—
    court's attitudes to mergers of,
      212   *see also* MERGERS AND
      ACQUISITIONS
    history of mergers in US, 209
    implication of power, 191
    internal growth, legality question,
      191, 198
  linked in common ownership,
    conspiracy within, 32   *see also*
    CONSPIRACY
  parent and subsidiaries, conspiracy
    between, 36   *see also* PARENT
    AND SUBSIDIARY;
    SUBSIDIARY COMPANIES

COMPANY DIRECTORS AND
    OFFICERS
  ban on exchange of, in US
    mergers, 232
  business judgment rule, in US, 21
  chairman's residence, jurisdiction
    issue, 312
  conspiracy involvement—
    independent interest as evidence,
      58–59
    multi-company activities, 59–60
    with corporation in US, 57–58, 64
  personal liability—
    in EEC, 23–24, 70–71
    in US, 19–23, 65

COMPETITION
  concentration, meaning, 22

COMPETITION—*cont.*
  elimination of, methods—
    acquisition, 226   *see*
      also MERGERS AND
      ACQUISITIONS ·
    buying-up of customer, 212
    division of market, 103, 129–
      131   *see also under* MARKET
    group boycott, 160   *see also*
      GROUP BOYCOTT
    illegal practices generally, 103
    joint ventures, 237, 242   *see also*
      JOINT VENTURES
    price-fixing, 89   *see also* PRICE-
      FIXING
    toehold acquisition, 224
  freedom principle—
    as basis of antitrust laws, 7, 17
    English Common Law, 18
  in research and development, 245–
    246
  intensity of, dependent on
    numerous competitors, 22, 210
  intent to restrict, in US law, 92
  market division, effect of, 133
  preservation for public benefit, 7
  promotion through mergers, EEC
    view, 234
  restraint of—
    EEC ruling against, 68
    justification, lower prices as, 157
    substantial reduction as US
      violation, 86
  restrictive practices—
    all-sales royalties, 287–288
    exclusive licences, 276
    mergers, illegal element in, 210
    non-use of patent, 290
    tying arrangements, 170, 172
    use of trademarks as, 262–263
    trade associations, 114

COMPETITORS
  agreement between—   *see also*
    AGREEMENT
    absence of, affecting practice
      legality, 70, 124, 163
    as conspiracy, 68
    associations of   *see* TRADE
      ASSOCIATIONS
    common buying agency, use of, 163

COMPETITORS—*cont.*
  common selling agency, use of, 96,
    108, 242
  co-ordination of activity as
    agreement, 73
  exchange of information among,
    114, 116, 123
  market division among, 128   *see also
    under* MARKET
  mergers of   *see* MERGERS AND
    ACQUISITIONS
  multiplicity of, competition
    dependent on, 210
  price-fixing among   *see* PRICE-
    FIXING

CONCENTRATION OF MARKET
    POWER
  EEC view of, 234, 235
  examples, 213–214
  meaning, 22
  mergers, views of, 232, 235   *see also*
    MERGERS AND
    ACQUISITIONS
  prevention of, in US, 213, 226

CONCERTED PRACTICE
  agreement distinguished from, 71,
    77
  as violation, EEC and US views, 76
  EEC Commission's intervention on,
    72–73
  EEC Court and Commission
    disagreement, 327
  example of legal problems of, 320–
    322
  exchange of information
    constituting, 118
  meaning, in EEC, 69, 70
  parallel conduct as, 74, 76   *see also*
    CONSCIOUS PARALLELISM
  parent and subsidiary, between, 70
  price-fixing action as, 73–74

CONDITIONS OF TRADE
  unfair, EEC ruling, 190

CONFIDENTIALITY
  importance in knowhow licensing,
    312

CONSCIOUS PARALLELISM
  European and US usage, 73
  example of, 320–321

CONSCIOUS PARALLELISM—*cont.*
  meaning, 67

CONSENT DECREE
  in US violation cases, 25–26

CONSPIRACY   *see also* GROUP
    BOYCOTT
  agent's involvement in, 61
  agreement, dependent in US on
    existence of, 69
  associations, within, 63
  cases in US, 32
  charge—
    company conduct to avoid, 68
    defence to, 50, 52   *see also*
      DEFENCES TO CHARGES;
      SINGLE TRADER DOCTRINE
  competitors' agreement as, 68
  "concerted practice" of EEC
    compared, 69
  corporate structure, within, 32–33
  corporation and its officers,
    between, 57–58
  distribution, over, 53
  EEC ruling comparable with US
    law, 68
  employee, with, 61
  end-result as legality test, 51
  essential elements of, 65
  evidence of, 66–67
  foreign element in, US law on, 76–
    77
  foreign subsidiaries and parent
    companies, between, 45
  holding company as, 235
  independent interest of director,
    58–59   *see also* COMPANY
    DIRECTORS AND OFFICERS
  "infra-enterprise", 33, 37
  interstate trade, affecting, 80–81
  liability, allocation of, 65
  licence, withholding of, 54
  meaning, 30, 34
  monopoly distinguished from, 64,
    66, 201–202
  offences relating to, 64
  patents, pooling of, 280, 282
  per se doctrine, 83   *see also* PER SE
    ILLEGALITIES
  test for—
    end result, 51

CONSPIRACY—*cont.*
test for—*cont.*
Attorney General's Committee, of, 67
effect on third party as, 50, 53, 55, 66
unreasonable restraint of trade as object, 64

CONSUMERS   *see* PUBLIC BENEFIT

CONTRACT
US term equated with EEC "agreement", 68

CO-OPERATION AGREEMENTS
exemptions granted, examples, 336–343

COPYRIGHT
legality decisions in EEC, 262, 263–264

CORPORATION   *see also* COMPANIES
acquisition of   *see* MERGERS AND ACQUISITIONS
activities of, legal boundaries, 65
consciously parallel behaviour, 32   *see also* CONSCIOUS PARALLELISM
formation of, as joint venture, 237
officers, conspiracy with, 34, 57

COURT OF JUSTICE   *see* EEC COURT OF JUSTICE

COURTS
attitudes—
competitors' exchange of information, 120
intracorporate entities, conspiracy among, 60
large companies as monopolistic, 202–203
market division, 129
mergers, 210
patent licensing, 279, 286
price-fixing, 31, 112
price information exchange, 125
prices stabilization, 99
single trader doctrine, 35, 37, 40, 50
vertical market limitations, 138-139
vertical restrictions of dealers, 148, 149

COURTS—*cont.*
delineations of relevant markets, 196–200
freedom of competition as main concern, 17
in EEC—
"concerted practice", meaning, 71
illegality declarations, retroactive, 28
in US—
cases in American foreign commerce, 150–152
conspiracy inferred from facts, 31
infra-enterprise conspiracy interpretations, 35
jurisdiction over foreign companies, 310–318
jurisdiction over foreign joint venturers, 244
justification of rulings, 42
orders halting mergers, 211
parent and subsidiaries' actions, cases, 52, 53
patent licence royalties, 282
patents, judicial attitude to, 260, 279
procedure, 25
restraints of trade not all bad, 86
undue or unreasonable restraint, interpretation, 84
powers, European and US contrasted, 91
statements and decisions as guidelines, 10–11

CUSTOMERS
discount systems, 332
refusal to deal with, 160
restriction on, boycott as, 160
secondary boycott, 167

CUSTOMS BARRIERS
removal as EEC aim, 14

DAMAGES, ACTIONS FOR
in EEC national courts, 26
in US—
company directors' liability, 19–23, 65
criminal suits by Federal Government, 21
third party suits, 24
threefold recovery, 23, 29

DEALER *see also* AGENCY;
DISTRIBUTOR; WHOLESALER
competitive products, dealing
restriction, 308
exclusive dealing agreement, 163–
164
location clauses, legality, 145, 146

DEFENCES TO CHARGES OF
VIOLATION
conspiracy—
associations as intracorporate
structures, 63
common ownership element, 64
group boycott as counter-measure
to pirating, 166
interstate trade not affected, 83
market division, competition
enhanced by, 130, 271
mergers necessary to survival, 210
parent ignorant of subsidiary's act,
52
price-fixing—
good intent, 95
neither intended nor effected, 94,
110
single trader doctrine, 55
reasonableness as justification, 88
restraint on competition justified,
85, 87
rule of reason, 174[n.] *see also* RULE
OF REASON
single trader doctrine—
parent and subsidiary, 55
US Supreme Court on, 57 *see
also* SINGLE TRADER
DOCTRINE
tying arrangement, lower prices
resulting from, 187

DEPARTMENT OF JUSTICE, US
examples of licensing clauses, 298
foreign joint ventures, 243
guidelines on mergers, 210–216
concentration in market,
prevention of, 213
conglomerate mergers, 215–216
justifiable mergers, 214
percentages of share of market,
214, 215, 216
vertical mergers, 215

DIRECTORS OF COMPANIES *see*
COMPANY DIRECTORS AND
OFFICERS

DISCOUNT SYSTEMS
EEC Commission, view of, 332

DISCRIMINATION IN TRADE
Spaak report on, 14

DISTRIBUTION
as major concern of antitrust laws,
160
division of territory *see under*
MARKET
exclusive—
acquisition of distributor
distinguished, 217–218
EEC law on, 136, 153–154, 330
rights, value of, 135–136[n.], 140
sales and purchase, covering,
330–331
trademark case in EEC, 265
franchise of dealers, legality,
140 *see also* FRANCHISE
AGREEMENTS
limitation as EEC illegality, 190
quota systems, cases involving, 328
selective agreements, exemptions
granted, 334–335
vertical chains, courts attitudes, 149

DISTRIBUTOR
acquisition of—
by manufacturer, 217
foreign company, involving, 223
advantages of dealing through, 311–
312
area of primary responsibility, 142,
145, 149
competing products, dealings in,
163
extra-territorial sales, levy on, 151
location clauses, 144–145
market division among, 131, 132 *see
also under* MARKET
price-fixing with supplier, 103
Schwinn principle, application, 145,
293
termination of distributorship, 152,
161
vertical territorial limitation, 134

DOMINANT POSITION
abuse of, 190–192 *see also* ABUSE
OF DOMINANT POSITION;
MONOPOLIES
deliniation of relevant market in
proceedings, 197
examples of companies enjoying,
192
licensor of knowhow, 315, 318
meaning in EEC, 189
mergers, EEC view of, 234
obtaining without abusing in EEC,
197
trademark ownership producing,
267
US prevention policy, 213
EEC COMMISSION
Competition Directorate, 16
jurisdiction—
action against mergers, 233
daily penalties, authority for, 24
decisions, interpretative, 10–11, 14
exemption from antitrust laws,
10, 319–343 *see also*
EXEMPTION FROM
ANTITRUST LAWS
fines, 23
rule of reason, 10, 90, 91
policy—
concerted practice to fix prices,
74
internal growth of company, 191
licence numbers marked on
products, 257–258
mergers, effect of, 234–235
monopolies, 92
national trademarks and patents,
253
EEC COURT OF JUSTICE
areas of disagreement with
Commission, 327, 331
cases and findings—
concerted practice, 320–321
copyright, 264
trademark infringements, 265–
266
fines reduced by, 327
policies of—
concerted practices and
agreements, 71
price-fixing practice, 75, 118

EEC COURT OF JUSTICE—*cont.*
relevant market delineation, 331
rule of reason in, 10, 90, 91
ultimate arbiter on violations, as, 26

EEC LAW
concerted practices, US influence,
77–78
copyright, decisions on, 262
dominant position, definition, 189
exclusive licences, 276–278
grants-back, intention on status of,
318
individual's role in violation
procedure, 24
industrial property rights licensing,
254–258
joint ventures, position of, 244
jurisdiction, extent of, 24, 265
knowhow, recognition of, 313
notification procedure, 26 *see also*
NOTIFICATION OF
AGREEMENTS
patents and trademarks policy, 253
principle underlying, 15
Treaty of Rome *see* ROME,
TREATY OF
tying arrangements, legality, 185
vertical agreements, legality, 134
US laws compared—
abuse of dominant position, 190
concerted practice and
conspiracy, 77–78, 322
conditional patent licences, 181,
185–186
conspiracy, 68, 77–78
contract and agreement, 68
differences in general, 14–15
distributor, agreed restraint on,
163
effect on trade as violation test, 76
exclusive distributors, 155
export of licensed products, 293
franchise agreements, 145, 157
group boycott, 160
intent, in concerted practice, 321
market division, 131
mergers and acquisitions, 233–235
monopoly and abuse of power,
196
patent licensing, 253–261
price-fixing intent, 106

EEC LAW—*cont.*
US laws compared—*cont.*
resale restrictions, 156
selection of distributors, 155–156
trademarks, tie-ins with, 185–186
tying arrangements, 185–188
vertical territorial restriction, 137,
153–154

EEC MEMBER STATES   *see*
MEMBER STATES OF EEC

EMPLOYEE   *see also* COMPANY
DIRECTORS AND OFFICERS
conspiracy with company, 61

ENGLISH LAW
free competition principle
originating in, 18

EVIDENCE
coercion of customer, 181
conspiracy, 58–59, 66–67
existence of agreement, 73
justifying restraint on competition,
87
legality of restraint, determining,
89–90
mergers indicating monopoly
attempt, 194
price-fixing, of—
beneficial results, 90
information exchange as, 117
legality, factors essential for, 108
requirement of, by court, implying
rule of reason, 88

EXCLUSIVE DISTRIBUTOR   *see
under* DISTRIBUTION

EXEMPTION FROM
PROHIBITION IN EEC
conditional, 333, 339
decision of Commission, 319–343
licensing agreements qualifying for,
333
US rule of reason compared, 10, 90

EXPORT
ban removal for exemption grant,
333, 340
licensed products, control of, 293
manufacturer's control of
wholesaler, 151

EXPORT—*cont.*
patent products from licensed
territory, 255
restriction of, EEC decisions, 327–
328

FAILING COMPANY
allowance for practices of, 147
merger involving, 214, 230

FEDERAL TRADE COMMISSION,
US
market entry by foreign companies,
228
mergers, challenge of, 211
opinion on practice legality, 10

FINES
in EEC—
cartel, imposition on, 320
companies, imposed on, 23, 320
daily penalties, 24
failure to notify agreement, for,
26–27, 327
reduction in EEC Court, 327
in US, imposed on directors, 21

FOREIGN COMMERCE   *see*
INTERSTATE TRADE

FOREIGN COMPANIES
joint ventures involving, 243, 244
licensee, restrictions on, 297
mergers involving, 223

FRANCHISE AGREEMENT
dealers, obligations imposed on, 155
exclusive, test for legality, 218
legality in Europe and US, 145, 157
meaning, 146
trademark, built around, 182

FUGATE, W. L.
quoted on—
parent and subsidiary companies,
37
single-trader protection, 49

GATT
effect of, 128

GRANT-BACK
improvement in patents, 303, 314–
318
US legal attitude to, 316–317

GROUP BOYCOTT
as illegal practice, 103, 106
coercion, legal effect of, 162, 164
definition, 160
secondary boycott, 167–168
US cases, 164–167

HARLAN, JUSTICE
on coercion, 175, 284

HORIZONTAL MERGERS *see*
under MERGERS AND
ACQUISITIONS

HORIZONTAL TERRITORIAL
LIMITATION
illegality, 133 *see also* MARKET

ILLEGAL PRACTICES *see also*
VIOLATION OF ANTITRUST
LAW
exchange of information, 113–127
failing or new company, allowances
for, 147
group boycott, 103, 106, 160–168
holding company as, 235–236
intent to control prices, 201
joint venture, legality test, 241
justification in lower prices, 157
list of, 103
market division by use of
trademarks, 271
market outlet restriction, practices
causing, 219
mergers, illegal effect of, 210
monopolization as—
EEC equivalent, 190
in US, 193
patent licensing violations, EEC
and US, 254–258
patents, illegal use of, 261, 262–272
trademark licence applications,
foreign, 269
tying arrangements, 173, 176

IMPORTS *see also* PARALLEL
IMPORTS
blockage by use of patents, 273, 274
duties elimination as EEC aim, 14,
128
patented products, flow in EEC, 253
quantity restriction, effect of, 128

INDEPENDENT INTEREST
of company directors, as conspiracy
evidence, 58–59, 64

INDUSTRIAL PROPERTY
RIGHTS
licensing agreements cases in EEC,
333
notification of agreements on, 185–
186
territorial distribution by, 158–159
tie-ins, European allowance of, 187
vulnerability to antitrust laws, 207–
208

INDUSTRY
effect of non-patented goods on,
287–288
industrial power as economic
threat, 212

INFORMATION EXCHANGE
alternative availability factor, 123,
124
legality, practices advised to secure,
123
prices exchanged among
competitors, 124–125
trade association activity, 114, 116

INFRA-ENTERPRISE
CONSPIRACY
meaning, 33–34
test of single entity, in EEC, 38

INTENT
evidence requirement in US, 321
market division, in trademark
cases, 267, 324
price fixing, relevance in, 106, 107,
108
restriction of competition, in US
law, 92

INTERNATIONAL LAW
Canadian and US on mergers, 235
problems, summary of, 2–3

INTERSTATE TRADE
effect on—
application of US law dependent
on, 104
appreciable restraint of tying
arrangements, 171–172
conspiracy, as test for, 77, 80

INTERSTATE TRADE—*cont.*
effect on—*cont.*
European and US views of, 187
patent licensing restrictions, 258
test for legality of restraint, 89
licensing clauses, examples, 298–309
meaning, 81
restraint of—
illegality, 103
patent licensing, effect of, 274
trademarks, 263
retailers' activities obstructing, 165
significance of, in EEC, 90
US law—
cases on Schwinn doctrine, 150–152
substantial effect, 82, 104

INTRACORPORATE CONSPIRACY
cases and examples, 53–54
no European equivalent, 70

INTRACORPORATE DOCTRINE *see also* SINGLE TRADER DOCTRINE
examples of, 50

JACKSON, JUSTICE
on parent-subsidiary conspiracy, 45–46

JOINT VENTURES
aircraft development example, 246–250
antitrust arguments against, 251
Clayton Act application to, 238
definitions, 237
exemption granted, example, 339
foreign companies, involving, 243
in EEC, 244
research and development, for, 245

KNOWHOW
confidentiality requirement in licence, 303, 313
examples of licensing problems, 316–318
licensing practice, 298–300
technical assistance, as, 312

LEVET, JUDGE
quoted on all-sales royalties, 287, 291

LIABILITY FOR VIOLATION
in EEC, 23–24
in US, 19–23, 65

LICENCES AND LICENSING *see also* INDUSTRIAL PROPERTY RIGHTS PATENTS; ROYALTIES PAYMENTS; TRADEMARKS
agreements, EEC decisions on, 333, 334
coercion in—
all-sales royalties, 280, 284, 287, 291
package licence, 282–283
tie-ins, 279
competitive products, dealing in, 308
conditional, of patents in Europe, 181
exclusive agreements—
exemption granted, examples of, 333
legality in EEC and US, 255, 276–278
grant by patentee, effect of, 289
improvement in processes, grants-back, 303, 314, 316–317
knowhow, licensing of, 299, 312
other purchases from specified source, 257
meaning, 284
package licensing, meaning in US 280n.
restrictions, UN recommendations, 296–297
Schwinn principle applied in, 293
terms of, rights in deciding, 284
trademarks, 182–184, 253
tying arrangements, affecting, 169
validity of patent, challenge of, 306
withholding as conspiracy, 54

McLAREN, Richard
quoted on—
co-ordinated actions of large firms, 51
grant-back clauses, 316–317
merger guidelines, 232–233
parent and subsidiary companies, 37

MANUFACTURER *see also* SUPPLIER

MANUFACTURER—*cont.*
acquisition of distributor, 217
control of distributor, 103, 134, 142–144
export by wholesalers, restriction on, 151
foreign, acquisition of distributor by, 223
right to choose distributors, 156, 161

MARKET   *see also* DISTRIBUTION; RELEVANT MARKET
area of primary responsibility, meaning, 141
concentration, US official views, 213–214
division—
  Addyston principle, 131
  among competitors, 103, 106
  clauses tending to cause, 144–145
  EEC cases on, 327
  foreign commerce, US cases on, 150–152
  horizontal and vertical, 131–132
  intent, in EEC cases, 324
  per se violation, as, 128
  vertical, meaning, 140
divisive practices—
  aggregated rebate systems, 332
  dealer location clause, 145–148
  exclusive agreements, 330
  generally, 131
  grant-back on patents, 314
  patent and trademark violations in EEC, 255
  patents, use of, 273
  Schwinn-type territorial limit, 137–138, 145, 293
  termination of distributorship, 152–153
  trademarks, by use of, 269–272, 329
dominant position, meaning in EEC, 189   *see also* ABUSE OF DOMINANT POSITION; DOMINANT POSITION
entry into—
  foreign entry into US, 224
  joint venture legality case, 238–241
  methods of, 227–228
  threat of, as factor in legality, 241, 251

MARKET—*cont.*
geographic—
  determination of, 200–201
  exclusive dealership within, 218
  licensing clauses, examples, 300–302
  patent licensing, exclusive, 255
  relevant, dispute over, 227   *see also* RELEVANT MARKET
  "section of the country", as, 213
oligopolistic, meaning, 232
percentage of share of, in merger control, 214, 215, 216
potential entrants, practices of, 227–228
power to control inferred from price-fixing, 111
reciprocal buying, 216
relevant   *see* RELEVANT MARKET
"section of the country" meaning, 222

MEMBER STATES OF EEC
copyright law, conflict in, 264
governments, competitive activities of, 15
national courts, damages actions in, 24
patent licensing disputes, 273–278
patents and trademarks in, 253

MERGERS AND ACQUISITIONS
as evidence of monopolization attempt, 194
business reasons for, 209–212
Canadian law, 235
coercion and reciprocity arising from, 231
competition, legal issue concerned with effect on, 225
conglomerate—
  meaning, 215
  reciprocity as likely danger of, 231
definitions, 237
EEC law, 233–235
"engaged in commerce" requirement, 223, 243
exchange of stock interests, 232
exclusive distributorship distinguished, 217–218
foreign companies, involving—
  attempt of US company, 222
  two, US view of merger of, 223

MERGERS AND ACQUISITIONS
—*cont.*
horizontal, meaning, 213
in US—
government action against, 211
historical view of, 209
joint venture similar to acquisition,
240
justification, reasons giving, 214
manufacturer and distributor,
between, 217
market entry by means of, 226–228
modern trends condoned, 8
share capital, all or part, 217, 220,
222
toehold acquisitions, 224
US market, foreign entry into, 224
US subsidiaries in foreign mergers,
228–229
vertical, meaning, 215
vulnerability to antitrust law, 207–
208

MITCHELL, John
on reciprocity in conglomerate
mergers, 231

MONOPOLIES AND
MONOPOLIZATION
comparison of laws on, 16
division of market as cause of, 130
grant-back clause, as element in, 317
holding company as attempt, 235–
236
in EEC—   *see also* DOMINANT
POSITION, ABUSE OF
DOMINANT POSITION
Rome Treaty, attitude of, 92
views on illegality, 7, 202
in US—
as objective of conspiracy, 64
as test of conspiracy, 60
attack on under Sherman Act, 8,
193–194
conspiracy distinguished from, 66
illegal elements, 192, 221
illegal practice, as, 16, 28–29, 189,
202
meaning, 66
penalties, 193
restraint of competition leading
to, 91

MONOPOLIES AND
MONOPOLIZATION—*cont.*
in US—*cont.*
trade restriction offences distinct
from, 194–202
mergers, tendency of, 210
patent licensing, status of, 259
tendency as illegal element in
grant-back clauses, 317
trend towards, in large companies,
202, 203
tying arrangements, effect of,
174   *see also* TYING
ARRANGEMENTS

MULTINATIONAL
CORPORATIONS
conspiracy definition, importance
of, 64–65
control measures in EEC, 233–234
growth and development, 2
patents, pooling of, 280
trademark licensing practices, 268

NEWSPAPERS
conspiracy cases involving, 59, 62

NOTIFICATION OF
AGREEMENT IN EEC
concentrations subject to, 235
failure, fine as penalty for, 327
procedure, 26–27, 91
industrial rights, bi-partite
agreements on, 185–186
validity until Commission
declaration, 322–323

OFFENCES   *see* ILLEGAL
PRACTICES; VIOLATIONS OF
ANTITRUST LAWS

PACKAGE LICENSING
mandatory, as US violation, 254

PARALLEL CONDUCT   *see also*
CONSCIOUS PARALLELISM
concerted practice, as, 74–76, 322

PARALLEL IMPORTS
prevention—
by discriminatory price-list, 325
effect of, 326
illegal methods, 265
trademarks practice in EEC, 262

PARENT AND SUBSIDIARY
conspiracy between, 57
licensing, international practices,
268
market division with foreign
subsidiary, 45
relationship—
competition not required, 65–66
concerted action, US policy on, 52
conspiracy, elements of, 65
distribution, concerning, 53
EEC ruling on separation, 70

PATENT
conditional licence, in Europe, 181
duration in US, 289, 305
duration of licence in EEC, 334
feedback of improvements, 303,
313 *see also* GRANT-BACK
foreign rights, 301–302
judicial view of, 260
jurisdiction over foreign owners in
US, 312
knowhow distinguished from, 315
licence— *see also* LICENCES AND
LICENSING
exclusivity, EEC attitude, 253
licensee, restrictions on, 280–281,
294
US violations, 254
misuse—definition in US, 280
establishment of, 285
national coverage in US and EEC,
253
non-use of, 290
number mark on product, 257–258
owners' rights in US, 178
parallel—
illegality, 275
meaning, 273, 274
rights, exhaustion of, 273, 275, 276
royalties payments, 256, 260–
261 *see also* ROYALTIES
PAYMENTS
sale of, US law, 296
trademark, distinguished from, 183
tying arrangement, as evidence of,
279

PENALTIES FOR
VIOLATIONS *see also* FINES
dual, under two legal systems, 320

PENALTIES FOR
VIOLATIONS—*cont.*
mergers declared illegal in US, for,
216
monopolization, imprisonment for,
in US, 193
Sherman Act, under, 29

PENCE, CHIEF JUDGE (US)
on conspiracy in single corporation,
42

PER SE ILLEGALITIES
categories of illegal practices, 103–
104
Europe and US, contrast between,
90–91
grant-back patent, status of, 315, 317
group boycott, 164
market division, 129, 133, 140
monopolization, in, 193–194
practices adjudged *per se*, 11
practical applications of principle,
102
price-fixing, 105–107, 110
royalties based on non-patent
products, 287, 291
Schwinn rule on, 137–139, 147, 151
test of, 103
tying arrangement, 171

PIRATING OF DESIGN
as counter to boycott charge, 166

PRICE DISCRIMINATION
meaning, 127

PRICE-FIXING
as illegal practice—
agreement as illegal element, 105
circumstances establishing
violation, 30
condemnation widespread, 31
in US, 103
common buying agency, by, 96–97
courts' decisions, disparity of, 11
defences to charge—
good intent, 95
neither intended nor effected, 110
no power to control market, 94
single-trader doctrine, 55
directors, consequences for, 22
evidence of, information exchange
as, 117–118

PRICE-FIXING—*cont.*
  in EEC—
    court findings, 73, 118
    legality, attitude to, 90, 126
  in US—
    as illegal practice, 103
    examples of, 64, 97, 311
    government procedure in cases,
      25
    grant-back, coupling with, 314
    judge's view of, 22
    oil companies' case, 97, 107
    intent—
      agreement, purpose of, 89
      conscious parallelism, inferred
        from, 321
      controlling power combined
        with, 101, 111
    licensor, by, 293
    parent and subsidiaries, between,
      53, 55–56
    patented products, 254, 256–257
    power to control—
      courts' presumption of, 109
      inferring market control, 94, 111
    property sales example, 64
    reasonable, attempt to justify as, 88
    stabilization of prices *see under*
      PRICES
    test of, inquiry questions, 107
    trade associations' activities, 73, 115
    trusts, origins of, 7–8

PRICES
  effect on, of large corporations, 212
  natural movement of, 112–113
  reduction of, EEC attitude to
    justification grounds, 157
  stabilization of—
    evidence of intention, 108–109
    exchange of information,
      through, 124
    illegality, whether indicating, 124
    resulting from conspiracy, 121–122
  unfair imposition of, in EEC, 190
  uniform, effect on competition,
    EEC case, 323

PRIVATE INDIVIDUALS
  freedom to compete, 28
  procedure for redress—
    in EEC, 24, 26, 27
    in US, 24–25

PRODUCTS
  competitive—
    availability of, in legality test, 218–
      219
    dealings in, 258, 308
  compulsion of lessees to use, 178
  franchisee, obligations on, 182
  interchangeability factor in relevant
    market, 213
  licensed—
    mark of patent number or
      trademark on, 257–258
    quantity limitation clauses, 257
  non-patented, restriction on output
    of, 290
  royalties payments based on, 279–
    292
  patented—
    competition with non-patented,
      290
    limitation on use of, 307–308
    restriction on sales of, 254
  private labels, use of, 271
  relevant markets for, 196–200 *see
    also* RELEVANT MARKET
  research and development costs,
    245 *see also* RESEARCH AND
    DEVELOPMENT
  tying arrangements, supplied
    under, 169, 279

PROOF OF ILLEGALITY
  in US courts, 104

PUBLIC BENEFIT
  all-sales royalties, effect of, 291
  competition control, effect of, 7, 91
  EEC view of—
    as evidence, 22
    distributor agreements, in, 157
    rationalisation of small
      companies, 202
  exemptions granted, factor in, 337
  free competition, in, 7
  inventions and patent licences, 289
  monopolies, discouragement of, 130
  rule of reason, link with, 165
  secrecy in knowhow licensing,
    318
  selection of dealers by
    manufacturers, 156
  stabilization of prices, 121

PUBLIC BENEFIT—*cont.*
  tying arrangements, from, as
      defence, 187
  US view of—
    as evidence, 22
    irrelevant in price-fixing case,
        110–111
    no defence to charges, 92–93, 103

REASON, RULE OF *see* RULE OF
    REASON

RECIPROCITY
  illegal elements in US, 232
  meaning, 230, 231

REFUSAL TO DEAL
  legality, factors affecting, 161–162

RELEVANT MARKET
  definition of term, 213
  delineation of—
    acquisition by supplier of
        distributor, in, 218
    co-operation agreements, in, 342
    merger, in defence of, 210
    merger effect, in measuring, 212
    need for, 196–197
  EEC views, 196–198, 331
  joint venture case, importance in,
      251
  meaning, 22
  price-fixing case in EEC, 325
  "section of the country", meaning
      in US, 213
  tying arrangement, significance in,
      174
  US view, 199–200

RESALE PRICE FIXING
  as illegal practice, 103, 126
  EEC copyright case, 263–264
  non-complying dealers, boycott of,
      161–162
  sale-network bans, through, 324

RESEARCH AND
    DEVELOPMENT
  competition restriction in, 334
  costs as reason for joint ventures,
      245
  improvements by licensee, 303–304,
      314
  joint ventures for, 237^n, 246–250
  patent products, analysis of, 261

RESTRAINT OF TRADE
  conspiracy with a view to, 35, 64
  EEC decision on, 319–333
  foreign commerce, cases involving,
      150–152
  intention as illegal element, 101–102
  legality, evidence to determine, 90
  monopoly offences distinguished
      from, 66, 194–202
  parent and subsidiaries' actions, 48,
      52
  practices, restrictive—
    exchange of information, 119
    group boycott, 160–168
    preferential routing, 172
    price fixing with subsidiary, 56
    trade association activities, 122
  public benefit from, 86
  trade, meaning, 79
  unreasonable—
    meaning and importance, 84
    tying arrangement, illegal
        element, 173–174
  violation of Sherman Act, as, 28–29,
      101–102

RETAILERS
  group boycott by, 164–165
  restriction on sales to, 138

ROBINSON, CHARLES W.
  on transnational enterprises, 12

ROME, TREATY OF *see also* EEC
    LAW
  conspiracy, ruling on, 68
  first antitrust laws, 13
  market division, attitude to, 273
  monopolies, provisions on, 16, 92
  trademarks, national laws on, 263

ROYALTIES PAYMENTS
  all-sales, 280, 284, 287, 291
  alternative payment schemes, 291–
      292
  companies' views of, 260–261
  computation of, 290
  expiry of patent, after, 334
  knowhow licensing in US and EEC,
      313
  licensed products, for, legality, 256
  sales by licensee, amounts related
      to, 254

ROYALTIES PAYMENTS—*cont.*
small company's view of patent, 260
taxation in US, 295

RULE OF REASON
attempts by courts to codify, 11
courts' requirement of evidence in, 88
European and US courts contrasted, 91
group boycott, applied to, 167
interpretation difficulties, 11, 101
price-fixing legality, in judging, 112
public benefit as justification, 165
US legislation, in, 85, 174[n.]

SALES   *see also* DISTRIBUTION;
RETAILERS; WHOLESALERS
agencies, 96, 108, 242
aggregated rebate systems, 332
conditions fixed by Trade Associations, 336
exclusive agreements, 330
restriction by patentee, 254

SHARE OF MARKET   *see also*
MARKET
percentage figures in merger control, 214, 215, 216

SCHWINN PRINCIPLE
summary of, 137–140, 145, 293

SINGLE-TRADER DOCTRINE
association of businesses, 64
conspiracy, relevant to, 35
courts' attitudes in US, 39
manufacturer and agent as one, 139
parent company and subsidiary, 36
weakness in theory of, 50

SPAAK REPORT
problems dealt with in, 14–15

SPECIALIZATION AGREEMENTS
exemption granted, 337–338

STANDARDS AND SPECIFICATIONS
patent licensing, in, 257

STATUTE OF LIMITATION
purpose in EEC, 320

SUBSIDIARY COMPANY   *see also*
PARENT AND SUBSIDIARY
conspiracy among, 34, 36

SUBSIDIARY COMPANY—*cont.*
control of, 49
EEC test of single entity, 38
foreign, US case, 42–45
foreign mergers, involved in, 228–229
infra-enterprise conspiracy, between, 34
jointly owned, in EEC, 342
jurisdiction over foreign, in US, 311–312
meaning, in US, 36
obedience held not conspiracy, 53
single trader status, 49   *see also*
SINGLE TRADER DOCTRINE

SUPPLIER   *see also*
MANUFACTURER
acquisitions involving, 215   *see also*
MERGERS AND ACQUISITIONS
exclusive distributor agreement, effect of, 217–218

SUPREME COURT, US
cases and findings—
joint venture, 251
market division by trademark, 271
patents and royalties payments, 280
refusal to deal, 161–162
trademarks, use of, 269–272
vertical market limitations, 137–140
policy of—
control of subsidiaries, 57
director's liability to prosecution, 22
foreign companies, treatment of, 21
market division, legality, 131–132
patent licensee, restrictions on, 281
patent misuse, establishment of, 284
subsidiary companies in conspiracy, 41
wholesalers, selection of, 157–158
tests for legality—
coercion in misuse of patent, 281, 283
information exchange, in practice of, 120, 121
monopoly, for existence of, 196

TAXATION
  relevance in US to patents sales and
    licensing, 295

TECHNICAL ASSISTANCE,
  (KNOWHOW)   *see also*
  KNOWHOW
  secrecy and licensing problems, 303,
    313–318

TECHNOLOGY
  licensing of, 298

TERMINATION OF
  DISTRIBUTORSHIP
  manufacturer's right, 152, 161

THIRD PARTY
  EEC national courts, in, 26
  group boycott of, 160–161
  injury to, as conspiracy test—
    associations, actions of, 63–64
    distributorship termination, 53
    independent dealer's complaint,
      54–55
    parent and subsidiary action, in,
      65–66

TIE-INS   *see under* TYING
  ARRANGEMENT

TRADE, INTERSTATE— *see*
  INTERSTATE TRADE

TRADE
  meaning, 81
  restraint of   *see* RESTRAINT OF
    TRADE
  trading practices   *see* BUSINESS
    PRACTICES

TRADE ASSOCIATIONS
  development in Europe and US, 115
  discount systems, EEC view of, 332
  exhibitions for control of, 340–341
  general description of, 113
  price-fixing by, 73–74
  sales conditions fixed by, 336

TRADEMARKS
  antitrust law, conflict with, 182
  exclusive distribution agreement,
    265
  franchise built around, 182
  market division by use of, 269–272,
    329

TRADEMARKS—*cont.*
  national coverage in US and EEC,
    253
  obtaining, methods of, 267
  parallel imports in EEC, 262
  patent, distinguished from, 183
  registration, mark of, 257–258

TRANSNATIONAL
  ENTERPRISES
  competition, effect on, 12

TRUSTS
  origins among large US companies,
    7–8

TYING ARRANGEMENTS
  as *per se* illegal practice, 103, 106, 176
  business practice, viewed as, 178–184
  definition, European, 185
  definition, US, 169
  examples of, 303, 305
  franchise agreements, with, 182
  legality question, EEC, 190
  legality question, US, 279
  monopoly, tendency toward, 179
  patent licensing, clauses in, EEC,
    257
  patents as evidence, 178, 279
  tie-ins—
    as abuse of dominance in EEC,
      187–188, 279
    circumstances allowing legality in
      US, 184, 271–272
    commercial effect of, 179, 181
    exemption from need to notify in
      EEC, 186
    illegal, US example of, 294
    patent misuse in US, 286–287

UN CONFERENCE ON TRADE
  AND DEVELOPMENT
  licence restrictions,
    recommendations, 296–297

UNIFORMITY OF ACTION   *see
  also* CONCERTED PRACTICE;
  CONSCIOUS PARALLELISM
  in test for conspiracy, 67

UNITED STATES FEDERAL
  TRADE COMMISSION   *see*
  FEDERAL TRADE COMMISSION

UNREASONABLE
RESTRAINT   *see under*
RESTRAINT OF TRADE

US ANTITRUST LAWS   *see also*
names of illegal practices e.g.
CONSPIRACY; MONOPOLY
abuse of dominance in EEC
compared, 190
application of, by courts, 279
Attorney General's Committee   *see*
ATTORNEY GENERAL'S
COMMITTEE
Canada, agreement with, 235
EEC laws compared   *see under*
EEC LAW
exclusive dealing agreements,
164   *see also under*
DISTRIBUTION
grant-back arrangements, 303, 313–
318
illegal practices   *see* ILLEGAL
PRACTICES
joint venture, government view of,
237–238
jurisdiction—
foreign mergers, 222, 228–229
scope of, 310
licensing clause with foreign firms,
301
"long arm" statute, 311
monopoly as illegal practice, 189,
193–196   *see also* MONOPOLIES
multinational corporations, 2, 64–
65
patents—
exclusive rights, (255)
licensing violations, 254
sale of, 296
royalties, payment of, 304   *see also*
ROYALTIES PAYMENTS
third party actions for damages, 24
trademark law, conflict with, 182
tying arrangements, 169–184
violations   *see also* VIOLATIONS
OF ANTITRUST LAWS
government action, 211
individual states, action by, 105
liability for, 19–23, 65   *see also*
LIABILITY
procedure for plaintiff, 24–25

US GOVERNMENT   *see also*
DEPARTMENT OF JUSTICE;
FEDERAL TRADE COMMISSION;
SUPREME COURT
competitive activities of, 15
legal action by—
mergers, federal procedure
against, 211
powers of individual states, 105
policy of—
joint ventures, 237–238
patent licensing, 259
trademarks and patents, 253

VERTICAL AGREEMENTS
European and US law, 137, 153–154
mergers, 215
territorial limitations, legality, 133

VIOLATIONS OF ANTITRUST
LAW
attitudes generally adopted—
distributorship termination, 152
patent, non-use of, 289
practices illegal in EEC and US,
104   *see also* ILLEGAL
PRACTICES
price-fixing, 105–127
trade associations' activities, 113–
127
in EEC—
in absence of agreement, 70
patent licensing, 254–258
in US—
competition, substantial
reduction of, 86
consent decree, 25–26
defendant, tactics of, 25
facilities refused to third party,
52
government procedure, 25
information exchange among
competitors, 117
meaning, in Sherman Act, 28, 29
monopoly as crime, 193
patent licensing, 254
per se violations   *see* PER SE
ILLEGALITIES
restraint of trade, practices
causing, 101–102

VIOLATIONS OF ANTITRUST
  LAW—*cont.*
  in US—*cont.*
    Sherman Act offences, 194–202
    territory allocation by trademark,
      269
    trademark offences, 268, 269

WHOLESALERS
  boycott of, 164–165
  competition among, 156
  control of exports by, 151
  resale price fixing, participation, 162
  selection of, and franchise, 157

Printed by J. W. Arrowsmith Ltd., Bristol BS3 2NT